P!NK

SONG BY SONG

P!NK

SONG BY SONG

STEVE BISHOP

FONTHILL

First published in Great Britain in 2026 by
Fonthill
An imprint of
Pen & Sword Books Ltd
Yorkshire – Philadelphia

ISBN 978-1-03615-639-8

A CIP catalogue record for this book is available from the British Library.

Typeset in Sabon LT Std 10/13 by
SJmagic DESIGN SERVICES, India.
Printed and bound in the UK by CPI Group (UK) Ltd, Croydon, CR0 4YY

MIX
Paper | Supporting responsible forestry
FSC® C013604

The Publisher's authorised representative in the EU for product safety is Authorised Rep Compliance Ltd., Ground Floor, 71 Lower Baggot Street, Dublin D02 P593, Ireland.
www.arccompliance.com

For a complete list of Pen & Sword titles please contact
PEN & SWORD BOOKS LIMITED
George House, Units 12 & 13, Beevor Street, Off Pontefract Road,
Barnsley, South Yorkshire, S71 1HN, England
E-mail: enquiries@pen-and-sword.co.uk
Website: www.pen-and-sword.co.uk

or

PEN AND SWORD BOOKS
1950 Lawrence Rd, Havertown, PA 19083, USA
E-mail: uspen-and-sword@casematepublishers.com
Website: www.penandswordbooks.com

Contents

Introduction

Alecia Beth Moore—better known as P!nk—has been one of the music industry's most dynamic and outspoken voices for over twenty-five years. Authentically herself, her raw emotion, outspoken individuality, and 'genre-agnostic' approach to music have set her apart from her contemporaries and ensured her longevity.

Born on 8 September 1979, in Elkins Park, Pennsylvania, P!nk grew up in a 'middle-class' family. Her father, James 'Jim' Moore, was a Vietnam War veteran and musician, while her mother, Judith Moore, was a nurse. Her older brother, Lieutenant Colonel Jason Moore, was born in 1977. Diagnosed with asthma as a child, P!nk developed a natural talent for three activities that not only helped strengthen her lungs but also shaped the course of her life—dance, gymnastics, and music. While music became her primary focus, gymnastics was her first love, and today, her live performances incorporate all three.

On her VH1 *Behind The Music* special, her father, Jim Moore said: 'She got into all the different choral groups in school choirs and singing groups. Music is where she gravitated to. It was a natural thing to her; she would grab something and pretend it was a microphone.'

When P!nk was 9 years old, her parents separated. After her father left, P!nk began to use music both as an escape and as an outlet for her emotions, which became apparent to her parents. Jim Moore said: 'I think music became for her a hiding place and it was a place for her to get away from the arguing, to get away from the unhappy part of her life.'

P!nk began taking vocal lessons when she was 10. At a recital at Germantown Academy, Philadelphia, she performed a cover of Madonna's 'Oh Father' in front of 1,500 people. Moving into her teenage years, she also began to explore writing, starting with poetry that would eventually become lyrics to songs. Judith recalled finding her diaries and being unsure about whether she needed to intervene. She said: 'Her initial writings were always very introspective. Some of it was very black and very deep and almost worrisome. But it was her outlet and her way of venting these feelings.'

Other changes were also happening, as P!nk made new friends and decided to take control of her appearance. Rebelling against her mother, she began to get into trouble with law enforcement authorities and was moved to Lenape Middle School. It was here that her cover of Simon and Garfunkel's 'Bridge Over Troubled Water' at an evening recital brought her to the attention of local music teacher Joseph Ohrt. Having been told to dress in a more feminine manner, P!nk turned up in a dress accompanied by Dr. Martens boots.

P!nk joined a rock group called Middleground when she was 13, which became her first band and expanded her musical knowledge. Whilst many of her friends were listening to R&B and pop, and P!nk herself was a huge Madonna fan, the band took inspiration from the likes of Aerosmith and Janis Joplin. She also enjoyed skating, and was determined to master it, to prove a point to the boys around her who said she couldn't compete. Middleground was short-lived; they disbanded after losing a 'battle of the bands' competition to rivals The Jetsists.

At 14, P!nk moved to Central Bucks High School West, where Ohrt became her music teacher and mentor, encouraging her to take further solo parts in school recitals. However, outside of school, P!nk's rebellion continued. She began sneaking out to Philadelphia clubs, hoping to be spotted by a talent scout. She was initially recruited as a dancer but soon became a backing vocalist for hip-hop group Schools of Thought. This success did nothing to reduce the tension between herself and her mother. With another group of new friends immersed in the underground club scene, P!nk was using drugs to escape her pain, even going as far as selling them. She added that her fear of needles prevented her from using heroin, even though her friends did. Tragically, she eventually lost her friends Tim Russell and Sekou to drug use.

It was around this time that P!nk was spotted performing and joined Basic Instinct, a new girl group that had been signed to MCA Records. However, this was also short-lived, as within just weeks of joining, P!nk was asked to leave by the other members. In an early interview with MTV, she said: 'Because I was white, they said I didn't fit in. Whatever.' The group split completely one month later, without releasing any music.

By the summer of 1995, things had deteriorated at home to the point that P!nk's mother asked her to move in with her father, Jim. Later that year, P!nk's life changed significantly. During an all-night rave at Club Fever in Philadelphia on Thanksgiving, P!nk met Scratch and his friends at an open mic event and won over the crowd with a performance of 'Real Love' by Mary J. Blige. However, she overdosed later that same night. Scratch told her: 'Come back tomorrow, I'll give you a guest spotlight. But you can never touch drugs again.' From then on, P!nk said: 'I never took drugs again, ever.'

Once P!nk officially left school to pursue music, she continued performing regularly and auditioning for opportunities, being offered the chance to sing hooks for Scratch 'n' Smoove. It was at one of their gigs that producers working with a new all-girl R&B trio called Choice, who had recently had a member leave, asked her to audition.

P!nk told *The Philadelphia Inquirer* that she sang '50 or 60 songs' at the McDonald's at 30th Street Station (which has since closed) for them. She recalled: 'I was like, "I can sing Whitney, I can sing Mary, I can sing Green Day, I can sing Janis Joplin, I can sing Billy Joel, Phantom of the Opera... What genre are you looking for? I can do that!"'

Before even meeting the rest of the group, she was asked to join as the new lead vocalist on a thirty-day trial. Within a month, Choice had sparked a record label bidding war, and in the summer of 1996, they signed to LaFace Records.

Choice only officially released one song, but because of that record contract, Alecia Beth Moore went on to sign a solo deal, choosing to go by the pseudonym P!nk. She has released nine solo studio albums, a greatest hits compilation, and an album with Dallas Green as one half of You+Me. In addition to co-writing most of her songs, she has also become a prolific songwriter for other artists, including Cher and Celine Dion. P!nk has cemented her place as one of the most successful live performers of her generation, incorporating cover versions of songs into her shows to honour the artists and influences that have shaped her sound.

P!nk: Song by Song examines the tracks she has recorded or performed, including every track from her studio albums, compilations, one-off singles, guest appearances, and live performances. As a songwriter, P!nk has an extensive catalogue of unreleased material; some of these songs have been recorded by others, whilst others have become available online through illegal leaks from various sources. Many remain unavailable to the public but have been registered on licensing catalogues, such as ASCAP (American Society of Composers, Authors and Publishers) and BMI (Broadcast Music, Inc.). These are included where it's likely P!nk recorded a demo.

1

Choices (1996–1998)

Choice were founded in 1996 by Joe 'P' Priolo and Carl Carr, consisting of three girls including Chrissy Conway and Sharon 'Sheri' Flanagan (now Sharon Sable). Following the departure of their third member later that year, P!nk (still known as Alecia at the time) was approached to audition. Although they originated as a vocal harmony group, P!nk became their lead vocalist with Conway and Flanagan as backup singers.

Flanagan recalled to *The Press of Atlantic City* in 2006: 'We sang and it instantly meshed. There were sparks. It worked really well. Chrissy, Alecia, and I laughed a lot. We could turn an airplane ride into our own comedy show. When we weren't laughing, we were usually singing gospel in our kitchen. I remember the three of us being deeply moved by our voices together. It was something very special.'

During P!nk's thirty-day trial in the group, where they rehearsed and recorded some initial demos together, they came to the attention of various record labels, sparking a bidding war between Stonecreek Recording (who had Boyz II Men on their roster) and LaFace Records. On day twenty-eight of the thirty-day trial, they signed with the latter and began working with Antonio 'L.A.' Reid and Kenneth 'Babyface' Edmonds on their debut album. Reid said in 2002: 'What I saw in Choice was Alecia. And that's why I signed them. She came into my conference room, and she just started to wail. Her personality was so, so contagious.'

Choice spent the next two years rehearsing for eight hours a day and flying around the USA to work with various producers. P!nk told *The Face* magazine in 2002: 'It was two long years of recording and spending major money, and at the time I didn't realise it was all recoupable, so I didn't give a shit.'

Following an underwhelming performance of three songs at the record company's Christmas party in 1997, the group's future was in jeopardy.

Reid recalled in VH1's *Driven*: 'People said: "What is this? And what is on L.A.'s mind?" Alecia stood out. And everybody had the same comment – "Not sure about the group, but the girl is incredible." Afterwards, I had conversations with

Alecia and said, "I'm not sure about the group, I think you're incredible." I really would love for you to take a stab at it solo. She had deep reservations about it, she was very loyal to the group.'

Before 'There You Go' was released, early press releases gave the official reason for Choice's disbanding as the members having different goals—'one wanted to sing Broadway tunes, the other wanted to make alternative records, and P!nk wanted to do it all.'

In 2003, P!nk told *Yahoo! Music* how much she loved being in Choice. She said: 'I loved being in a group… I was in a band. Bands are different. But groups… I love harmony, I love harmonising, there's nothing like it. When you are with two girls and you all live together and sing together and breathe together and cry together, the sound that you three can make together, it's beautiful. We used to sing gospel songs and rock and every kind of song, and it was just beautiful… being in a group is hard, but it was cool in my situation because we all wanted to do different things.'

While the Choice album remains officially unreleased, two of the songs the group recorded were released on P!nk's debut album, *Can't Take Me Home*. 'Let Me Let You Know' and 'Love is Such a Crazy Thing' were both re-recorded, with the latter featuring the original backing vocals from Conway and Flanagan. The entire album, believed to have tentatively been called *Choices*, leaked online in September 2023.

Album Tracks

'Players'

Written by Kenneth 'Babyface' Williams
Produced by Kenneth 'Babyface' Williams
Includes a sample of 'Dreams' performed by Fleetwood Mac and written by Stevie Nicks
Duration: 4:27

'Players' was recorded in one of Choice's first sessions after signing to LaFace Records, written by Babyface. Re-recorded for *Can't Take Me Home*, it was played for journalists before the album was finished, referenced in a January 2000 *Vibe* magazine article by Tracy E. Hopkins.

'Stay'

Written by Daryl Simmons
Produced by Daryl Simmons
Duration: 4:51

R&B ballad 'Stay' was written and produced by Daryl Simmons, who won the Grammy Award for Best R&B Song in 1993 for writing 'End of the Road' with

Babyface and L.A. Reid. The song was a #1 hit for Boyz II Men in the USA, UK and Australia.

Once LaFace Records confirmed that Choice's album would not be released, Simmons sent 'Stay' to Destiny's Child, who recorded and released the song on their second studio album, 1999's *The Writing's on the Wall.*

'I Love My Boo'

Written by Kenneth 'Babyface' Williams and Jon-John Robinson
Produced by Kenneth 'Babyface' Williams and Jon-John Robinson
Duration: 3:51

'I Love My Boo' is a collaboration between Babyface and Jon-Jon Robinson, who had worked with TLC on 'Let's Do it Again' from their multi-platinum selling album, *CrazySexyCool*, and K-Ci and JoJo on their single, 'How Could You.'

'Just to Be Loving You'

Written by Daryl Simmons and Alecia 'P!nk' Moore
Produced by Daryl Simmons
Duration: 4:34

A collaboration between P!nk and Daryl Simmons, 'Just to Be Loving You' marked the first time LaFace Records acknowledged P!nk's songwriting talent. In an early press release, she said: 'Daryl asked me to write the chorus to 'Just to Be Loving You.' I thought that was so cool, because no one had even asked me if I wrote. So I just closed my eyes and out it came. I wrote that, and it was the beginning of my writing career.'

A clip of the song plays in P!nk's episode of VH1's *Driven*. It is rumoured that the song was re-recorded for *Can't Take Me Home*, but this is unconfirmed.

'Make Cool'

Written by Alonzo 'Lonnie' Jackson, Taura Latrice Stinson and De'Andre Lamont Griffin
Produced by Alonzo 'Lonnie' Jackson
Duration: 3:57

A hip-hop-influenced mid-tempo track, 'Make Cool' was written by Alonzo 'Lonnie' Jackson and his then-wife, Taura Stinson (formerly Taura Jackson), with De'Andre Griffin. Jackson and Griffin produced the 1994 album *Anna's Boy* by Young Woo (Gregory Kendricks), whilst Stinson was part of Emage, an R&B trio who released an album entitled *Soul Deep* in 1994.

'Make Cool' was reportedly originally pitched to TLC.

'Gotta Be You and Me'

Written by Sean 'Sep' Hall, Nate Butler and Stone Stafford
Produced by Sean 'Sep' Hall
Duration: 4:19

'Gotta Be You and Me' was written by Sep and Nate Butler, who went on to write 3LW's 2000 hit singles, 'No More (Baby I'ma Do Right)' and 'Playas Gon' Play.'

'My Love is Gone'

Written by Errol Johnson, Joseph 'Joe' Priolo and Alecia 'P!nk' Moore
Produced by Errol Johnson
Duration: 4:18

Errol Johnson and Joseph 'Joe' Priolo wrote 'My Love is Gone' for Choice, after having success with singles for Whitehead Bros. in 1994. After Choice disbanded, they continued to write with Chrissy Conway, collaborating on 'Not This Time' for 3LW's debut album and ZOEgirl's 'No You.'

A clip of 'My Love is Gone' played on P!nk's first VH1 *Behind the Music* episode.

'Chitty Chitty Bang Bang'

Written by Kenny 'K-Smoove' Kornegay, Darryl '88 Fingas' Young and Kelly Price
Produced by Kenny 'K-Smoove' Kornegay and Darryl '88 Fingas' Young
Duration: 4:44

'Chitty Chitty Bang Bang' is one of two songs co-written and produced by K-Smoove and 88 Fingas, who worked with R&B duo Changing Faces on their self-titled debut album. The song was reportedly considered to be the album's first single.

Kelly Price, who sang backing vocals on many Mariah Carey singles, contributed to the melody and lyrics of 'Chitty Chitty Bang Bang.' The title references the 1964 children's novel, *Chitty Chitty Bang Bang*, about a magical car of the same name, adapted into a hit movie in 1968.

'If I Ever See Heaven Again'

Written by Diane Warren
Produced by Daryl Simmons
Duration: 4:21

'If I Ever See Heaven Again' was given to Choice by Diane Warren, known for writing hits such as Celine Dion's #1 single, 'Because You Loved Me,' Monica's

'For You I Will' and Toni Braxton's 'Un-Break My Heart,' amongst many other classics.

When the Choice album was shelved, Warren sold the song to Swedish artist Jessica Folcker, who released it on her debut album, *Jessica*, in 1998, with new production from David Kreuger and Per Magnusson.

The song was later recorded again, by girl group i5 (the 'i' standing for 'international' as each of the five girls came from a different country). After supporting Britney Spears on tour, they released the song on their 2000 debut album.

'Don't Go Breakin' My Heart'

Written by Christopher 'Tricky' Stewart, Sean 'Sep' Hall and Thabiso 'Tab' Nkhereanye
Produced by Christopher 'Tricky' Stewart and Sean 'Sep' Hall
Duration: 4:45

'Don't Go Breakin' My Heart' was co-written and co-produced by Christopher 'Tricky' Stewart, who met L.A. Reid after working on 'Treat U Right' for BlackGirl in 1994.

Stewart later had a huge hit with 'Case of the Ex,' recorded by Mýa, who joined P!nk on 'Lady Marmalade.' He also discovered Blu Cantrell, who released two albums under Reid's mentorship, and worked with Britney Spears on her 2003 album, *In the Zone*.

'Can't Wait Another Day'

Written by Kenny 'K-Smoove' Kornegay, Darryl '88 Fingas' Young and Gordon Chambers
Produced by Kenny 'K-Smoove' Kornegay and Darryl '88 Fingas' Young
Duration: 3:40

'Can't Wait Another Day' is the second song on the album to feature production from K-Smoove and 88 Fingas, with Gordon Chambers joining them as a co-writer.

Chambers co-wrote the 1994 single, 'If You Love Me,' for R&B girl group, Brownstone, which reached the top 10 in the USA and UK and was nominated for a Grammy Award for Best R&B Performance by a Duo or Group with Vocal in 1996.

'Living in My World'

Written by HOP Productions (John Howcott and Donald Parks) and Ezekiel Lewis
Produced by HOP Productions (John Howcott and Donald Parks)
Duration: 5:53

One of the first Choice songs to leak online, 'Living in My World' was originally credited as an unreleased P!nk demo from the *Can't Take Me Home* sessions.

In 2017, P!nk was played a clip of the song on BBC Radio 1 and said: 'I like that song, I do a really good little ad-lib moment in that song.'

'Leaving for the Last Time'

Written by Raphael 'Tweet' Brown and Ralph B. Stacy
Produced by Raphael 'Tweet' Brown and Ralph B. Stacy
Duration: 5:14

Originally recorded for Choice's debut album, 'Leaving for the Last Time' was re-recorded for *Can't Take Me Home*, appearing on a four-track pre-release CD sampler that was sent to radio DJs around the USA. It was also referenced in the same January 2000 *Vibe* magazine article that mentions 'Players' being on P!nk's 'tentatively self-titled soul-pop disc, due out in March.'

Other Songs

'Key to My Heart'

Written by Joe 'P' Priolo and Carl Carr
Produced by Joe 'P' Priolo and Carl Carr
Recorded at Cream Production Studios, New Jersey
Duration: 5:45

'Key to My Heart' is the only song officially released by Choice, appearing on the soundtrack to the 1996 movie, *Kazaam*, starring American basketball legend, Shaquille O'Neal. Written and recorded for the movie, the song wasn't due to appear on Choice's debut album.

'I Know I Never'

Written by Joseph 'Joe' Priolo, Alex Cantrall and Myron Davis
Produced by Joseph 'Joe' Priolo

Joe Priolo uploaded a one-minute clip of 'I Know I Never' to YouTube in June 2016. In a comment, he mentioned that Choice had recorded approximately twenty songs in total, with thirteen being selected for inclusion on their debut album. Alongside 'Key to My Heart,' 'I Know I Never' was also not due to appear on the album.

2

Can't Take Me Home (1999–2000)

Released:	4 April 2000 (USA and Canada) 14 April 2000 (Europe) 17 April 2000 (UK) 29 May 2000 (Australia) 18 September 2000 (UK Special Edition)
Chart Position:	USA: 26 Canada: 19 UK: 13 Australia: 10 Germany: 85

After they decided not to release *Choices*, LaFace Records gave P!nk an ultimatum—leave Choice, after which they would sign her as a solo act, or be held hostage in the contract indefinitely.

P!nk told Howard Stern: 'I went home and called my dad, and said, "I'm fucked." He said, "Well, let's talk about this… when you were a little girl and you pictured yourself up on stage, what did you picture?" I said, "I pictured myself." He said, "Well, sometimes we have to do hard things." I went into a room with the managers who managed all three of us, and they said, "You have to do it." Then they went in the room with the other girls and said, "She's cunning and out to break your heart." Everyone disappeared. I had no record deal. I had no management.'

Concerned there would be 'interference of contract,' LaFace Records made P!nk wait several months before signing her as a solo artist. She spent time living in the Bronx writing. Six months or so passed before she came to the attention of EMI Publishing's Brian K. Jackson, who offered her a deal. P!nk negotiated a $1 million contract, including part-ownership under her own company, Pink Panther Music, LLC.

On learning she was now the recipient of a publishing deal, the managers of Choice claimed that they had not officially resigned or been fired and were now entitled to fees. Her father, James T. Moore, took over as soon as they left, and she signed to LaFace Records as a solo artist. Shortly after, she reportedly went to their offices and declared to L.A. Reid, 'I'm Mr. Pink,' referring to the character in the Quentin Tarantino movie, *Reservoir Dogs*. However, as with all folklore, there are multiple origin stories for just why Alecia chose to adopt the pseudonym.

In 2001, she told MTV: 'I went to camp when I was young. I was six or seven and I had my first crush going on. We all went swimming but I didn't have a bathing suit. So, I just swam in my underwear. No big deal. When it was time for the kids to put their dry underwear back on, I was like, "Aw, shucks, I don't have any - I'll just put my shorts back on." My crush, Devin, decided that he was going to pull my pants down, and there was my ass. Can I say that? Oh, well, I said it already. Anyway, I got embarrassed, and I turned pink. I mean, I turned bright pink. And he looked at me and said, "Pink." I never lived it down.'

A little while later, in a fan web chat, she gave a briefer explanation: 'It was always my nickname when I was a little girl. My friends named me that because I was the only girl in my clique.'

In 2002, British magazine *The Face* asked her for 'the truest version' of how she became known as P!nk. referring to her former bodyguard Matt Epps, who died in 2014. She said: 'Sure, if your ears can handle it. For the first year of my friendship with Matt, he kept begging me, "Please, can I see it? Please can I see it, I've never seen a white girl's thing!" And he was so freaking relentless, but he's so harmless. I'm like "Matt, no!" And I'm so sick of telling him no that one day I'm like, "You know what? Come here!" And I shoved his face down there and I was like, "See it? Take a good look, because you're never going to see it again!" And he had this revelation. He was like, "Oh my God! It's pink!" So they started calling me Pink. I was the only white girl in our whole clique, and *Reservoir Dogs* was our favourite movie, so I became Mr. Pink, and Matt was Mr. Blonde and there was Mr. White, and we were all a bunch of thugs going around the city terrorising people.'

Regardless of the truth, 'Pink' became 'P!nk' to give a distinctive artist name that would avoid trademark conflicts. However, despite having both a record and publishing deal, P!nk was still working at a petrol station to fund her lifestyle while working on her debut solo album. After being discovered by Reid's son, Reid agreed to cover her salary so she could quit the job.

P!nk's debut album, originally planned to be self-titled, followed the direction that was started with Choice, introducing her to the world through a blend of soul, R&B and hip-hop. Whilst the sound is very much indicative of the era, the lyrics contain the seeds of the rebellious spirit and attitude that would later define her career, reflected in the defiant album title, *Can't Take Me Home*.

P!nk said: 'It's crazy. My favourite word is eclectic. It's really hard for me to categorise it. To explain myself in a nutshell, I'm eclectic and versatile. I love like all kinds of music. Even over the hard hip-hop tracks you can hear the influences from rock and gospel and opera and alternative. There's a lot of influences going on in my brain and that came out in the album so I'm really happy about that.'

However, during promotion for *M!ssundaztood*, she reflected: 'People embraced this pink-haired freak, pissed-off girl with a bad attitude problem, writing songs about bad relationships. But it wasn't mine. I didn't get to push all the buttons.'

Reid added: 'She did things that she didn't want to do, she sang songs that she really didn't want to sing. Musically, I didn't think she was satisfied, but we did the best that we can do under the circumstances – and we ended up getting what we really needed which was a couple of great songs that became hit singles.'

P!nk performed the album's three singles, 'There You Go,' 'Most Girls' and 'You Make Me Sick,' alongside two album tracks ('Split Personality' and 'Stop Falling'), across the USA as one of the support acts on *NSync's *No Strings Attached* tour. Although she followed in the footsteps of Britney Spears, who had also supported *NSync, P!nk was otherwise marketed as her opposite.

In addition to comparisons to her young female contemporaries, *Can't Take Me Home* attracted commentary around P!nk's race as a white woman singing R&B and hip-hop. P!nk told *Launch*: 'We all came from the same place: God. That's how I explain it, we're all pink on the inside. Whatever you want to call it. I don't care. If you respect me, I respect you. And if you're ignorant, then I don't have anything to do with you, basically.'

Can't Take Me Home went onto sell over 2 million copies in the USA alone, but despite its commercial success, P!nk distanced herself from it in later years. She continued to perform songs from the album in her live shows from 2001 to 2013, culminating in a medley of its singles on *The Truth About Love tour*.

In 2019, P!nk reflected on the album in an interview with *Variety* magazine, saying: 'A lot of it was me: there are a few songs that came from my time in the Bronx, like "Hiccup," "Is it Love" and "Can't Take Me Home." "Split Personality" was mine - I wrote that on the beach in Miami. I was really young. I was on my own. And I was making music. I thought my shit didn't stink. So, yeah, it was really fun!'

Album Tracks

'Split Personality'

Written by Kenneth 'Babyface' Edmonds, Terence 'Tramp-Baby' Abney and Alecia 'P!nk' Moore
Produced by Kenneth 'Babyface' Edmonds
Recorded at Brandon's Way, Los Angeles
Duration: 3:59

The album's opening track, 'Split Personality,' explores P!nk's internal conflict and struggle for self-acceptance. The song features two versions of P!nk—one singing and one commenting and providing feedback to the other.

In an interview with MuchMusic Canada, P!nk said: 'I think everybody has different sides to them. Everybody has their tough, you know, outer exterior, like nobody can touch us. And then we go home and take it off and cry and look in the mirror and, watch *Care Bears* and pet our puppies.'

She added to MTV: '"Split Personality" is just me. I was in the car the other day, driving, and somebody cut me off and I was about to kill them. That's where it came from. That song's going to let the world know how many issues I really have.'

In 2023, P!nk told *Vulture*: 'That was the first song I had written alone. It was sunrise in Miami. I later sang it to L.A. Reid, and he was like, "Yeah, that's no good." I was living in Atlanta at the time, and I went out to Los Angeles to work with Babyface. I sang it to him and he goes, "Where have you been hiding this song?" I'm like, "Well, L.A. told me it was shit." And he said, "Excuse me while I go call L.A." Then he helped me record it. It felt like a real accomplishment to have someone like Babyface, who can't fit all of his plaques in his studio, tell you that he wants to help you record a song of yours that you love. It was a first for me. Back then, they didn't want me to write. Pop stars didn't; they just got handed songs and were told how to sing them. I was like, "This is bullshit," so I started writing my own songs.'

Although not on the soundtrack album, 'Split Personality' appears in the 2001 Disney movie, *The Princess Diaries*.

'Hell Wit Ya'

Written by Kevin 'She'kspere' Briggs, Kandi Burruss, Alecia 'P!nk' Moore and Darius Green
Produced by Kevin 'She'kspere' Briggs
Recorded at Triangle Sound Studios, Atlanta
Duration: 2:58

'Hell Wit Ya,' co-written by P!nk, is a fiery breakup anthem that dismisses a disrespectful ex-boyfriend. In addition to being a member of the R&B girl group Xscape, Kandi co-wrote two Billboard Hot 100 #1 hits with She'kspere while working on her debut album. 'No Scrubs,' the lead single from *FanMail*, TLC's third album, reached #1 in April 1999, followed by 'Bills, Bills, Bills', the lead single from Destiny's Child's second album *The Writing's on the Wall*, which topped the chart in July.

In 2012, P!nk reflected on 'Hell Wit Ya' to *The Los Angeles Times*, saying: 'What is this song?! I can't even remember what the chorus is! Oh my gosh... She'kspere. This was with Kandi. I was like 2 years old. I was so mad at my ex-boyfriend during this whole record.'

'Most Girls'

Written by Kenneth 'Babyface' Edmonds and Damon Thomas
Produced by Kenneth 'Babyface' Edmonds
Recorded at Brandon's Way Recording, Los Angeles
Duration: 4:59 (Radio Edit: 4:14)
Released as a single in June 2000
Music video directed by Dave Meyers
Chart Position: USA: 4; Canada: 2; UK: 5; Australia: 1

'Most Girls' was written by Babyface and Damon Thomas, who wrote 'These Are the Times' by R&B group Dru Hill. Coincidentally, as P!nk was making her debut, their lead singer Sisqó was launching his solo career, leading to both artists appearing as support acts during select dates of *NSync's *No Strings Attached* tour.

In an appearance on *The Queen Latifah Show*, P!nk said: 'Pop culture, the whole bling-bling thing, is putting a lot of both negative and positive messages out there. But if you listen to my lyrics, that's exactly what I'm talking about in "Most Girls." I'm not like most girls. Most girls want a man with money, cars, and all that. But I'm saying I'm not most girls. I tell girls through my music, don't be like most girls. Care about how a man treats you, not what he can give you, because you can get it for yourself.'

Directed by Dave Meyers, the music video for 'Most Girls' stars P!nk as a kickboxer training in the gym and fighting. She also performed the song at the 2002 American Music Awards, with an introduction including lookalikes of Britney Spears, Christina Aguilera, and Jessica Simpson.

In an interview after the awards, P!nk said: 'I had three lookalikes on stage with me. People were seriously pissed at me because they said, "That's our princess! How could you go against our princess?" That is America's dream. But that's exactly what I was saying, I don't ever want to be America's dream. My point was to make a joke of the entire situation.'

'Most Girls' charted higher than its predecessor in the UK and USA, where it had a CD single release backed by remixes from Skribble and Anthony. It became P!nk's first #1 single in Australia and charted at #24 in the Netherlands; however, the single was not released in many parts of Europe, including Germany and France.

'There You Go'

Written by Kevin 'She'kspere' Briggs, Kandi Burruss and Alecia 'P!nk' Moore
Produced by Kevin 'She'kspere' Briggs
Recorded at Triangle Sound Studios, Atlanta
Duration: 3:23
Released as a single in January 2000
Music video directed by Dave Meyers
Chart Position: USA: 7; Canada: 6; UK: 6; Australia: 2; Germany: 65

P!nk's debut single, 'There You Go,' addresses an ex-boyfriend who refuses to move on. The second of two collaborations with She'kspere and Kandi that appear on the album, given the duo's massive success with TLC and Destiny's Child, it was the obvious choice for the first single.

Promoting the single, P!nk told MTV: 'I was pissed off when I wrote it, again. I'd been with the same person for about four years, and I was really mad at him. Everybody wants the upper hand in a relationship and I figured, "Guess what? I get to put it on the radio. I'm just gonna write a song about you, and then the whole world's gonna know." But we're fine now. I'd always wanted to have the upper hand in that relationship and the only way I could have that was through the song.'

P!nk collaborated with Dave Meyers, who had previously directed videos for Ginuwine, Kid Rock, Juvenile, LL Cool J and Eve, on the music video. This marked the beginning of a long-lasting creative relationship, which P!nk predicted when she told MTV: 'Dave Meyers is the best. He is the only director I ever want to work with in my life. We were all exhausted, but we had so much fun. I got to crash a motorcycle through somebody's window. I crashed two motorcycles. That's why I'm wearing pants the whole video. I had cuts and bruises all over my legs. I scared the crap out of everybody. They had insurance policies all over the place!"

In a 2019 interview with *Billboard* magazine, P!nk revealed she was high on cannabis during the video shoot: 'I smoked a lot of weed and Dave Meyers kept coming up to me and saying, "Can you wait to smoke that next blunt before the beauty shot?" I was like, "What do you mean?" He was like, "I really want you to be able to open your eyes." I was like, "My eyes are open!" I think this is the prettiest I've ever looked and will ever look.'

'There You Go' was a commercial success and instantly established P!nk as an artist. It became the sixteenth biggest single of the year in the USA, was certified Platinum in Australia, and sold over 200,000 copies in the UK.

'You Make Me Sick'

Written by Anthony President, Brainz Dimilo and Marthony 'Mark' Tabb
Produced by Kenneth 'Babyface' Edmonds, Anthony President and Brainz Dimilo
Recorded at Brandon's Way Recording, Los Angeles
Duration: 4:10
Released as a single in December 2000
Music video directed by Dave Meyers
Chart Position: USA: 33; UK: 9; Australia: 25; Germany: 88

'You Make Me Sick,' the third and final single to be taken from *Can't Take Me Home*, is a slick R&B track that finds P!nk caught between desire and self-control, acknowledging her attraction to a man she knows is toxic.

Her third collaboration with Dave Meyers, P!nk told *NME* magazine that the music video was a fun and stress-relieving experience: 'All that glass you see break? I got to do that every take. I had more glass, every take. I'm like, "I could get used to this!"'

In a 2023 interview with *Vulture*, P!nk reflected on the video: 'That was my third video ever. Mario, my co-star in it, was a really good friend of mine, so I felt comfortable with him. I mean, he's the guy who would come over and help me hang curtains back in the day. He was just a sweetheart, and he's super-hot also. I'm like, "Look, my friend's cute. Let's use him." And I got to destroy a mall, and there was a mall Santa. It was sort of *War of the Roses*, which is a movie from 1989 that I love, and it's kind of like my marriage. We're not that violent, but we want to be. It was a fun thing; there was an upside-down car. Director Dave Meyers is just a genius. It's crazy the stuff we get to do. I feel like a stuntwoman most of the time.'

'You Make Me Sick' reached the UK top ten, and top 30 in Australia, backed by remixes from Dub Conspiracy and El-B.

'Let Me Let You Know'

Written by Christopher 'Tricky' Stewart, Sean 'Sep' Hall and Robin Thicke
Produced by Christopher 'Tricky' Stewart and Sean 'Sep' Hall
Includes elements of 'Cease the Bombing' written by Neal Creque and performed by Grant Greene
Recorded at Boss Productions, Atlanta
Duration: 4:45

The album's first ballad, 'Let Me Let You Know' was originally recorded by Choice for inclusion on their debut album at the same time as 'Don't Go Breakin' My Heart'. P!nk re-recorded the song for the album, adding new backing vocals from Nycolia 'Tye-V' Turman, while keeping the original production.

'Let Me Let You Know' was co-written by Robin Thicke, prior to the launch of his solo career and many years before achieving global success in 2013 with 'Blurred Lines' featuring T.I. and Pharrell.

Choice's recording of the song leaked online, along with the rest of their unreleased album, in 2022.

'Love is Such a Crazy Thing'

Written by Lamont Maxwell, Daron Jones, Jason Boyd, Marvin Scandrick, Michael Keith, Quinnes Parker and Courtney Sills
Produced by Lamont Maxwell and Daron Jones
Recorded at Doppler Studios, Atlanta
Duration: 5:13

'Love is Such a Crazy Thing' is another slower moment on *Can't Take Me Home*, with P!nk singing about the emotional highs and lows of falling in and out of love. Lamont Maxwell and Daron Jones co-wrote and produced the song, having previously worked with R&B group 112 on their 1996 debut album.

Like 'Let Me Let You Know,' 'Love Is Such a Crazy Thing' was initially recorded for *Choices*. Whilst P!nk re-recorded her vocals for this version, both Chrissy Conway and Sheri Flanagan are credited as background vocalists on the track. Though commercially unavailable, Choice's original recording was released on a LaFace Records promo CD in July 1998, entitled *The Platinum Family: Black Music Month Sampler*. Their original recording leaked online in full in 2022.

'Private Show'

Written by Carsten 'Soulshock' Schack, Kenneth Karlin, Andrea Martin, Ivan Matias
Produced by Carsten 'Soulshock' Schack and Kenneth Karlin
Recorded at Record Plant, Los Angeles
Duration: 4:15

'Private Show' is a collaboration with Danish producers Soulshock and Karlin, described by *Arena* magazine in 2001 as 'probably the best R&B producers in the world.' In addition to writing and producing the USA Billboard Hot 100 #1 singles 'Before You Walk Out of My Life' by Monica in 1995 and 'Heartbreak Hotel' by Whitney Houston featuring Faith Evans and Kelly Price in 1998, the duo also worked with 2Pac.

'Can't Take Me Home'

Written by The Specialists (Harold Frasier), Steve 'Rhythm' Clarke, Alecia 'P!nk' Moore and Lafferon 'Boo' Miles
Produced by The Specialists (Harold Frasier) and Steve 'Rhythm' Clarke
Recorded at Soundtrack Recording Studios, New York
Duration: 3:38

The album's title track, 'Can't Take Me Home,' expresses P!nk's frustration with a boyfriend who is only interested in a physical relationship despite claiming to have deeper feelings for her. Originally titled 'Can't Take Me Home to Mama,' after inspiring the album's name, it was abridged. Lafferon Miles was omitted from the album booklet credits but is registered as a co-writer on the song's BMI and ASCAP registrations.

P!nk arranged this song herself and described it as one of her top three songs on the album, telling MTV: 'I wrote it when I was very pissed off. I was with someone of a different race, and he didn't want to take me home to his mother because he didn't think that his mother would approve of me, basically.'

The Specialists filed a lawsuit against P!nk and Sony Music in 2013, following an administrative error in 2004, which resulted in them not receiving royalties for this song or 'Hiccup,' as they had not supplied valid contact details for a representative. The Supreme Court of the State of New York dismissed the case later that year.

'Stop Falling'

Written by Will Baker, Pete Woodruff and Alecia 'P!nk' Moore
Produced by Will Baker and Edward 'Pete' Woodruff
Recorded at Doppler Studios, Atlanta and Purple Dragon Studios, Atlanta
Duration: 5:52

'Stop Falling' is another of the few ballads on *Can't Take Me Home*, written by P!nk with childhood friends Will Baker and Pete Woodruff, who worked together on the USA Billboard Hot 100 #1 single 'Lately' for the girl group Divine in 1998.

P!nk described the song to MTV, saying: 'It's a ballad I wrote about being too young. I'm not looking for love. I'm not looking for all the stress that it brings. I'm looking for better days, and either give me everything or nothing at all.'

Reflecting on the album in later interviews, P!nk has continued to reference 'Stop Falling' as one of her favourites, telling *Vulture* in 2017: 'I wrote it all myself, basically, with the help of a piano player. I was 18. I loved singing that song, and I love that vocal. That was a young vocal that I liked.'

She added in 2023 that the song helped her begin to discover her musical voice, saying: 'I think "Stop Falling" on the first record was that first moment where I started figuring out who I was. There's a purity and immaturity to it that's kind of painful to listen to. I feel very motherly toward my younger self. I wish the me now had been around for her then. I wish I could give her a hug. That girl really needed it.'

'Do What U Do'

Written by P.A. (James 'Mello' Hollins, Kawan 'K.P.' Prather and Maurice 'Big Reese' Sinclair) and Ezekiel Lewis
Produced by P.A. (James 'Mello' Hollins, Kawan 'K.P.' Prather and Maurice 'Big Reese' Sinclair)
Recorded at Patchwerk Recording Studio, Atlanta and Doppler Studio, Atlanta
Duration: 3:58

'Do What U Do' is an upbeat track about being authentically yourself, co-written and co-produced by Southern hip-hop trio P.A. (an abbreviation of Parental Advisory), who released two albums in the 1990s and were part of the Dungeon Family alongside Outkast.

Although P!nk did not co-write the song, it expresses her anti-homophobic views in the line, 'boy-girl, girl-girl, boy-boy, whatever, you should do what you do,' helping establish her as a prominent LGBTQIA+ ally.

'Hiccup'

Written by The Specialists (Harold Frasier), Steve 'Rhythm' Clarke), Alecia 'P!nk' Moore and DeLouie Avant
Produced by The Specialists (Harold Frasier) and Steve 'Rhythm' Clarke
Recorded at Soundtrack Recording Studios, New York
Duration: 3:32

'Hiccup' is a second collaboration with The Specialists and Steve 'Rhythm' Clarke, written about the frustration of miscommunication in a relationship. Alongside 'Can't Take Me Home,' 'Hiccup' was also included in The Specialists' 2013 lawsuit against P!nk and Sony Music.

Talking to *Yahoo! Music*, P!nk said The Notorious B.I.G. inspired the song and that it was initially a joke. She said: 'I was listening to Biggie and he says something about females - that they're irritating like the hiccups, or something like that - and I wrote a song called "Hiccup" because I was so inspired by that. I thought that was so funny and so cool, the way he did that in his rhyme. I was like, "Wow!" So I wrote a song about hiccups. I was joking when I wrote it. It was a joke to me.'

'Is It Love'

Written by The Specialists (Harold Frasier), Steve 'Rhythm' Clarke, Alecia 'P!nk' Moore and Aaron Phillips
Produced by Steve 'Rhythm' Clarke
Co-Produced by Alecia 'P!nk' Moore
Recorded at Unique Recording Studio, New York
Duration: 3:38

'Is It Love' closes *Can't Take Me Home* with a mid-tempo moment of reflection, as P!nk questions a relationship, asking, 'Is it love, or just a curse?'

In addition to co-producing the track, P!nk arranged 'Is It Love' with Aaron Phillips. Phillips went on to co-write Demi Lovato's hit single, 'Heart Attack,' in 2013.

Other Songs

'Play How You Want'
Cuban Link featuring P!nk

Written by The Neptunes (Pharrell Williams and Chad Hug) and Felix 'Cuban Link' Delgado
Produced by Felix 'Cuban Link' Delgado
Duration: 3:39

Cuban Link is a Cuban-American rapper and original member of the hip-hop collective Terror Squad, who disbanded in 2000 following the death of Big Pun. At the time, Cuban had finished his debut album for Atlantic Records, entitled *24K*, featuring a duet with P!nk entitled 'Play How You Want.' The album's release was cancelled due to label politics involving fellow Terror Squad member Fat Joe, who had signed Cuban.

'Play How You Want,' co-written by The Neptunes—Pharrell Williams and Chad Hugo—was issued as a promo 12" single in 2000, featuring P!nk singing the hook. She sings: 'It's P!nk and Cuban Link, this is the club with a Latin swing, so if you with it baby, blaze up a blunt, drink till you're drunk, ain't no rules where we're from.'

The album leaked online, as a promotional CD-R acetate had been sent to certain press outlets. Cuban spoke about 'Play How You Want' to 97.7 Outlaw FM in 2022, saying: 'The one with P!nk, that was a crazy joint.'

'Nobody Liver'
Benzino featuring P!nk

Written by Hangmen 3 (Jeffrey Neal, John Bynoe and Raymond 'Benzino' Scott) and Alecia 'P!nk' Moore
Produced by Hangmen 3 (Jeffrey Neal, John Bynoe and Raymond 'Benzino' Scott)
Duration: 2:45

Before becoming a reality TV personality known for appearing on *Love and Hip Hop: Atlanta* and *Marriage Boot Camp*, Raymond 'Benzino' Scott was a founding member of rap groups, including the Almighty RSO and Made Men. He recorded his debut solo album, *The Benzino Project*, over two years, being released in October 2001.

P!nk co-wrote and appears on 'Nobody Liver,' performing the song's chorus.

Unreleased Songs

'We're Thru'

Written by Carl E. 'Chucky' Thompson, Phillip Aaron and Alecia 'P!nk' Moore
Produced by Carl E. 'Chucky' Thompson
Duration: 3:37

Chucky Thompson produced 'We're Thru' for *Can't Take Me Home*, having previously worked with some of P!nk's favourite performers, including Mary J. Blige on her influential album, *My Life*. The song is a duet with Dante Thomas, who released his debut album, *Fly*, in 2001 through Elektra Records.

P!nk recorded a second version of the song with Preston Creed, who was also trying to launch his career at the same time as her; a demo of this version of the track leaked online in 2004, while the original recording with Dante Thomas leaked in 2011.

Chucky Thompson sadly passed away from COVID-19, aged 53, in August 2021.

'Streets of Philly'

Written by Will Baker, Pete Woodruff and Alecia 'P!nk' Moore
Produced by Jonathan 'Mookie' Morant

Registered on ASCAP, 'Streets of Philly' is reportedly a very personal song that P!nk presented to producer Mookie before her debut album was completed.

In his book, *The Happy Has Been: A Memoir of Music and Life in 6 Degrees*, Mookie says: 'She said "Okay, Mook, let's make some noise."' P!nk had an idea she'd been holding onto since first getting her record deal. 'I have the lyrics/ melody for a song I wrote about growing up in Philadelphia, 'Streets of Philly." She suggested a track with a raw beat that still needed to be edgy, 'Can we do guitars?' That's all I needed to hear. I jumped up and onto the drum machine, programming a hard-hitting beat, and then I left the rest to her in the vocal booth.'

The song is currently unavailable to the public.

Catalogue Registrations

'Final Goodbye'

Written by Steve 'Rhythm' Clarke and Alecia 'P!nk' Moore

'The Truth Hurts'

Written by Steve 'Rhythm' Clarke and Alecia 'P!nk' Moore

'Why'

Written by The Specialists (Harold Frasier), Steve 'Rhythm' Clarke, Alecia 'P!nk' Moore and Lafferon 'Boo' Miles

'Last Laugh'

Written by Anthony President and Alecia 'P!nk' Moore

'I'm No Scrub'
Written by Anthony President and Alecia 'P!nk' Moore

'Stop Me'
Written by Rodney 'Darkchild' Jerkins, Brian Smith and Alecia 'P!nk' Moore

'Puppy Dog'
Written by Will Baker, Pete Woodruff and Alecia 'P!nk' Moore

'Mama Said'
Written by Anthony Dent and Teron Beal

3

M!ssundaztood (2001)

Released:	20 November 2001 (USA and Canada) 26 November 2001 (UK) 3 December 2001 (Australia) 25 January 2002 (Europe) 28 January 2002 (UK) 26 November 2002 (USA and Canada—Deluxe CD/DVD)
Chart Position:	USA: 6 Canada: 5 UK: 2 Australia: 14 Germany: 5

After the success of *Can't Take Me Home*, P!nk began to overhaul key elements of her career, developing a clearer vision of what she wanted to achieve and the kind of artist she aspired to become. In 2001, P!nk met Roger Davies, renowned for managing Australian artist Olivia Newton-John, as well as his transformative work with Tina Turner, establishing her as a global touring sensation. Having previously been managed by her father, P!nk asked Davies and former Bros bass player Craig Logan, who worked alongside him, to share management duties and guide her into this new era.

In addition to the change in management, P!nk deliberately expanded her sound from the R&B of her debut to a more pop-rock sound, collaborating with producers of her choice, such as Dallas Austin and Linda Perry. The result was *M!ssundaztood*, a massive global success that marked her breakthrough as an artist showcasing songs that reflected her struggles and emotions.

Sessions for the album started with Dallas Austin, who had worked extensively with L.A. Reid and LaFace Records artists such as TLC, for whom he wrote and produced two USA Billboard Hot 100 #1 singles—'Unpretty' and 'Creep.' P!nk and Austin had a session to work on songs for her debut album, but Austin cancelled after one session, saying: 'I don't feel this kind of music for you.' P!nk knew he had also worked with Madonna on her 1994 album, *Bedtime Stories* and was determined to reunite with him for *M!ssundaztood*. She assumed he thought she was 'a little troublemaker with bright fuchsia hair and a bad attitude.'

Austin told VladTV: 'She was like, "You're going to do my album this time, just like we said the first time. And I'm ready to do whatever you want to do. And I'm not leaving until you do the record." And I said, "Well, I know what it should sound like." We did "Just Like a Pill" and another, first. L.A. didn't like them. He said, "We can't take her without it being R&B." I think finally, he played "Just Like a Pill" for a few people at the label, and they were like, "Are you crazy? The song's amazing." And then he called me back.'

After setting out the album's identity with Austin, which P!nk described as 'real music you can live or die to, songs that make you want to stand up and change your life,' she set about working with one of her dream collaborators.

In a letter posted on her website to fans, P!nk wrote: '4 Non Blondes' *Bigger, Better, Faster, More!* was one of my favourite albums and I used to sit on the corner in Doylestown with my two friends that played guitar and we'd sing, "What's Up?", "Drifting" and "Spaceman". Sometimes we'd get hassled by the cops – once we got arrested, I never understood the whole "disturbing the peace" thing. The lead singer of that band was a girl named Linda Perry, and that's who I called.'

Talking to *Rolling Stone* magazine, P!nk said she found Perry's number in a contact book owned by make-up artist Billy B and called her directly. She said: 'I left her a ten-minute message about how much I loved her and how she owes me because I got arrested singing her music out of my window at 3:30am in the morning, and how I'm gonna stalk her if she doesn't return my call. She called back five minutes later and said, "You're fuckin' crazy - you should come over." So I jumped in my truck. When I got there, we sat and looked at each other for a while and didn't know what to do. Then she went to the piano, I picked up a microphone, and "Eventually" was written five minutes later. That's how the next month and a half went. I just didn't leave. I camped out on her furry rug. We had a goal of writing twenty-five songs. We got to twenty. She became a really, really good friend, and I treasure her. You don't meet a lot of people in L.A. who are so raw and honest.'

Perry told *The Face* magazine in 2002: 'She wanted to make a more honest, open record, to express her feelings more clearly and to put music to it that wasn't like what was going on. That's what caught my ear. I thought that was a pretty bold step. She's the one that kept me confident because when she was singing it, I believed every fucking word.'

In an interview with *Rolling Stone* magazine in 2019, Perry recalled that she told P!nk the album was going to be a success. She said: 'We were sitting one day, and I said, "This album's going to be huge." P!nk laughed at me. But I was like, "It's going to be a groundbreaking record and change things for you." She didn't believe me. But we completely changed her format, and it worked.'

As well as Perry, P!nk brought producer Damon Elliott, Dionne Warwick's son, on board to make her 'beats bang.' She said: 'During a *Moulin Rouge* rehearsal, I met a producer named Damon Elliott. He was with Mýa, and we just clicked right away and decided to make some music together. I also had a lot of fun whooping his ass at pool – he'll try and tell you he beat me, but don't listen to him, he's lying!'

After writing songs with Austin and Perry, P!nk had a session with Scott Storch, who had produced some of her favourite songs, including 'You Got Me' by the Roots featuring Erykah Badu and 'Let Me Blow Your Mind' by Eve and Gwen Stefani. In the letter on her website, she said: 'Scott is a sweetheart from my hometown, Philadelphia. The song he produced for me is "Family Portrait". That particular song is closest to me (although they all are). My mum cried for 4 days when she listened to it. There was this big gap of denial in my family over the whole divorce thing. I'm sure it was the same for some of you out there. I suppose I wanted to talk about it, and through a song is the best way I know how.'

Despite being reassured by his team after they heard 'Just Like a Pill,' L.A. Reid remained reticent about the album's direction. Talking to *The Face* magazine, P!nk added: 'He thought I was abandoning my fans, and "if it ain't broke, don't fix it." What I'm doing is natural. I haven't changed who I am, I haven't changed my beliefs, I haven't changed anything other than producers. So, this is what I'm going to do, and if you guys don't like it, then I'd like to go back to work in McDonald's. Because I will not make another album that is producer-driven, and that is a fact. I won't do it.' Reid ultimately caved in, with P!nk recalling he said, 'Fine, I'm going to give you the opportunity to fail.'

M!ssundaztood was officially completed in August 2001, with promotional photos shot by controversial photographer Terry Richardson. 'Get the Party Started' was released as the first single in October—just a month after the horrific terror attacks of 11 September. On her website, P!nk wrote: 'Recent events have reminded me how precious and short life is, and how petty a lot of the things we worry about are. Sometimes it takes a tragedy to bring us together. Sometimes it just takes music.'

Following the attacks, international plans for *M!ssundaztood* were postponed until early 2002. It was released in the USA, Canada and Australia before the end of 2001, with import copies shipped to stores across Europe to satisfy fan demand. As a result, P!nk's lead European label, BMG UK and Ireland, decided to reorder the album's tracklist and add 'Catch-22,' which was only available via digital download using the original album's enhanced CD functionality. The revised order was used for most international editions of the album, even becoming the standard in Australia when the album was re-pressed in early

2002. However, the original running order was reinstated when the album was issued on 12" vinyl for the first time in 2017.

M!ssundaztood went on to become P!nk's best-selling album to date, selling over 12 million copies worldwide, and is certified 5x Platinum in the USA, 5x Platinum in Canada, 6x Platinum in the UK, 4x Platinum in Australia, and 2x Platinum in Germany. It was nominated for Album of the Year at the 2002 Billboard Music Awards, Best Album at the MTV Europe Music Awards 2002, and Best International Album at the BRIT Awards in 2003. It also earned a Best Pop Vocal Album nomination at the 45th Grammy Awards in 2003.

Reflecting on the album to *Variety* magazine in 2019, P!nk said: 'That album was a huge turning point in my life. But before it came out, I was being told that it's going to completely fail. Still, I was stoked to be given the opportunity to fail... *M!ssundaztood* was my life's work. Then it comes out and sells 15 million records. I'm, like, "Holy shit!"'

Album Tracks

'M!SSUNDAZTOOD'

Written by Linda Perry and Alecia 'P!nk' Moore
Produced by Linda Perry and Damon Elliott
Recorded at The Enterprise, Burbank
Duration: 3:36

M!ssundaztood opens with the title track, a collaboration with both Linda Perry and Damon Elliott, the son of Dionne Warwick, who met P!nk whilst she was working on 'Lady Marmalade.' Elliott, who had previously worked with Destiny's Child and Flesh-n-Bone from the group Bone Thugs-n-Harmony, said he and P!nk became closer after the video shoot. He spoke to the *Hollywood at Home* podcast in 2022, saying: 'After working with her on vocals and stuff, we kind of fell in love as a producer-and-artist relationship and spent every breathing moment together.'

P!nk told MTV that the song reflects how she feels in the music industry, which is why she named the album after it. She said: 'I named the album *M!ssundaztood* because I feel very much like I'm misunderstood at times. I say the wrong things. I tell the truth, which tends to get me in trouble. And I'm a very eclectic person, so I feel that's misunderstood as well. Everything I do, I just... I've always said that since I was small.'

The song opens with a spoken word intro, where P!nk says, 'Go Damon, Go Linda, Go P!nk.' She freestyles over the end of the track, which Elliott infers sounds like she is constipated, to which P!nk responds, referring to a laxative brand in the USA: 'No, this ain't no damn Ex-Lax commercial, this is my first single, man!'

'Don't Let Me Get Me'

Written by Dallas Austin and Alecia 'P!nk' Moore
Produced by Dallas Austin
Recorded at Pinetree Studios, Miami Beach and DARP Studios, Atlanta
Duration: 3:31
Released as a single in February 2002
Music video directed by Dave Meyers
Chart Position: USA: 8; Canada: 20; UK: 6; Australia: 8; Germany: 10

'Don't Let Me Get Me' is P!nk's first collaboration with Dallas Austin, exploring P!nk's battles with anxiety and self-doubt, and her frustration with the music industry and media. She references L.A. Reid, who signed her, and Britney Spears, to whom the media compared her.

P!nk sings: 'L.A. told me, "You'll be a pop star, all you have to change is everything you are",' with Reid telling VH1: 'I absolutely did not say that to her, but she was poking fun at me. And I think she does prove a point here, you can be a popstar, and have a brain, and have some creativity, and have some depth, and have some feelings, and not be afraid to bear those feelings.'

Talking to *Rolling Stone*, P!nk explained the exact elements that Reid and the label tried to change. She said: 'My outspokenness and my eating manners. I'd gone to my first industry dinner, where they pay $8000 a plate. The next day I got a call from the label asking me to take etiquette classes. They tried to convince me that it's better to know the rules and then break them. I said, "If I know them and break them, I'll just have a guilt trip."'

With Britney Spears becoming the most prominent female pop act to have emerged from the era, she was a consistent reference for the media when talking about new and emerging acts, even though P!nk was quite clearly a very different artist. P!nk sings: 'Tired of being compared to damn Britney Spears, she's so pretty, that just ain't me.' Talking to *Women's Health* magazine in 2019, P!nk said: 'I've always said I like Britney. I swear to God, I've stuck up for Britney since the beginning. She and I have talked about it. My point was, "Stop comparing me to her, because we're different animals."'

Chosen as the second single from *M!ssundaztood*, the music video for 'Don't Let Me Get Me' was shot in January 2002 in Los Angeles and Malibu, with scenes of P!nk at school shot at the Susan Miller Dorsey High School. Directed by Dave Meyers, L.A. Reid does not appear but is portrayed by actor Ted Lyde.

Talking to MTV at the video shoot, Meyers said: 'What's absolutely unique about P!nk is she's done every single one of her videos since the beginning of her career with me. Now that she's really starting to define herself as an artist, her ideas are getting more and more specific. So, the concept of the video is kind of a collaboration between me and P!nk. I really wanted it to take place in school We're taking 15 scenes or so from P!nk's life, starting back in high school volleyball and moving our way through a classroom and into L.A. Reed's office, the girls' locker room… the song is the first time that P!nk's really been vulnerable.'

P!nk added: 'The song is basically about feeling inadequate and wanting to get away from yourself. Any truth is good, whether it hurts or not, so me looking in the mirror standing next to what most people would call a "perfect girl", I have those feelings - I think every girl does - and it's important for girls to know that I'm up here, I'm doing my thing. I am a strong individual; I've gained that strength over the years... but I still look at my myself in the mirror and try to pat my hips...'

'Don't Let Me Get Me' became another global hit for P!nk, charting in the top 10 in many territories and becoming her first #1 single on the USA Billboard Pop Airplay (previously known as Mainstream Top 40) chart. Despite the song's success, P!nk told *The Los Angeles Times* in 2012 that she hated performing the song. She said: 'I wish I could burn that song and never sing it again.'

'Just Like a Pill'

Written by Dallas Austin and Alecia 'P!nk' Moore
Produced by Dallas Austin
Recorded at Pinetree Studios, Miami Beach
Duration: 3:57
Released as a single in June 2002
Music video directed by Francis Lawrence
Chart Position: USA: 8; Canada: 4; UK: 1; Germany: 2

A dark and emotionally charged song about addiction and unhealthy relationships, 'Just Like a Pill' was the first song P!nk finished with Dallas Austin and one of the first songs she completed for *M!ssundaztood*. Released as the third single, it became P!nk's first solo UK #1 single and has become one of her most recognisable hits.

Dallas Austin told *Songwriter Universe* that his personal experiences inspired the song: 'It was really about me and my ex at the time. We were out there taking pills that made you feel good... and when we broke up, instead of that pill making me feel better, it made me feel ill.'

P!nk shot the music video for the song with director Francis Lawrence in April 2002. Talking to VH1, she said: 'This one's very dark and artsy, and I have black hair, which is very fun. I loved it.' However, the video featured an elephant called Nelly, which made P!nk uncomfortable, leading her to vow never to feature animals in her videos again, strengthening her engagement with People for the Ethical Treatment of Animals (PETA).

Appearing on MuchMusic Canada, P!nk elaborated: 'We used an elephant called Nelly that I feel really bad about because I'll never do it again. I promise I'll never do it again. Nelly came with her trainers, and I got into a fight with the trainer because we're in this warehouse and it was hard-floored, and Nelly had to keep getting down on her knees so I could kneel in front of her and I could tell she wasn't enjoying it. And I was like, "this is so wrong, this is so wrong, please let her go. We'll come up with something else. I can't have Nelly in pain like this. Please let her go." And they wouldn't let her go.'

The song was censored for its release as a single, removing the reference to the pain-relief opiate morphine, replacing it with a repeat of 'life support.' Additionally, 'bitch' was replaced with an edit of the word 'switch', cut to sound like 'witch.' Despite the single's success, it was not released in Australia, where the label opted to send the song to radio to boost album sales.

In 2012, P!nk reflected on the song in an interview with *The Los Angeles Times*. She said: 'This was with Dallas Austin, in Miami, we wrote this. The first thing that comes to mind with this? When I used to be on drugs, I should write a song about it. When you're young, you think your ideas are so clever. I loved the video, I… loved it. Still one of my favourites. I dyed my hair black. My hair has to match my heart. So dramatic!"

'Just Like a Pill' has been covered by other artists, including Cascada, who recorded a Eurodance version of it for their 2007 album *Perfect Day*. In December 2013, Canadian duo Tegan and Sara performed a live cover of the song for P!nk at Billboard's Women in Music event, held in her honour.

'Get the Party Started'

Written by Linda Perry
Produced by Linda Perry
Recorded at LP Studios, Sherman Oaks and Larrabee Studios, Los Angeles
Duration: 3:12
Released as a single in October 2001
Music video directed by Dave Meyers
Chart Position: USA: 4; Canada: 11; UK: 2; Australia: 1; Germany: 2

'Get the Party Started' was written by Linda Perry while she was learning how to use recording software ProTools, taking inspiration from the 'current' sounds she was hearing on radio and MTV. Deciding the song sounded more 'pop' than would fit her solo record, she sent it to Madonna's A&R team, who rejected it.

Describing how the song was written in *Backstory Song*, Perry said: 'I was just like, I'm going to think of every cliché possible. The words just showed up. And then I did go back after I laid a vocal down and then I started writing down what I was saying because I was just saying so much craziness. And then I made it make sense and then I just lay down the vocal. I was laughing because I knew it was a hit. I was just like, "this is so awesome", because I didn't think at all. To me, I was just playing and having fun. I wasn't trying to write a song, I was just trying to understand what this equipment did. And then literally a week later, get a phone call from this girl, P!nk. I went and met her and we just got along so well. And then I left her with "Get the Party Started". I said, "Hey, I just wrote this song. I don't know if you're interested. But here." And I gave her an MP3, and then she called me probably three or four days later and L.A. Reid said, "It looks like we have our first single." And then that's kind of how we started. And then she came here to my house. We just wrote like 15 or 16 songs and eight of them ended up on the album.'

Talking to Planet Rock TV in the UK, P!nk said: 'It was just infectious. I loved it. I needed the party song. It was right after 11 September. Everybody was depressed. I was like, "This is it, this is now, this has got to come out." It's the perfect transformation between *Can't Take Me Home* and *M!ssundaztood*. It's the bridge I need. "Give this song to me now, or I will kill you!" So I got it! It's definitely much more me than it is her, it's just funny!'

In an interview with MTV announcing the album's release, she described the song as 'techno-ish, with a hip-hoppy attitude. It's all about what happens on the way to the club instead of what happens at the club.' The song's lyrics were the subject of controversy, as rumours abounded that P!nk was singing, 'I'm coming up', in reference to taking ecstasy. P!nk was asked about the reference in a 2017 interview with *Q* magazine in the UK but was unable to clarify. She said: 'You'd have to ask Linda Perry if it's about ecstasy. I don't know what she meant with it. I still don't know if it's "I'm coming out" or "I'm coming up" - I don't even know what I sang.'

P!nk reunited with Dave Meyers for the music video, shot in late September in Los Angeles, with Perry making a guest appearance as a bartender. In the video, P!nk is shown getting ready for a party and overcoming obstacles to get to the venue, such as stealing and falling off a skateboard after her car's tank empties and being refused entry. When she finally arrives, she is joined by dancers Georvohn Lambert and Kevin Federline, who later married and had two children with Britney Spears. The video won P!nk her first solo MTV Video Music Awards in 2002, receiving Best Female Video and Best Dance Video, with her performing 'Just Like a Pill' at the ceremony.

'Get the Party Started' became P!nk's biggest hit thus far, reaching #1 in Australia and just missing the top spot in the UK, Germany, Austria and Switzerland. Climbing to #4 on the USA Billboard Hot 100, it became her joint highest-charting single, matching 'Most Girls,' and being certified Gold. At the MTV Europe Music Awards 2002, it won Best Song and was nominated for Best Female Pop Vocal Performance at the 45th Grammy Awards in 2003.

A remix of 'Get the Party Started' by Rockwilder, who had worked with P!nk on 'Lady Marmalade,' featuring Redman, was included on the single, sampling 'Sweet Dreams (Are Made of These)' by Eurythmics. Adaptations of this remix have gone on to become the version used on P!nk's tours, including the *I'm Not Dead* tour in 2006–2007 and the *Summer Carnival* in 2023–2024, where C+C Music Factor's 'Gonna Make You Sweat' was also incorporated.

'Respect' featuring Scratch

Written by Linda Perry and Alecia 'P!nk' Moore
Produced by Linda Perry and Damon Elliott
Recorded at LP Studios, Sherman Oaks and Sony Studios, Santa Monica

Duration: 3:25
Scratch appears courtesy of MCA Records

'Respect' is a funky, up-tempo anthem of female empowerment and self-respect, with a feminist message of reducing jealousy and envy between women. Scratch, best known for being a member of The Roots, appears on the track, using his voice and loop machines to replicate the sounds of turntablism.

Talking to VH1 about how she gained the respect of others, which inspired the song, P!nk said: 'I started early with everything in my life. Being out in the streets and being with a lot of different kinds of people - you just learn the hard way. And I've always been a tomboy, so I had the privilege of growing up with guys and not having to be their girlfriend, so they didn't have anything to hide from me. So, I got to know the real deal and what they talk about, and how they look at women and blah blah blah. I learned the mentality. I don't agree with a lot of it, but I think a lot of women - you know the way we portray ourselves - we only get as much respect as we command.'

P!nk had a longstanding friendship with Scratch, having been 'the hook girl' for his act, Scratch 'n' Smoove. In December 2007, he filed a lawsuit against her, using his legal name of Kyle Jones, claiming he was not paid for his work on 'Respect.' In the case, he admitted that a final fee had not been agreed on, with a spokesperson for P!nk's management company saying: 'There's nothing to say on this matter, as it is an unjustified lawsuit.' The case was settled outside of court.

'18 Wheeler'

Written by Dallas Austin and Alecia 'P!nk' Moore
Produced by Dallas Austin
Recorded at Pinetree Studios, Miami Beach and DARP Studios, Atlanta
Duration: 3:44

'18 Wheeler' is a rock-infused anthem co-written and produced by Dallas Austin, describing P!nk's resilience. The song is censored on all editions of the album, removing the word 'fuck' at the end of 'I won't give a...'

In the song, P!nk sings the lyric, 'you can hang me like a slave', which Austin says she was apprehensive about singing. In an interview with VladTV, he said: 'When we did "18 Wheeler", there's a line that says, "You can hang me like a slave, I'll go on the ground." She's like, "You're going to get me killed out here." I said, "No, no, no, no, I'm just giving you enough edge to be different than everybody else."'

P!nk also affirms, 'You know I'm not that kind of girl that'll lay there, let you cum first.' *Rolling Stone* magazine asked her about this lyric and questioned what kind of girl she is. She said: 'I know what I want. And I'm not giving out any favours. I got to get mine. That's the kind of girl I am.'

'Family Portrait'

Written by Scott Storch and Alecia 'P!nk' Moore
Produced by Scott Storch
Recorded at The Enterprise, Burbank
Duration: 4:58 (Radio Edit: 3:49)
Released as a single in September 2002
Music video directed by Sophie Muller
Chart Position: USA: 20; Canada: 49; UK: 11; Australia: 11; Germany: 8

'Family Portrait' is a sincere mid-tempo song about P!nk's experience growing up as a child of divorced parents following their separation when she was young. In the lyrics, she begs her father not to leave and blames herself for their split, promising to be better in order to keep her family together. The song is based on a poem she wrote when she was 9 years old, with additional writing and production from Scott Storch, who had previously worked with Dr. Dre and The Roots.

Speaking to MTV about the song, P!nk said: 'This song is really personal to me. And I wrote it not thinking. When I write, I don't think about the consequences or what people are going to think when they hear it. I just write. And I write what I think moves me. What's going to move the producer. And it was cool. And then I started letting people come in to listen to it. And I just felt really strange. I didn't like the feeling at all. People liked it, but I mean, most of the people that heard that song cried. So that's... I don't know. My mum cried for four days when she heard that song, but I like to write. I like to upset people and make points and break down barriers and all that sort of stuff.'

The song became the fourth single from *M!ssundaztood*, at P!nk's insistence, with a video directed by Sophie Muller. In the video, P!nk is followed by her younger self, who tries to get her attention and interrupts her therapy sessions. Young P!nk is played by Kelsey Lewis, who was 7 years old when she starred in the video. Lewis went on to become a DJ and skydiver but tragically died in a paragliding crash in October 2024.

On VH1's *Driven*, P!nk's mother, Judith Moore, said: 'To listen to it was difficult. I never realised until I listened to that song and listened to all the words, just how much the divorce had affected her. It opened up dialogue for us, and I'm grateful that we've had an opportunity to rebuild some of our bridges.'

Reflecting to *The Telegraph*, she added: 'I have hurt my parents several times with my lyrics. The thing I realise now is that I signed up for this life and they didn't, so me being as honest as I am and as open, maybe that wasn't always fair. I was a daddy's girl and I was devastated when he left because my mum and I never really got along. But it was also, "God what a relief." You spend the first 9 years of your life afraid of what's going to happen in your house and then you just have quiet. I flinch now when people fight. I can't handle it. My mum and I now have the coolest relationship. I call her almost every day. We just needed some years and age and wisdom.'

'Family Portrait' became another top 20 hit for P!nk, being certified 2x Platinum in Australia and Silver in the UK. It was also released commercially as a DVD Video single in the USA, featuring the 'Don't Let Me Get Me' music video, selling over 25,000 copies.

'Misery' featuring Steven Tyler

Written by Richard 'Richie Supa' Goodman
Produced by Marti Frederiksen and Richard 'Richie Supa' Goodman
Recorded at Drive By Studios, North Hollywood
Duration: 4:33
Steven Tyler appears courtesy of Columbia Records

Featuring Aerosmith's Steven Tyler, 'Misery' is a bluesy rock duet exploring the theme of misery and emotional pain in relationships. The song was written and co-produced by Richie Supa, best known for his work with Aerosmith and Richie Sambora of Bon Jovi.

In a *Billboard* magazine interview about the album, P!nk said: 'I met Steven at a Y100 radio show and I basically threw myself at him. I figured he'd either have me thrown out or he'd love me. He looked at me and told me I reminded him of Janis Joplin. It was either the biggest compliment of a lifetime or the biggest insult. I begged him to do a song with me, and he was all for it. He actually brought the song to me - a friend of his wrote it. I heard it, and I loved it. We're harmonising together, and it was just an experience of a lifetime.'

She added to Planet Rock TV in the UK: 'Steven Tyler is amazing. He has the spirit of a 12-year-old - a very smart 12-year-old. But his energy is contagious, and he's just got stories for days. And he told me he's going to teach me everything it took him 30 years to learn in a year. So, I'm being a sponge right now, learning how to glue furniture to the ceiling. But he's awesome. Just singing with him in the studio, I love his voice. Voices, to me - I'm a singer and a lyricist, and I just... voices like that drive me crazy. And he's got it.'

There are two versions of 'Misery' with original pressings of *M!ssundaztood* in the USA and Canada featuring an initial mix where P!nk sings the song's second verse. Later pressings feature the final version, with Tyler singing it instead.

'Dear Diary'

Written by Linda Perry and Alecia 'P!nk' Moore
Produced by Linda Perry
Recorded at LP Studios, Sherman Oaks
Duration: 3:29

'Dear Diary' is an introspective confessional, with P!nk reflecting on herself and hoping to be understood, even if only by her diary. Speaking to *Variety* magazine in 2019, P!nk said the song, written with Linda Perry, was inspired by Choice's former managers.

She explained: 'This publisher, Brian K. Jackson, walked in and said: "What would it take to get you to sign a publishing deal?" I'm broke at this point, I have like $20. And I go, "$1 million!" I was joking. And he goes, "OK, I'll see you on Monday." I was like, "Huh? Shit, I should have said $2 million!" And right as I was signing, my managers, that I haven't seen in like 6 months walked in, and I said, "What the fuck are you guys doing here?" And they go, "You never fired us. By the way, little girl, when you want to fire people, you have to put it in writing. So we're taking this advance." And they took all my money.'

'Eventually'

Written by Linda Perry and Alecia 'P!nk' Moore
Produced by Linda Perry
Recorded at LP Studios, Sherman Oaks
Duration: 3:34

'Eventually' is a bittersweet ballad in which P!nk explores the theme of karma catching up with those who have used her, but who are ultimately not there for her when she needs them. P!nk wrote the song with Linda Perry on their first day working together, after the initial awkwardness had subsided.

Speaking to Planet Rock TV, P!nk said: 'I'm sitting here looking at her, she's looking at me, and she's like, "I don't know what to do with you." I'm like, "I don't know what to do with you either." I'm like, "Just play something." She started playing on the piano, I took the microphone, and 10 minutes later, "Eventually" was written. And that was the first song on the record. And everyone was like, "What are you doing? She was a one-hit wonder. She's not producing anymore, blah, blah, blah, blah, blah." I was like, "Whatever."'

'Lonely Girl' featuring Linda Perry

Written by Linda Perry
Produced by Linda Perry
Recorded at LP Studios, Sherman Oaks
Duration: 4:20

'Lonely Girl' was written and produced by Linda Perry, inspired by a brief hospitalisation that P!nk had during their recording sessions. Perry appears on the song, turning it into a duet, as she asks P!nk questions such as, 'Do you even know who you are? Do you even know what you have?'

Talking to MTV, P!nk said: 'I was at her house, we were writing a song, and I have ulcers, and my stomach hurts sometimes and that happened. I was in a lot of pain, and I was curled up on the floor, and I left to go to the hospital, and she wrote this song about me because she thinks everything is internalised, and we create our problems for ourselves and all these things, so that's what happens. And I came back the next day and listened to it. And I was just like, "Wow. I can't believe my idol for however many years just understands me that well to write a song about me." It was a really strange experience. It was probably the most touching thing that anyone's ever done for me because I kind of felt understood and it scared me.'

'Numb'

Written by Dallas Austin and Alecia 'P!nk' Moore
Produced by Dallas Austin
Recorded at Pinetree Studios, Miami Beach and DARP Studios, Atlanta
Duration: 3:06

'Numb' was co-written and produced by Dallas Austin, with P!nk singing about the end of an abusive relationship, comparing herself to the local anaesthetic, Novocaine.

'Gone to California'

Written by Linda Perry and Alecia 'P!nk' Moore
Produced by Linda Perry and Damon Elliott
Recorded at LP Studios, Sherman Oaks
Duration: 4:34

'Gone to California' is P!nk's farewell to the 'City of Brotherly Love'—the Greek translation of Philadelphia—as she explains why she is leaving to pursue the opportunities available in California.

In an interview on *Jabba's Morning Glory*, P!nk explained that her family situation influenced her desire to leave. She said: 'Definitely… wanting to get out. That's where "Gone to California" came from, because that was my dream. I listened to way too much Mamas and the Papas.'

'My Vietnam'

Written by Linda Perry and Alecia 'P!nk' Moore
Produced by Linda Perry and Damon Elliott
Recorded at LP Studios, Sherman Oaks
Duration: 5:20

'My Vietnam' uses the Vietnam War, of which P!nk's father, James T. Moore, was a veteran, as a poignant metaphor for her personal battles and struggles.

In an interview with *Billboard* magazine after the New York terror attacks on 11 September 2001, P!nk said: 'It's eerie to listen to that after the fact, because

I wrote it four months ago. It was just about life, but now it's taken on a whole new meaning.'

In the lyrics, P!nk references her parents, singing, 'Daddy was a soldier, he taught me about freedom, peace and all the great things we take advantage of' and 'Momma was a lunatic, she liked to push my buttons.' Her mother, Judith Moore said she confronted P!nk about those lyrics, saying: 'We had some long conversations after that.'

The song includes an interpolation of 'The Star-Spangled Banner,' performed by Jimi Hendrix at Woodstock '69, as the song ends.

Bonus Tracks

'Catch-22'

Written by Linda Perry and Alecia 'P!nk' Moore
Produced by Linda Perry
Recorded at LP Studios, Sherman Oaks and Larrabee Studios, Los Angeles
Duration: 3:51

'Catch-22' was included on all versions of *M!ssundaztood* with the revised international tracklist, credited as a bonus track. It also appears on the 2017 and 2018 12" vinyl re-release of the album, which uses the original USA and Canada tracklist, printed as 'Catch 22.'

The song opens with a spoken word message, where P!nk welcomes the listener to a flight that's about to take off. Pretending to be a flight attendant, she continues the message during the song before ending it with a post-landing message with a twist. P!nk says: 'We realise you have many choices and on behalf of P!nk Airlines, we'd like to thank you for flying with us. We hope you have a wonderful stay wherever your destination may be and remember.... be careful when retrieving your items, as during the flight they may have shifted and might fall on you or your neighbour's head and knock you the fuck out...'

Other Songs

'Lady Marmalade' with Christina Aguilera, Lil' Kim and Mýa

Written by Bob Crewe and Kenny Nolan
Produced by Missy Elliott and Dana 'Rockwilder' Stinson
Duration: 4:14
Released as a single in April 2001
Music video directed by Paul Hunter
Chart Position: USA: 1; Canada: 13; UK: 1; Australia: 1; Germany: 1

'Lady Marmalade' first became famous when it was recorded by funk-rock group Labelle, who took it to #1 on the USA Billboard Hot 100 in 1975. Known for its French-language line, 'Voulez-vous coucher avec moi ce soir?' which translates to 'Do you want to sleep with me tonight?' the song became iconic. Outside of the USA, Italian pop star Sabrina recorded the song in 1987, with British girl group All Saints taking it to #1 on the UK singles chart in 1998.

In 2001, Australian filmmaker Baz Luhrmann returned the song back to mainstream attention when he included 'Lady Marmalade' in a medley in his jukebox musical movie, *Moulin Rouge!* Ron Fair, who signed Christina Aguilera, met with Lurhmann to discuss ideas for a single that would help establish the movie soundtrack, which would be released on Jimmy Iovine's Interscope Records, suggesting a diverse collaboration between 'the greatest pop singers from each continent in the world.'

He recalled to *Billboard* magazine: 'I wanted the greatest K-pop girl, the greatest European singer, the greatest American singer.' His music supervisor, Laura Wasserman, suggested combining every different genre in America instead and the concept for 'Lady Marmalade' was born.

After Missy Elliott agreed to produce the track, Wasserman approached Christina Aguilera's manager, Irving Azoff. Wanting everyone to receive equal payment for the song, she said: 'I found out that Christina Aguilera loves Missy and Lil' Kim, and so I got Lil' Kim to agree, and then Christina was like, "I really wanna do this!" We went to P!nk, and someone else in the department had a relationship with her. We got her on board. They all sort of said they would do it if the other one would do it - and tried to get one to say yes before the other. We got them all together, and then Interscope was like, "We want to have Mýa in there!"'

Mýa recalled to *Cosmopolitan* magazine in 2021: 'P!nk had more of the rock and roll and alternative aspect happening. Christina had pop. I had the R&B, hip-hop thing. Kim was rap all the way. Missy was a full-on entertainer.'

Each artist recorded their vocals separately, meeting for the first time on 17 March 2001 for the music video, directed by Paul Hunter and featuring choreography by Tina Landon. P!nk made no secret of the fact that there was some tension on the set of the music video between her and Christina Aguilera, performing with a blow-up doll of Aguilera on her *Try This* tour, and telling *Buzzfeed* in 2023: 'It wasn't very fun to make. I'm all about fun and it was like, a lot of fuss, and there were some personalities. Kim and Mýa were nice.'

She later added on *Who's Talking to Chris Wallace?*: "Back then, our personalities did not mix at all and that was OK. We hugged it out and kissed it out and we have many times since.' P!nk and Christina have since worked together on *The Voice* USA as well as recording a duet in 2017, which is currently unreleased.

'Lady Marmalade' was a huge global success, becoming P!nk's first #1 in many countries. The music video won Best Video of the Year and Best Video from a Film at the 2001 MTV Movie Awards in June, where the quartet performed the song live. They also reunited the following year to perform it with Patti Labelle at the 44th Grammy Awards, where it won Best Pop Collaboration with Vocals.

'What You Wanna Do'—Naughty by Nature featuring P!nk

Written by Naughty by Nature (Anthony 'Treach' Criss and Vinnie Brown) and J-Nod Ettienne
Produced by Naughty by Nature (Anthony 'Treach' Criss and Vinnie Brown) and J-Nod Ettienne
Recorded at Millennium Studios, New Jersey and Larrabee West, California
Duration: 4:45

P!nk provides vocals on the track, 'What You Wanna Do,' from *Iicons*, the sixth studio album by the American hip-hop act, Naughty by Nature. The album is their first and only release as a duo, following the departure of their third member, DJ Kay Gee, and was recorded whilst they were signed to the same label as P!nk, Arista Records. After changing record companies, the album was released in May 2002.

Treach told MTV: 'P!nk, she's real cool. We met up at a party - it was all us, Lil' Kim, Junior M.A.F.I.A. Through that I was like, "I really like your style." She was like, "I've been a fan of yours." It was an exchange of numbers, and next thing we knew we did a song for a project that's coming out and we did it for our album. The hook was already there. She came in, added her flavour, her riffs and turned it around. It's a smoker'.

Vinnie added: 'P!nk is really talented. She got in there, she knew what to do - how to construct and add on and stack. She heard certain things and changed certain pitches. She didn't need no vocal coach.' P!nk is credited as an arranger for her work on the song.

Unreleased Songs

'Curse'

Written by Dallas Austin and Alecia 'P!nk' Moore
Produced by Dallas Austin
Duration: 2:44

'Curse' is registered on ASCAP from P!nk's sessions with Dallas Austin. The song appears on an EMI Music Publishing CD of demo recordings, entitled 'The Curse.' The CD also features early versions of 'Just Like a Pill,' '18 Wheeler' and 'Don't Let Me Get Me' and a demo of 'Sex on My Sleeve.'

Although the CD has been sold on record collector websites, the song has not yet leaked.

'Sex on My Sleeve'

Written by Dallas Austin and Alecia 'P!nk' Moore
Produced by Dallas Austin
Duration: 3:25

'Sex on My Sleeve' is registered on ASCAP from P!nk's sessions with Dallas Austin. The song appears on an EMI Music Publishing CD of demo recordings, credited as 'Sex on My Sleeze.' The CD also features demos with Debra Killings and 'Hit 'Em Up Style (Oops),' which became a hit for Blu Cantrell.

Although the CD has been sold on record collector websites, the song has not yet leaked.

Live Performances

'What's Up?'

Written by Linda Perry
Duration: 5:50 (*Live from Wembley Arena, London, England* Performance)

'What's Up?' was written by Linda Perry for her band 4 Non Blondes in 1993; the song became a huge hit in Europe, reaching #3 in France, #2 in the UK, and #1 in Germany, Austria, Sweden, Belgium and the Netherlands.

A rock song with an anthemic chorus, Perry recalled to *Billboard* magazine in 2020: 'It's a very personal punk-folk song based on frustration. I was writing about what it was like to be a human in this world, whether it was emotional blindness, or I was just needing help, or the obstacles that got in our way. But it was also an anthem for kids about not going away, and the purity and simplicity of that song is what took it to where it's still going today.'

Having performed the song at open mic nights before she was signed to a record label, 'What's Up?' is the song that inspired P!nk to track down Linda Perry to collaborate with her on *M!ssundaztood*. P!nk added the song to her 2002 *Party* tour and has performed it frequently throughout her career, including on her 2004 *Try This* festival date, the *I'm Not Dead* tour throughout 2006 and 2007, the 2010 *Funhouse Summer Carnival* tour and the 2024 leg of her *Summer Carnival* tour.

A recording of P!nk performing the song can be found on her *Live from Wembley Arena, London, England* DVD, filmed on 4 December 2006. In 2010, P!nk made a surprise appearance during Perry's performance of the song at the Los Angeles Gay and Lesbian Center's *An Evening with Women* event.

'I Love You'/ 'You're All I Need to Get By' Medley

'I Love You' Written by Mary J. Blige and Sean 'Puffy' Combs
'You're All I Need to Get By' Written by Nickolas Ashford and Valerie Simpson
Duration: 3:15

P!nk's 2002 *Party* tour features a medley of two of her favourite soul songs. The first, 'I Love You' is a cover of the 1995 single by Mary J. Blige from her album, *My Life*. The second is the 1968 classic, 'You're All I Need to Get By,' made famous by Marvin Gaye and Tammi Terrell but also interpolated into the 1995 song, 'I'll Be There for You/You're All I Need to Get By,' by Method Man featuring Mary J. Blige.

'Janie's Got a Gun'

Written by Steven Tyler and Tom Hamilton
Duration: 3:50

P!nk performed 'Janie's Got a Gun' at MTV's *mtv:ICON* honouring Aerosmith in April 2002, as well as on her *Party* tour. The song, which tells the story of a young girl who seeks revenge against her abuser, won Best Rock Performance by a Duo or Group with Vocal at the 32nd Grammy Awards In 1990.

P!nk spoke about her love for Aerosmith throughout the promotion for *M!ssundaztood*, particularly how thrilled she was that Steven Tyler agreed to duet with her on 'Respect.'

Janis Joplin Medley ('Summertime'/ 'Piece of My Heart'/ 'Me and Bobby McGee')

'Summertime' Written by George Gershwin, Ira Gershwin and DuBose Heyward
'Piece of My Heart' Written by Jerry Ragovoy and Bert Berns
'Me and Bobby McGee' Written by Kris Kristofferson, Fred Foster
Duration: 3:55

P!nk acknowledged Janis Joplin as one of her biggest inspirations in interviews as far back as 2000, telling MTV: 'She was so inspiring by singing blues music when it wasn't culturally acceptable for white women, and she wore her heart on her sleeve. She was so witty and charming and intelligent, but she also battled an ugly-duckling syndrome. I would love to play her in a movie.'

On her 2002 *Party* tour, P!nk performed a medley of three classic Joplin hits—'Summertime,' 'Piece of My Heart' and 'Me and Bobby McGee'—accompanied by photographs of the 1960s icon, hippies, and the peace movement. 'Summertime' is from the 1935 opera, *Porgy and Bess*, and was originally released by Abbie Mitchell. Joplin recorded her version in 1968 for the album *Cheap Thrills*, released by Big Brother and the Holding Company, the rock band for whom she provided vocals.

'Piece of My Heart' is a further cover, originally recorded by Erma Franklin in 1967. Also recorded for *Cheap Thrills*, it has become one of the most recognisable Janis Joplin singles.

'Me and Bobby McGee' was written by country songwriter Kris Kristofferson and recorded by Roger Miller in 1971. Joplin recorded a cover of the song for her second solo album, *Pearl*, which was released after her death in January 1971. 'Me and Bobby McGee' reached #1 on the USA Billboard Hot 100, making it her most successful release.

P!nk has performed the songs both in other medleys and on their own, including 'Me and Bobby McGee' for at her Sessions@AOL recording in 2003. A variation of the medley was included on her 2004 *Try This* festival dates, swapping 'Me and Bobby McGee' and 'Piece of My Heart.' A further medley containing 'Piece of My Heart' and 'Me and Bobby McGee' was included on her *I'm Not Dead* tour in 2007. P!nk also performed 'Me and Bobby McGee' on its own during many dates of her 2023 *Summer Carnival* tour, and at the FireAid benefit concert in Los Angeles, which took place in January 2025.

Songwriting Credits

'Take a Picture'—Mýa

Written by Damon Elliott and Alecia 'P!nk' Moore
Produced by Damon Elliott
Additional Production by Ron Fair and Mýa Harrison
Recorded at Enterprise Studio, Burbank; Rob Bryton Studio, Toronto, Canada and Interscope Studio, Santa Monica
Contains elements of '(Lay Your Head on My) Pillow' performed by Tony! Toni! Toné! and written by Timothy Christian Riley, D'Wayne Wiggins and Raphael Wiggins
Duration: 3:29

R&B artist Mýa's third album, *Moodring*, was released in July 2003, debuting at #3 on the USA Billboard albums chart. Having worked with her on 'Lady Marmalade,' an unused demo from *M!ssundaztood* that P!nk wrote with Damon Elliott was given to Mýa to record. 'Take a Picture' is a reflective song about wanting to capture a moment, so it lasts forever.

Mýa' told *Idolator*: 'We had a bond creatively that came out of "Lady Marmalade." It was our link. And people don't know this, but P!nk and I actually met when we were both 16 years old in Philadelphia. I was recording my first album, and we were working with the same producers, so I originally knew her as Alecia.'

'If You're Gonna Fly Away'—Faith Hill

Written by Linda Perry and Alecia 'P!nk' Moore
Produced by Byron Gallimore and Faith Hill
Recorded at Henson Recording Studios, Hollywood
Duration: 3:48

Country singer Faith Hill attempted to crossover further into the pop market with her fifth studio album, 2002's *Cry*. 'If You're Gonna Fly Away' was written and recorded by Linda Perry and P!nk for *M!ssundaztood* but did not make the final cut. Jeff Aldrich, who led A&R for *Cry*, thought the song would be perfect for Faith Hill, so she recorded it with Byron Gallimore.

In an interview with *Music Connection* magazine, P!nk spoke about Mýa and Faith Hill performing songs she had written, admitting that she finds giving away songs difficult. She said: 'It's just really hard for me to give one of my songs away, because the way I sing and the way I do my thing, it's really hard to let go and have somebody else sing it a different way – although I love what they did. I mean, I'm a fan of theirs; I wouldn't have given my song to anybody. I would have to seriously believe in them.'

Catalogue Registrations

'Déjà Vu'

Written by Scott Storch and Alecia 'P!nk' Moore

'Girl on the Side'

Written by Linda Perry and Alecia 'P!nk' Moore

'Justice'

Written by Linda Perry and Alecia 'P!nk' Moore

'I Will'

Written by Marti Frederiksen and Alecia 'P!nk' Moore

4

Try This (2002–2003)

Released:	7 November 2003 (Europe)
	10 November 2003 (UK)
	11 November 2003 (USA, Canada and Australia)
Chart Position:	USA: 9
	Canada: 8
	UK: 3
	Australia: 8
	Germany: 2

P!nk's artistic evolution from *Can't Take Me Home* to *M!ssundaztood* marked a bold shift from soul and R&B to pop-rock, earning both critical acclaim and commercial success, with over 13 million copies of the album sold worldwide. With such global success comes pressure; however, P!nk used the freedom it afforded her to present something unexpected. In *Try This*, she embraces her punk rock influences, working with Tim Armstrong, who was part of influential punk groups Rancid and Transplants.

P!nk started writing the album with Linda Perry but found it different to the sessions they had for her second album. She said: 'I started with Linda, because she's my favourite. But it was just totally different and a little strange. I love working with Linda; me and Linda, when we work together, it's really personal and it's really heartfelt, and we do a lot of good stuff. But I knew there was something else coming. Then I met Tim and, all of a sudden, everything was perfect again. I just love him as a person. He's super, super versatile. I was kind of intrigued because he came up to me and said, 'I'd love to work with you,' and I thought, "Hmm, that would be interesting." And then when I heard his stuff, it was like, "Whoa..." So when I heard this music, I was like, "This could be interesting. It's worth a shot." I didn't really have any expectations. Linda and I had done about 10 or 11 songs, but when I met

Tim, it took on a whole new energy and life force. It was so easy; two weeks later, we were done.'

P!nk added in the album's press interview that the collaboration felt like fate. She said: 'Usually in my life, the only time that the universe comes together is right when I'm about to record a record. It just works, every other time it sucks. We worked together on eight songs. It was so easy and just endless fun, it was great. People think because I worked with Tim, it's a punk rock record, and it's completely not. He was totally open to pop melodies and my kind of thing, and he wanted to come over to my side of the world for a second.'

After writing with Armstrong for around two weeks, P!nk joined him and the Transplants as they went on tour with the Foo Fighters, recording songs on their tour bus. She said: 'I went out and rode in the back of the bus and we kind of recorded live. We did the drums and the guitars and the bass and everything in the back of the bus. I never expected to be doing anything like that. But I like the easiness of it, and the freshness - just the rawness and the vibe. It was really cool.'

Talking about the album's title, P!nk said: 'I named the album *Try This* because I believe that in this world there are leaders and there are followers, and I hope to be a leader. I don't set out like "I'm going to be different", I just go with what's in my heart. And it's a really good feeling when you go against the grain. I wish more people would do it.'

Comparing the album to *M!ssundaztood,* she said: 'I was in a different place when I made that record, I was taking a big chance and going against what everybody was telling me to do because I really wanted to, and I needed the freedom to speak my mind. This time around I had the freedom to do whatever I wanted to do, which was a little uninspiring, but good at the same time. I didn't really want to be so complaining on this record. I wrote songs about other people. There's definitely a lot of lighter energy.'

Alongside collaborating with Tim Armstrong, P!nk teamed up with Billy Mann for the first time on the album's second single, 'God is a DJ,' marking the beginning of her longest-running musical partnership.

After 'Trouble' charted at #68 and *Try This* charted at #9 in the USA, P!nk was asked about the era's success in an interview with *The Ledger*. She said: 'I don't judge myself on how well my songs do at radio, or how much my album sells. A failure and a success is all how you look at it. I've been creative to my highest potential at this point of my life, and I'm super proud of myself for making it this far. I've basically reached all the goals that I set out for myself. Now it's just about having fun and causing chaos and doing what I want to do.'

P!nk admitted the album was rushed in 2005, telling *Billboard* magazine: '*Try This* was my rebellion against deadlines. Fine, you want your fucking records, I'll write 10 songs in a week, and you can press it and put it out. I don't have to think about it, I don't have to get emotionally invested. I was tired of talking about divorce. I was tired of talking about my life and talking about being lonely. I walked out of half of my interviews crying. I needed to coast for a while, and that's what I did.'

Try This was a success in Europe and Australia, where P!nk toured the record, even adding a summer festival leg from June to August in Europe. John Fleckenstein, Chief Operating Officer at RCA Records, told *Music Week* magazine in 2023: 'When she took a pivot on *Try This*, the American market wasn't accepting of the music and so she pivoted overseas... people were saying, "You're crazy, she's a pop artist, you can't put her on European festivals like Rock Am Ring!" She showed that she could actually pull that off. It transformed her international career.'

P!nk said that the transition to *Try This* was the biggest lesson of her career so far, telling *The Los Angeles Times* in 2012: 'I was rebelling for no reason... had I stayed on my path and not worried so much about what other people said I couldn't do I would have probably been all right. But anything I was gonna do after *M!ssundaztood* was going to be a failure. After something that big, anything is gonna suck to people.'

Album Tracks

'Trouble'

Written by Tim Armstrong and Alecia 'P!nk' Moore
Produced by Tim Armstrong
Additional Production by John Fields
Recorded at Steakhouse Studios, North Hollywood; The Transplants' Bus; Mansfield Lodge, Hollywood and Crackertracks, Los Angeles
Duration: 3:13
Released as a single in September 2003
Music video directed by Sophie Muller
Chart Position: USA: 68; Canada: 2; UK: 7; Australia: 8; Germany: 7

'Trouble' is the first single from *Try This*, evolving P!nk's sound by combining pop, punk, and rock. A rebellious, fun anthem, P!nk said in an interview with *Music Connection* magazine: 'It's not like a high-concept song. When I heard the music for "Trouble", I just started singing it, and it felt good. It's a fun, attitude song; it's just about being a badass and causing chaos, which I love to do.'

Talking to *VH1* about her songwriting and how 'Trouble' was written, she added: 'Usually I write about one incident or one happening. But this is just a mixture of all kinds of stuff about being a badass, having fun, causing trouble.'

The music video, directed by Sophie Muller, sees P!nk causing havoc in a 'Wild West' saloon, with a guest appearance from Jeremy Renner as the town's evil sheriff. Talking about the video to *The Sun* newspaper, P!nk said: 'Actually, I hate western films, but I really like the attitude of the time. Back in the Wild West, somebody could shoot you and take your horse, and it was as simple as that. There weren't any lawsuits. When I think of the word "trouble", what better way to represent it than with the Wild West and bar fights? It was actually a trip to Las Vegas that inspired that video. I like to think of it as the modern day in a western setting.'

Shot on a ranch in Newhall, California, where the TV show *Little House on the Prairie* was once filmed, the video also features the Pussycat Dolls and Robin Antin as saloon girls. P!nk did the video's stunts herself, working with Chuck Borden as the stunt coordinator.

'Trouble' reached the top 10 across Europe and Australia, with the CD single featuring two non-album bonus tracks, 'Delirium' and 'Free.' In February 2004, the song won Best Female Rock Vocal Performance at the 46th Grammy Awards. Tim Armstrong also recorded and released a cover of the song in 2012 under the alias Tim Timebomb.

Reflecting on 'Trouble' in a 2012 interview with *The Los Angeles Times*, P!nk said: 'I love this song too. I recorded it in a tour bus when I was running down the road. That's my punk rock moment. I won a Grammy for it! Then they dissolved the category the day after. It's like, "Really?" This is hard for me to not take that personally. Could you have waited like a week?'

'God Is a DJ'

Written by Billy Mann, Alecia 'P!nk' Moore and Jonnie 'Most' Davis
Produced by Billy Mann and Jonnie 'Most' Davis
Recorded at Steakhouse Studios, North Hollywood
Duration: 3:44
Released as a single in November 2003
Music video directed by Jake Scott
Chart Position: UK: 11; Australia: 24; Germany: 44

'God Is a DJ' is an up-tempo track that celebrates life and music as a form of salvation, co-produced by Billy Mann, marking the start of one of P!nk's longest-lasting collaborative relationships. In the album's track-by-track commentary, P!nk said of Billy Mann: 'He's an amazing, amazing guy, super talented. And I heard this music and I thought, "Wow, that's cool." He actually came to me. I got to the song and then we finished it together.'

Asked about the song when talking to Capital FM in the UK, she added: 'It was actually Billy Mann's idea, and I just helped him finish it really. It was the one song on the album that I didn't create from the very start, but I just liked the message behind it. I read this book called *The Alchemist* and I so believe in that - taking what you have. I liked it – the message – take what you have and do the best with it. I like the metaphors and stuff.'

Talking to *Seventeen* magazine about the lyrics of 'God Is a DJ,' P!nk said: 'I've kind of had the ugly duckling syndrome since I was little... but you take what you got and use it. You know whatever it is, you find something that works for you and go for it. We all have our issues. But I think that's really important with girls - there's something we're all good at and it would be so much better if we concentrated on what we're good at and not what society wants us to be like, look like, talk like, act like. I think that everyone's gotten really comfortable, but women still have a long way to go as far as our fight for equality - especially in other parts of the world.'

In 2017, Billy Mann recalled to *Variety* magazine: 'This was the first song that Alecia and I wrote together, sitting in her truck after the first time we met. We drank some whiskey and blasted the idea in its infancy. We finished it days later. Like most of my songs with her, they are not obvious formula records, but find strange, unexpected cultural footholds and stay strong.'

The song became the second single from *Try This*, released to radio in the USA in November 2003, accompanied by a music video showing P!nk and her friends getting ready for a night out and travelling on the subway to a nightclub. Although the song did not chart in the USA, it was featured in the hit movie, *Mean Girls*, starring Lindsay Lohan, and appears on the film's soundtrack.

'Last to Know'

Written by Tim Armstrong and Alecia 'P!nk' Moore
Produced by Tim Armstrong
Recorded at Steakhouse Studios, North Hollywood and The Transplants' Bus
Duration: 4:03 (UK Radio Edit – 3:52)
Released as a single in April 2004
Music video directed by Russell Thomas
Chart Position: UK: 21; Germany: 66

'Last to Know' was the third single to be lifted from *Try This*, released exclusively in the UK and Europe. In the lyrics, P!nk aggressively calls out a guy she went on a date with who stood her up and failed to attend her concert despite her leaving him a complimentary ticket at the door. She blames his behaviour on the fact that she wouldn't have sex with him on the first date, singing, 'I wouldn't go home with you, I wouldn't put my heels in the air for you.' The song was censored for release as a single, removing the phrase 'stupid fuck', abbreviating it to 'stu…'

In an interview with *Q* magazine in 2004, P!nk confirmed that the lyrics are autobiographical, when asked about 'going all the way on the first date.' She said: 'I did that a couple of times and it was really disappointing. You need to know somebody; you need to know what they like and they need to know what you like. Sex is only fun if you can be fucking open, so you either have to know the person or be wasted.'

The music video for the song was directed by Russell Thomas, featuring concert footage from P!nk's *Try This* tour, which saw her playing arenas across Europe in early 2004. The song charted just outside the top 20 in the UK, reaching #66 in Germany, #48 in Austria, #46 in Switzerland, and #40 in the Netherlands.

'Tonight's the Night'

Written by Tim Armstrong and Alecia 'P!nk' Moore
Produced by Tim Armstrong

Recorded at Steakhouse Studios, North Hollywood; The Transplants' Bus, Mansfield Lodge
Duration: 3:56

A high-energy track about living in the moment and having a great night out, 'Tonight's the Night' embodies the carefree, fun attitude P!nk says she wanted *Try This* to showcase.

In an interview with Italian magazine, *Tribe*, P!nk said that the lines, 'Hit the town with brass knuckles, while all the good people stare, I hope I don't end up in jail, but then again I don't really care,' are about not tolerating inappropriate behaviour from drunk people.

She said: 'When you go to a pub or to a club, you have to understand that some drunk people don't behave appropriately, especially to women. You can choose to react the same way or not - I do. If I'm with my friends and a drunk man is rude, I pour a glass of beer on his head. I'd like to punch him too, but I can't, because we'd end up in court and that would be expensive!"

'Oh My God' featuring Peaches

Written by Tim Armstrong, Alecia 'P!nk' Moore and Merrill 'Peaches' Nisker
Produced by Tim Armstrong
Recorded at Steakhouse Studios, North Hollywood; The Transplants' Bus, Mansfield Lodge and Battery Studios, New York City
Duration: 3:44
Peaches appears courtesy of XL Recordings

Featuring Canadian electroclash artist and provocateur, Peaches, 'Oh My God' is an unapologetic celebration of sexuality.

In a promotional video for *Try This*, P!nk said: 'It's my sex song. And I worked with Peaches on that because I love Peaches. I think she's great and raunchy and sexy and hot and incredibly talented. And we got together on that, and it took us about 15 minutes and then we went shopping.'

Talking to *Music Connection* magazine, she added: 'What happened was, this person I know was just telling me his problems, and he was really attractive to me. It's kind of a play on words, like "Oh my God, go a little slower, what was that again? Tell me your problem, you got all the problems I think I can solve" – kind of a play on words. I just wrote the song and I was like, "Hmm, if I could have one person on my album, who could it be?" And I said, "It would be Peaches!" So I e-mailed her, "Please come be sexy with me on this song", and she did. I'm honoured, because she's hot.'

In a 2021 interview with *Stereogum*, Peaches reflected on working with P!nk. She said: 'P!nk was exploring her sexuality, or deciding to explore it, on the album, and just wanted me to... she was like, "Your record is part of this whole exploration." She was so humble; she was so sweet. She's great.'

'Catch Me While I'm Sleeping'

Written by Linda Perry and Alecia 'P!nk' Moore
Produced by Linda Perry
Additional Production by John Fields
Recorded at Casa de P!nk, Sherman Oaks; Enterprise Studios, Burbank; Mansfield Lodge, Hollywood; Vibatorium, Los Angeles and Crackertracks, Los Angeles
Duration: 5:03 (Radio Edit: 3:57)

'Catch Me While I'm Sleeping' is a reflective ballad, written with Linda Perry, which P!nk has performed live just once, as part of her *CD:UK Spotlight* special, aired in the UK on 4 November 2003. The song was planned as a single in the USA, with a promotional CD containing a radio edit sent out to radio stations, but was recalled when the song's release was cancelled.

In an interview with *Music Connection* magazine, P!nk said that the song was originally written for *M!ssundaztood*, explaining: 'There were way too many songs. That's the most heartbreaking part of making albums - having to whittle them down. So I kind of put that one away and people started hearing it and other people wanted to record it, but I became rather possessive and decided to put it on my new album.'

'Waiting for Love'

Written by Linda Perry, Alecia 'P!nk' Moore, Eric Schermerhorn, Paul Ill and Brian McLeod
Produced by Linda Perry
Recorded at Casa de P!nk, Sherman Oaks and Enterprise Studios, Burbank
Duration: 5:28

'Waiting for Love' is a soaring, heartfelt track about longing for emotional connection, co-written with Linda Perry, guitarist Eric Schermerhorn, drummer Brian McLeod and bass player, Paul Ill. The trio had previously worked with Tina Turner, while she was recording with Guy Chambers in London.

'Save My Life'

Written by Tim Armstrong and Alecia 'P!nk' Moore
Produced by Tim Armstrong
Recorded at Steakhouse Studios, North Hollywood and The Transplants' Bus
Duration: 3:16

Although not originally written about her own experiences, 'Save My Life' became one of the more personal songs on *Try This*. In the lyrics, P!nk tells the story of a girl who has returned to taking drugs, leaving behind her boyfriend and success, but who is asking for help.

Talking about the song in a promotional video for *Try This*, P!nk said: 'It was the first song I wrote with Tim Armstrong, and I wrote it about a couple friends of mine. So, part of it is in third person and part of it's not, because I can relate to crying out to God for somebody to save my life. It's a really personal song and one of my favourites… I cannot pick a favourite song on this album.'

She later added to MTV: 'I'm very close to "Save My Life", which was supposed to be called "Back On Drugs", but we had to change it for Walmart. That's just a story about somebody I'm really sad for right now. The song is light, but there's a lot of pain in it.'

'Try Too Hard'

Written by Linda Perry and Alecia 'P!nk' Moore
Produced by Linda Perry
Additional Production by John Fields
Recorded at Casa de P!nk, Sherman Oaks; Enterprise Studios, Burbank and Mansfield Lodge, Hollywood
Duration: 3:14

'Try Too Hard' is another song from P!nk's sessions with Linda Perry, critiquing society's obsession with image and superficiality and how others change under the pressure to conform before acknowledging she is guilty of doing it too.

'Humble Neighborhoods'

Written by Tim Armstrong and Alecia 'P!nk' Moore
Produced by Tim Armstrong
Additional Production by John Fields
Recorded at Steakhouse Studios, North Hollywood; The Transplants' Bus; Mansfield Lodge, Hollywood and Crackertracks, Los Angeles
Duration: 3:52

'Humble Neighbourhoods' is an uptempo track in which P!nk raps about travelling all over the world on tour.

In the promotional video for *Try This*, P!nk said: '"Humble Neighborhoods" is super fun. It's another song I wrote with Tim. I like to rap. I always wanted to be a rapper and have an entourage, so I'm on my way.'

'Walk Away'

Written by Tim Armstrong and Alecia 'P!nk' Moore
Produced by Tim Armstrong
Recorded at Steakhouse Studios, North Hollywood and The Transplants' Bus
Duration: 3:39

'Walk Away' is another collaboration with Tim Armstrong. P!nk sings about her relationship with Carey Hart, referencing how easy he finds it to give up and leave when things get complicated in a relationship. In the lyrics, she sings: 'I gave you three years of my life, you always said I'd be your wife,' but by the end of the song, she takes control and decides to end the relationship herself.

'Unwind'

Written by Tim Armstrong and Alecia 'P!nk' Moore
Produced by Tim Armstrong
Recorded at Steakhouse Studios, North Hollywood and The Transplants' Bus
Duration: 3:12

P!nk wrote 'Unwind' with Tim Armstrong about one of her biggest inspirations, Janis Joplin, who died in 1970 at just 27 years old. In the lyrics, P!nk references Joplin's love for the whiskey Southern Comfort and her desire to be loved.

Talking about the song, P!nk said: 'Tim had this melody in his head and I just wrote that song about Janis Joplin. But then when I looked at the lyrics, it was like, "Wow, this song is really about me too." So I turned it around, saying it from my point of view. And I have a deep spiritual connection to Janis, and I don't know why, how, or when, but I've always been extremely attracted to her energy and her pain and her voice and her life. And I just think she was one of the most amazing women that ever lived.'

'Feel Good Time' featuring William Orbit

Written by Beck Hansen and William Orbit
Produced by William Orbit
Recorded at Guerilla Canyon Studios, Los Angeles; House of Blues Studio, Los Angeles; Sam West Studio, London, UK and Enterprise Studio, Los Angeles
Includes a sample of 'Fresh-Garbage' performed by Spirit and written by Jay Ferguson
Duration: 3:56
Released as a single in May 2003
Music video directed by Dave Meyers
Chart Position: USA: 60; UK: 3; Australia: 7; Germany: 16

'Feel Good Time,' originally titled 'Real Good,' was written by William Orbit and Beck around a sample of the 1968 song 'Fresh-Garbage' by rock band Spirit. It served as the lead single from the soundtrack to *Charlie's Angels: Full Throttle*, the sequel to director McG's successful 2000 film adaptation of *Charlie's Angels* and was also included on all editions of *Try This* outside of the USA and Canada.

The song was written in 2002 when British producer, William Orbit, known for his work on two Madonna albums—1997's *Ray of Light*, and 2000's *Music*—flew to Los Angeles to collaborate with Beck. Initially intended for an album of collaborations that Orbit was planning (later released in February 2006, entitled *Hello Waveforms*), Beck told MTV that the song had a 'Latin fuzz guitar over percolating dance beats.'

P!nk had been approached to write and record a new track for the soundtrack, asking to make a cameo in the movie in return. After hearing Orbit's demo recording of 'Real Good' featuring Beck's vocals, the film's music team asked him to collaborate with P!nk During their sessions, Orbit played her 'Real Good' and she asked to cover it, rather than write something new.

Discussing the track, P!nk said: 'They approached and just wanted me to do the single, and I said "Okay, if I'm gonna do the song, I want to be in the movie", and then I had a little part. It was a really difficult part. I played the tough-as-chick with an attitude. William Orbit and Beck made this song, and I heard it and I thought it was awesome and I stole it from them and now it's mine. I don't usually do other people's songs, I usually write my own, but it was cool because it's something I never would have come up with. I like the whole feel of it, and I love Beck.'

Beck later confirmed to *The Colorado Daily* that P!nk's vocals were added over his, saying: 'P!nk wanted to cover my song, but in the end, she just sang over my original for the single. It's kind of nice having a number one song on MTV vicariously.'

The music video, directed by Dave Meyers, premiered on MTV's *Making the Video* on 19 May 2003. It blends footage of the movie with scenes of P!nk at an export terminal at Los Angeles International Airport and Westward Beach in Miami, featuring motocross racing stunts and beachside explosions.

'Feel Good Time' was nominated for Best Pop Collaboration with Vocals at the 46th Grammy Awards, ultimately losing to 'Whenever I Say Your Name' by Sting & Mary J. Blige. The single, which included remixes from D-Bop and Boris & Beck, reached #7 in Australia and #3 in the UK.

In August 2003, William Orbit played alternative versions of the song on his 'Superchunk' radio show, including a version featuring Beck's vocals. Beck's original demo also leaked online in early 2008.

'Love Song'

Written by Damon Elliott and Alecia 'P!nk' Moore
Produced by Damon Elliott
Recorded at Enterprise Studios, Burbank
Duration: 2:29

'Love Song' is a stripped-back, poignant ballad written with Damon Elliott. In it, P!nk vocalises her fears about falling in love and writing her first love song, ultimately ending with optimism.

In the *Try This* electronic press kit, P!nk confirmed she wrote the song about her then ex-boyfriend, Carey Hart. She said: 'I wrote "Love Song" about a special someone in my life. It's probably my most vulnerable moment on the record because I don't like being vulnerable and in love. I'm not comfortable with it yet. No, I mean it's a pretty song. I just hope it doesn't turn into a wedding.'

P!nk and Hart split as the album was being finished, which P!nk sings about on 'Walk Away,' however, they reconciled in 2004 and became engaged in June 2005. 'Love Song' is the final listed track on all versions of *Try This*, with 'Feel Good Time' preceding it in Europe and Australia, and 'Free' in Japan.

'Hooker'

Written by Tim Armstrong and Alecia 'P!nk' Moore
Produced by Tim Armstrong
Recorded at Steakhouse Studios, North Hollywood; The Transplants' Bus; Mansfield Lodge, Hollywood and Crackertracks, Los Angeles
Duration: 3:06

'Hooker' is an unlisted hidden track on all CD editions of *Try This*, appearing after a period of silence at the end of the album. It is listed on the album's 2017 and 2018 12" vinyl releases, with the song's lyrics and credits also being included for the first time. A sharp, biting track about betrayal, the song features sarcastic, blunt lyrics, with P!nk singing, 'You ain't nothing but a hooker, selling your fucking soul.'

Asked about the song by *Music Connection* magazine, P!nk said she would never reveal who she is singing about, drawing a comparison to Carly Simon's refusal to identify the person who inspired her hit, 'You're So Vain.' P!nk said: 'It was inspired by someone I really don't like. But I'm taking Carly Simon's position on that song and will never tell anyone who it's about. I'm sure people will make their own assumptions.'

Bonus Tracks

'Delerium'

Written by Linda Perry and Alecia 'P!nk' Moore
Produced by Linda Perry
Recorded at Casa de P!nk, Sherman Oaks and Enterprise Studios, Burbank
Duration: 3:40

'Delerium' sees P!nk narrating a story about a delusional woman who believes she has a new boyfriend, but the relationship exists only in her imagination. With an earworm of a hook, the song was included as a Japanese bonus track on *Try This* and was also a B-side to 'Trouble.'

'Free'

Written by Linda Perry, Alecia 'P!nk' Moore, Eric Schermerhorn, Paul Ill and Brian McLeod
Produced by Linda Perry
Recorded at Casa de P!nk, Sherman Oaks and Enterprise Studios, Burbank
Duration: 6:38

'Free' is one of the longest songs in P!nk's catalogue, co-written and produced by Linda Perry at the same time as 'Waiting for Love.' Through the song, P!nk expresses her longing to break free from societal expectations, relationships, and her own insecurities, pleading, 'Can you relate? Would someone help me please? I want to be free.' 'Free' was also included as a bonus track on *Try This* in Japan and appeared on the 'Trouble' CD single.

Other Songs

'We Will Rock You' Pepsi 'Gladiators' Soundtrack Remix 2004—Beyoncé, Britney and P!nk

Written by Brian May
Produced by Brian May and Roger Taylor
Duration: 3:10

Pepsi asked P!nk to join forces with two other global female icons—Beyoncé and Britney Spears—on a new version of Queen's 'We Will Rock You' with both Brian May and Roger Taylor of Queen, and Enrique Iglesias appearing in the commercial. The campaign, directed by Tarsem Singh and shot in Rome in a small section of an unused colosseum, was not aired in North America, with Singh recalling Pepsi telling him that 'it wouldn't work for the American audience.' A premiere took place at the National Gallery in London on 26 January 2004, at which all three stars appeared.

P!nk said: 'My favourite thing was the fact that us girls were all supposed to fight each other, and instead we band together, as females should. And we turn it around and overthrow the king… and hand out drinks to all.'

In a February 2022 interview with *People* magazine, P!nk reflected on the experience: 'What a weird deal that was. You're flying us to Rome to shoot in a fake coliseum down the street from the real Colosseum. We could have gone to Canada. I don't understand. That's Pepsi money. Beyoncé is the prettiest person you could ever stand in front of. She glows like a goddess. People think I was picking on Britney on "Don't Let Me Get Me" but I've always felt like a big sister to her. I wish her well. I cover her in light all day long.'

The song was released on a series of promotional CDs, one giving equal billing to all three stars as well as specific individual editions for Beyoncé, Britney and P!nk.

'Tell Me Why'
Rah Digga featuring P!nk

Written by Dorsey 'Megahertz' Wesley, Rashia 'Rah Digga' Tashan Fisher and Alecia 'P!nk' Moore
Produced by Dorsey 'Megahertz' Wesley
Duration: 4:07

Rah Digga, a respected hip-hop rapper and 'the first female of the Flipmode Squad', was set to release her second album in 2004, following the success of her 2000 debut, *Dirty Harriet*. However, after Flipmode Entertainment was absorbed into J Records, release plans for the album *Everything is a Story* were postponed and eventually left in limbo. P!nk features on the album track, 'Tell Me Why,' where she sings about trying to overcome ignorance and negativity.

'Tell Me Why' leaked online in 2005. Rah Digga officially self-released *Everything is a Story* on Payloadz.com in 2009.

'Shine'
Lisa Marie Presley featuring P!nk

Written by Linda Perry and Lisa Marie Presley
Produced by Eric Rosse
Duration: 4:10

Released in April 2005, Lisa Marie Presley's second studio album, *Now What*, saw her writing with Linda Perry, inspired by her work with P!nk on *M!ssundaztood*. P!nk, who was close friends with Lisa Marie, provides vocals on the track, 'Shine.' Their friendship began when P!nk first moved to California; Lisa Marie gifted her and Carey a dog called Elvis (named after her father), with P!nk describing him as 'the love of her life.' Elvis passed away in 2007, after accidentally drowning in the pool where he often swam.

Lisa Marie Presley passed away unexpectedly in January 2023. P!nk posted a heartfelt tribute on her Instagram, writing: 'Oh, this one hurts my heart. Lisa Marie, you were one of a kind. Funny as shit, smart as a whip, sensitive, talented, witty, mean, loving, generous, judgmental but always right, loyal, and you adored your children. My heart breaks for you and your beautiful family and your children. The world lost a rare gem today. May your soul rest in peace, friend.'

Unreleased Songs

'Bad Bad Day'

Written by Damon Elliott and Alecia 'P!nk' Moore
Produced by Damon Elliott
Duration: 4:05

An unreleased collaboration with Damon Elliott, P!nk finds positivity in 'Bad Bad Day,' despite feeling sad. In the lyrics, she sings about the things that have made her day bad, such as feeling tired, bad sex and traffic. As she cheers herself up, she references rapper 50 Cent's hit single, 'Candy Shop,' and sings, 'I could be sad all day, but I don't feel like it, no!' The song's demo leaked online in July 2008.

'I Can't Help It'

Written by Damon Elliott and Alecia 'P!nk' Moore
Produced by Damon Elliott
Duration: 3:32

'I Can't Help It' features P!nk's signature humour, opening with the line, 'I love you so much I want to light you on fire, show you how hot you are.' Another collaboration with Damon Elliott, the song's demo leaked online in July 2008 alongside 'Bad Bad Day.'

Live Performances

'Weigh On My Mind'

Written by Tim Armstrong and Rob Aston
Produced by Tim Armstrong and Dave Carlock
Recorded in Tim's Basement
Duration: 1:36

'Weigh On My Mind' is an album track on Transplants' 2002 debut album, *Transplants*, written by band members Tim Armstrong and Rob Aston. The song discusses feeling overwhelmed by unresolved problems, whilst struggling to achieve the 'American Dream.'

P!nk joined Transplants live on stage to perform the song in June 2003 at the 11th Annual KROQ Weenie Roast at the Verizon Amphitheatre in Irvine, California. They followed the song with a duet of P!nk's single, 'Get the Party Started.'

'Mercedez Benz'

Written by Janis Joplin, Michael McClure and Bob Neuwirth
Duration: 1:40

'Mercedez Benz' is a short acapella song, first recorded by Janis Joplin for her 1971 album, *Pearl*. The song's lyrics evolved from a poem by Michael McClure, which Joplin and Neuwirth expanded and set to a melody.

P!nk first performed the song in June 2003 at an impromptu short concert for a local radio station in Grant Park, Chicago, responding to a fan request for 'more Janis.' She later added the song to her *I'm Not Dead* tour, performing it throughout 2006 and 2007.

'I Wanna Rock'

Written by Dee Snider
Duration: 1:44

'I Wanna Rock,' written by Dee Snider and released by his band Twisted Sister on their 1984 album, *Stay Hungry*, is a loud declaration of freedom and defiance. Snider told *Songfacts* in 2016: 'It was designed when I realised that Iron Maiden was having tremendous success with their sort of galloping metal rhythms, and then there was the anthemic thing that I like to do, which bands like AC/DC do, and one of my biggest influences, especially in that area, Slade. I thought that if I could combine the drive of a Maiden song with the anthemic quality of an AC/DC song, I'd have a fucking huge hit.'

P!nk performed an abridged version of the song after 'Lady Marmalade' on her 2004 *Try This* tour.

'Welcome to the Jungle'

Written by William 'Axl Rose' Bruce Rose, Saul 'Slash' Hudson, Michael 'Duff' McKagan, Steven Adler and Jeffrey 'Izzy Stradlin' Isbell
Duration: 4:25

'Welcome to the Jungle' opens the debut album from Guns N' Roses, 1987's *Appetite for Destruction*, and was released as their second single. Axl Rose said his experience stepping into a big city inspired the song.

In an interview with *Hit Parader* magazine in 1988, he said it was written after visiting a friend in Seattle, later telling *Spin* magazine in 1999 that it was about his first trip to New York. He explained: 'It's a big city, but at the same time, it's still a small city compared to L.A. and the things that you're gonna learn. It seemed a lot more rural up there. I just wrote how it looked to me. If someone comes to town and they want to find something, they can find whatever they want.'

P!nk included a cover of 'Welcome to the Jungle' on her 2004 *Try This* tour, using it to open the show's encore before performing 'Get the Party Started.'

Catalogue Registrations

'For Better or Worse'

Written by Damon Elliott, Alecia 'P!nk' Moore and Greg Curtis

'What the World Needs Now'
Written by Damon Elliott, Alecia 'P!nk' Moore and Greg Curtis

'Full Throttle'
Written by Linda Perry and Alecia 'P!nk' Moore

'Better Off Alone'
Written by Mark Hoppus and Alecia 'P!nk' Moore

'Human Condition'
Written by Tim Armstrong and Alecia 'P!nk' Moore

'That's How You Turn Me On'
Written by Billy Mann, Alecia 'P!nk' Moore and Jonathan S. Davis

'Grass is Greener'
Written by Alecia 'P!nk' Moore

'The Un-Love Song'
Written by Alecia 'P!nk' Moore

'Dream Sellers'
Written by Alecia 'P!nk' Moore

5

I'm Not Dead (2005–2006)

Released:	31 March 2006 (Europe and Australia) 3 April 2006 (UK) 4 April 2006 (USA and Canada) 16 March 2007 (Australia—Tour Edition CD/DVD) 12 November 2007 (USA and Canada—Platinum Edition CD/DVD)
Chart Position:	USA: 6 Canada: 2 UK: 3 Australia: 1 Germany: 1

Following the relatively lukewarm reception of *Try This* compared to its predecessor, *I'm Not Dead* saw P!nk collaborating with a blend of familiar and new creative partners. She reunited with Billy Mann, with whom she co-wrote the bulk of the album, as well as working with new producers such as Butch Walker and Greg Kurstin.

The album also sees P!nk work with Max Martin and Lukasz 'Dr. Luke' Gottwald for the first time, despite initial reluctance. Martin—known for being one of the world's most successful pop songwriters—had been behind most of Britney Spears' first three albums, as well as having worked with Backstreet Boys and *NSync. However, in 2004, he had huge success with 'Since U Been Gone,' recorded by Kelly Clarkson, marking an evolution of his sound. Gottwald confirmed to *Blender* magazine that they had actually written the song for P!nk, but that she was not in the habit of accepting songs written for her.

In 2016, when Max Martin won the Polar Music Prize in Sweden, P!nk spoke about her relationship with him, saying: 'I think the funniest part about our relationship is neither one of us wanted to work together originally… it's not that we didn't want to, it's just that we weren't jumping up and down. I brought three bottles of wine and we started on the first, and we were not going to write a song until we got through the first bottle.'

Between albums, P!nk changed record labels following internal reshuffles within Sony BMG, the new overarching company formed because of Sony Music and BMG merging. BMG had previously closed LaFace Records in 2001, promoting L.A. Reid to President/CEO of Arista Records, with P!nk moving with him. Reid exited Arista in 2004, with P!nk moving to a revived LaFace Records under the Zomba Label Group arm, led by Barry Weiss. Weiss was previously the president of Jive Records, part of the Zomba Music Group, which was bought by BMG in 2002. Under his management, he oversaw the launch and careers of artists such as Britney Spears, Backstreet Boys and *NSync.

P!nk also decided to explore acting, being attached to a Janis Joplin biopic, which was indefinitely put on hold. In an interview with *The Courier Mail*, she said: 'At this point, I've let it go back into the universe. If it comes back to me, that's great. If not, there's other things out there.'

She did, however, star in a horror film entitled *Catacombs*, credited as Alecia Moore and playing the character of Carolyn, an American student living abroad in Paris. Shannyn Sossamon stars as Victoria, who travels to Paris to see her sister. P!nk said: 'Shannyn is the most gorgeous girl in the world. The first day I wanted to go home, I wanted to kick a wall and get the first flight out of there. But I got more comfortable. I know that out of the 50 scenes I'm in, at least one of them is really good. See, I think my speaking voice is really irritating so that was a big leap for me to take, speaking on film. It was even more vulnerable than singing, because I know I'm good at that.'

Recording what would eventually become *I'm Not Dead* around filming the movie, P!nk said she was surprised by the direction it took, particularly as she had struggled with promoting *Try This*. In an interview with the *Manchester Evening News*, she said: 'I didn't expect to be so emotionally involved in this album because the last one was definitely a draining experience but, I was forced to be emotionally involved by the people that I started working with. I started with Billy Mann, who's amazing and has become like my spiritual brother. I guess I was just kind of at that place where I felt like I kind of had something to add to the world, I feel like there's a hole and I know how to fill it, people aren't talking trash anymore. I was just feeling really creative and really emotionally available again, and it came out great. I did forty something songs. At the beginning of the record I was like, 'I don't know if I have anything to say, I don't know if I can do this,' forty songs later they are like, "Okay that's good, you can stop there."'

In July 2005, LaFace Records sent clips of five new songs to audience feedback websites to test P!nk's new material, including the now-defunct RateTheMusic and SongPeople. As a result, clips of ''Cuz I Can,' 'U + Ur Hand,' 'Long Way to Happy,' 'Who Knew' and 'Nobody Knows' leaked online. Speaking of the leaks, her label spokesperson told MTV: 'P!nk is finishing up her new album, which will be released later this year. Yes, she is working with Butch Walker, however, the titles of those tracks can't be confirmed yet.'

The title, *I'm Not Dead*, was inspired by a personal awakening she experienced after her father, who is featured on the album's hidden track, suffered a heart attack.

The album is P!nk's only album to be released on the short-lived DualDisc format, featuring all 15 songs from the UK album on the DVD side.

Speaking to *Variety* in 2019, she reflected on the album, saying: 'I was 24 when I made *I'm Not Dead*. I remember I had a dream that I got shot in the head, and I was stuffing newspaper into the back of my skull. I woke up completely freaked out and decided that my dream interpretation was that I had to start reading *The New York Times*. And I did, every day. Then I turned 25 and felt like I had just woken up. I became involved in causes like People for the Ethical Treatment of Animals. I thought, "What's actually going on in the world? And what does it mean to be a girl? And what does it mean to be a woman? And who the fuck is this guy we're calling our President?" Then I wrote "Dear Mr. President" and "Stupid Girls".'

Album Tracks

'Stupid Girls'

Written by Billy Mann, Alecia 'P!nk' Moore and MachoPsycho (Niklas 'Nikey' Olovson and Robin Lynch)
Produced by Billy Mann
Co-Produced by MachoPsycho (Niklas 'Nikey' Olovson and Robin Lynch)
Recorded at The Magic Shop, New York City and Turtle Sound, New York City
Duration: 3:17
Released as a single in February 2006
Music video directed by Dave Meyers
Chart Position: USA: 13; Canada: 2; UK: 4; Australia: 4; Germany: 5

'Stupid Girls' was the first single lifted from *I'm Not Dead*, co-written and produced by Billy Mann, who had previously worked on 'God is a DJ.' A biting critique of societal pressures on women to conform to superficial standards, the song features playful yet scathing lyrics, while the music video parodies celebrity culture.

P!nk said she wrote the song after seeing a trend of women in the public eye downplaying their intelligence to become more famous. After writing the song, she began noticing other commentary on the subject, including Ariel Levy's 2005 book, *Female Chauvinist Pigs: Women and the Rise of Raunch Culture*, which examines whether women are indeed free or whether they are learning to put on a show of 'cartoonish images of female sexuality' as young girls.

In an interview with *GenQ* magazine, she said: 'It's about the epidemic, it's about everyone and no one. I live in L.A. and it's all around me, it's everything we see on television. I wrote it because I think there should be a choice, and there's not a choice being given right now. It's their way or the highway, and I'm the highway. It's a fun song; it's all in good fun.'

She added on *Friday Night with Jonathan Ross*: 'There's a new tabloid every six weeks that pushes this one force-fed image of what a woman is supposed to look like, how she should act, how many big words she's allowed to use. In order to be sexy, you have to be stupid. To be successful, be less challenging. Don't contribute anything to the world, because it's not cute. It's just all these stereotypes that I find so boring and nauseating. If I want to find a strong woman, I have to Google her. But if I want to know who's divorcing, I can just open up a magazine. What I was doing with "Stupid Girls" does go against my idea of feminism because feminism is about supporting other women first and foremost. But I can't support that behaviour, and that's where the conflict comes in for me. I'm still figuring it out.'

The video, again directed by Dave Meyers, features P!nk parodying a handful of female celebrities, including Jessica Simpson from her 'These Boots Are Made for Walkin'' music video, where she seductively washes a car in a bikini. P!nk also impersonates Paris Hilton and Nicole Richie, who were starring in a reality TV show called *The Simple Life* at the time, where they came across as too naïve and unintelligent to take part in 'real life.' Other celebrities who are parodied include Lindsay Lohan, Fergie and Mary-Kate Olsen. P!nk said: 'I don't think any of them are stupid. You can't be that successful and be stupid. I think it's an act, and that's the part I can't respect.' The video also shows P!nk on the operating table having plastic surgery to fit in.

To *The Independent*, P!nk said: 'I'm a work in progress. The point is, I'm a stupid girl too. But I'm trying to be better. I can respect anybody who can admit that they're wrong and is trying to be better. You can always be better. I'm all about options, and alternatives and choices. There's such a lack of tolerance for diversity in the world as it is, that I thought it would help if the rest of the women, and the rest of the girls, were represented as well. If it could be like: "If I'm smart and I read a lot of books and I spend my money on charity instead of shoes, I could be in the tabloids too. Or I could be important. Or I could have a cuter boy. Or I could change the world." You know, you need examples when you're young.'

Music videos for both 'Stupid Girls' and 'U + Ur Hand' were filmed in December 2005, with both considered as the album's lead single. Barry Weiss, president of the revived LaFace Records, admitted that seeing the video made the decision clear. In an interview with *Billboard* magazine, he said: 'God, did she hit a chord.'

P!nk added: 'The first single is always hard, because it's supposed to represent a record that pretty much is like the first single. But with me, my only consistent thread is my voice, not even my humour is the same. My albums are just so eclectic. It's not all just funny, it's not all deep. It's everything in between.'

A commercial success, 'Stupid Girls' returned P!nk to the top 15 of the USA Billboard Hot 100 and reached the top 5 in Australia and most of Europe. The song was also nominated for Best Female Pop Vocal Performance at the 49th Grammy Awards in 2007, with the video winning Best Pop Video at the 2006 MTV Video Music Awards.

'Who Knew'

Written by Max Martin, Lukasz 'Dr. Luke' Gottwald and Alecia 'P!nk' Moore
Produced by Max Martin and Lukasz 'Dr. Luke' Gottwald
Recorded at Decibel Studios, Stockholm, Sweden and Conway Recording Studios, Hollywood
Duration: 3:28
Released as a single in May 2007
Music video directed by Dragon (Samuel Bayer, Robert Hales and Brian Lazzaro)
Chart Position: USA: 9; Canada: 46; UK: 5; Australia: 2; Germany: 12

'Who Knew' talks about the pain of losing someone unexpectedly, written from P!nk's personal experience of losing a friend to a drug overdose. Written with Max Martin and Dr. Luke, it became the album's second single in May 2006 and was re-issued in the USA and Canada in June 2007.

The music video, directed by Dragon, was shot at a country fair and carnival in Los Angeles in April 2006. During the video shoot, P!nk said: 'The song stemmed from death. I lost a friend to an overdose. But then it went on to mean more than that. It sort of encompasses loss in general. You can lose a friend and they don't have to die. They just move on.'

Reflecting on the song to *Entertainment Weekly* magazine in 2012, P!nk said: 'I always wanted to write a song for a friend of mine, Sekou Harris, who overdosed on heroin and died. And I never knew how because I didn't want to force it and write some cheesy overdose song. Over the years it's become about so many different things for me, which is why I love that song. It's been about my dog that died, and Carey, and Linda Perry, and my grandmother. It's always about something else.'

In 2017, while talking to BBC Radio 1, she added: 'I wrote it 12, 13 years ago and it's just taken on different meanings. For a while I wrote it about my friend and then it was about somebody else and then I was thinking about my grandma and then I was thinking about my soon-to-be ex-husband and then my husband again and then another friend passed away. It's never lost its meaning.'

'Who Knew' was another huge hit single for P!nk, reaching #2 in Australia and becoming her second-longest charting single in the country, ultimately being certified 5x Platinum. In the USA, however, the single struggled to gain airplay and peaked at #18 on the Billboard Bubbling Under Hot 100 chart.

'U + Ur Hand' was released in September 2006, reaching #1 on the Billboard Pop Airplay chart, which led to a resurgence in P!nk's profile. In March 2007, ABC TV show *October Rain* used 'Who Knew' in an advertising campaign, with download sales of the single helping it climb to #95 on the Billboard Hot 100 by the end of the month. P!nk performed 'Who Knew' on *American Idol* in May 2007, having refused to change the lyrics to 'U + Ur Hand,' and it was re-released to radio the following month, eventually climbing to #9 and spending 36 weeks on the chart.

'Who Knew' has also been translated into Italian and released by Clara Moroni as 'Io Non Piango Piu' on her 2010 album *Bambina Brava*.

'Long Way to Happy'

Written by Butch Walker and Alecia 'P!nk' Moore
Produced by Butch Walker
Recorded at House of Blues Studio, West Hollywood and The Chateau Marmont, Los Angeles
Duration: 3:49

'Long Way to Happy' is a powerful anthem exploring the journey towards healing after experiencing trauma, written by P!nk and Butch Walker. The song was based on a poem she wrote about sexual abuse when she was 13 years old. In an interview with *The Independent*, P!nk said: 'I know a lot of people that have been abused and/or molested and/or fucked over by someone close to them. And I'm no exception. And that's that song.'

Butch Walker spoke about the song in more detail in his book, *Drinking with Strangers: Music Lessons from a Teenage Bullet Belt*. He explained: 'Flipping through the pages, I started getting chills as I absorbed her words. Quickly I came up with a chorus and soon was able to take her musings and retrofit them into a song.'

He expanded in an interview with *PopMatters*, saying: 'It was written about her having to deal with being raped as a teenager by a cop, which was brutal for her. We had never even known each other before she expressed this to me, and I said "Well, obviously when we go into the studio it's going to be pretty emotional, so let's make sure the vocal goes down naturally," and sure enough she was practically in tears when she sang it, and I don't blame her. I don't think you have to subscribe to the mentality that you have to bring the person to pain to sing and give a good performance. You've just got to let the song be the song and let it do the work. Some songs are meant to be taken lighter and some are not. She definitely let that one fly.'

'Nobody Knows'

Written by Billy Mann and Alecia 'P!nk' Moore
Produced by Billy Mann
Recorded at The Steakhouse, Los Angeles and Turtle Sound Studios, New York City
Duration: 3:59
Released as a single in November 2006

Music video directed by Jake Nava
Chart Position: UK: 27; Australia: 27; Germany: 17

'Nobody Knows' is one of P!nk's most vulnerable ballads, exploring her feelings of loneliness, isolation and depression. Co-written with Billy Mann, the song was released as the fourth single from *I'm Not Dead* in the UK and Europe, becoming an airplay hit to promote the album over Christmas.

P!nk shot a music video for the song in London in October 2006, directed by British director Jake Nava. The video shows P!nk in her hotel room at the May Fair Hotel, wandering through the streets of east London and performing at Brixton Academy, where she first took the stage in 2002.

Billy Mann said that P!nk's label president, Barry Weiss, called him to congratulate him on 'Nobody Knows,' saying the song was a smash. He told *Variety* magazine: 'It was never released in the USA as a single. On tour, she crushed it and people wept. It's a song about dealing with loneliness. Simon Cowell apparently loves the song and years ago, on *The X Factor* UK, at the last minute, he had a boy band sing "Nobody Knows" to win the competition. They were called One Direction.'

'Dear Mr. President' featuring Indigo Girls

Written by Billy Mann and Alecia 'P!nk' Moore
Produced by Billy Mann
Recorded at The Magic Shop, New York City and Tree Sound Studios, Norcross
Duration: 4:33
Indigo Girls appear courtesy of Epic Records
Released as a single in April 2007
Video from *Live from Wembley Arena, London, England* directed by David Mallet
Chart Position: Canada: 50; Australia: 5; Germany: 3

A politically charged acoustic ballad, 'Dear Mr. President' addresses the 43rd President of the United States of America, George W. Bush, criticising his policies on war, poverty, abortion, and LGBTQ+ rights. The powerful protest anthem was written by P!nk and Billy Mann, featuring the folk duo Indigo Girls.

Talking about the song at a press conference for *I'm Not Dead*, P!nk said: 'I was in New York on Martin Luther King Day, feeling very political, drained, and exhausted. I'd been watching the news and reading *The New York Times* every day – now I limit myself to once a week, because it's all I can take. I was overwhelmed by all the arguing on both sides of the fence, and we wrote the song. Then we knocked on the walls and said, "Hello, is this on?" I called my business manager and said, "I'll be audited every year for the rest of my life." But I think it's one of the most important songs I've ever written.'

Written as an open letter to Bush, the song was released in the wake of the backlash received by The Chicks (formerly known as Dixie Chicks) after lead singer Natalie Maines criticised Bush and the war in Iraq. In an interview with *The Courier Mail*, P!nk referred to the negative treatment they received, such as having their CDs burned and being removed from country radio playlists. She said: 'It might cause some problems, but my management and label are used to that with me. It shouldn't be brave, but I guess it is. I guess what happened to The Chicks really spooked everyone. Luckily country radio doesn't really support my career. I don't know why, I'm so country!'

P!nk invited Amy Ray and Emily Saliers—better known as the Indigo Girls—to contribute backing vocals to the track, telling *Diva* magazine that she was a long-time fan of the duo. She said: 'I've loved the Indigo Girls forever, and I thought it was very brave of them to be part of this with me. I called them up and told them that I worshipped the ground they walked on. I grew up listening to their album *Closer to Fine*, and when I wrote "Dear Mr. President", I told them they had to sing it with me. They taught me how to harmonise.'

Amy Ray reflected on the experience in an interview: 'I think her co-writer, Billy Mann, who's worked with her a lot, came up with the idea of having us on "Dear Mr. President" and approached us. We were big P!nk fans even then, so we were flabbergasted – like, no fucking way! We didn't even think she knew who we were. But then it all made sense. We got together and did the song, and she told us, "We've been listening to Indigo Girls for 30 years." Who knew? It's a song that we need right now, a letter to the President, asking some really important questions.'

By January 2007, P!nk told *The Herald Sun* that she was considering releasing 'Dear Mr. President' as a single from *I'm Not Dead*. She said: 'I didn't want it to be one of the first singles - I didn't want it to be a publicity stunt or use it to sell albums. But at this point, I'd like it to be a single because the album's already done what it's going to do. I'd like more people to hear it, if for nothing else than to light a fire under their toes.'

'Dear Mr. President' was released a single in Australia, Europe, and Canada, where criticism of President Bush was more widely accepted. A live performance, lifted from P!nk's *Live from Wembley Arena, London, England* DVD, was used to promote the song instead of a music video. The single reached the top 5 in Australia, being certified 3x Platinum, the top 3 in Germany and Switzerland, and #1 in Austria and Belgium.

'I'm Not Dead'

Written by Billy Mann and Alecia 'P!nk' Moore
Produced by Billy Mann and Al Clay
Recorded at Remote Control, Santa Monica
Duration: 3:46

Title track 'I'm Not Dead' is a defiant declaration of resilience, written by P!nk and Billy Mann. Describing the lyrics, 'I'm not dead, just floating,' in an interview with *The Independent*, P!nk said: 'It's the first song I've written that's sort of subtle, or poetic, if you want to say that. Usually it's very much more cartoon-y and blunt, the way I write songs. I don't really know diplomacy or subtlety.'

In the album's electronic press kit, P!nk said: 'I wrote a song called "I'm Not Dead" and it's about changing and growing and just being alive, you know, you look around, it's hard to have your blenders on these days, there is a lot going on in the world. I turned 25, I'm a quarter of a century, and I want to live and be here, and I learned how to ride a dirt-bike, and I'm learning different languages, and I just don't want to sit down and shut up. I want to live and be as responsible and irresponsible as I possibly can – all at the same time. So damn it, I'm not dead, I'm standing up, and I'm doing it."

She added to MTV: "Billy Mann and I were in the studio for a month down at the Magic Shop in New York and it was sort of the last day. And usually on the last day all you do is party and talk and listen to stuff, but this was sort of done in 15 minutes and it's just about relationships, and coming and going, and growing and changing, and just fear and just all of it.'

''Cuz I Can'

Written by Max Martin, Lukasz 'Dr. Luke' Gottwald and Alecia 'P!nk' Moore
Produced by Max Martin and Lukasz 'Dr. Luke' Gottwald
Recorded at Conway Recording Studios, Hollywood
Duration: 3:43

''Cuz I Can' is a cocky, defiant proclamation in which P!nk makes it clear that she plays by her own rules, with a heavy dose of humour. In the chorus, she sings, 'I don't play your rules, I make my own, tonight, I'll do what I want 'cuz I can' before a choir chants, 'Ice cream, ice cream, we all want ice cream.'

A further collaboration with Max Martin and Dr. Luke, in an interview with MTV, P!nk acknowledged the song's lyrics might seem hypocritical. She said: 'I'm a walking contradiction. I'm a hypocrite sometimes.'

The song was released as a radio-only single in Australia and New Zealand in October 2007, reaching #2 on the Australian airplay chart and #9 in New Zealand.

'Leave Me Alone (I'm Lonely)'

Written by Butch Walker and Alecia 'P!nk' Moore
Produced by Butch Walker
Recorded at House of Blues Studios, West Hollywood and The Chateau Marmont, Los Angeles
Duration: 3:18
Released as a single in March 2007

Video from *Live from Wembley Arena, London, England* directed by David Mallet
Chart Position: UK: 34; Australia: 5

In 'Leave Me Alone (I'm Lonely),' P!nk captures the paradox of craving love but needing space, acknowledging her indecision.

In an interview with MTV, P!nk said: 'This is me. This is absolute me. "Go away, come back. Get off me! Get back on!" That's a fun song live. It was really fun to write because I love Butch Walker, who I did it with. I was feeling that way, I get really cramped, and I'm a walking complex. But every girl needs her space, and that's just about that. It's just a funny take on "I love you."'

The song was released as the fifth single from *I'm Not Dead* in the UK and Australia, with the Australia-exclusive CD single, featuring audio from the *Live from Wembley Arena, London, England* DVD, helping it achieve 2x Platinum certification. The performance from the DVD was circulated to promote the song instead of a music video.

'U + Ur Hand'

Written by Max Martin, Lukasz 'Dr. Luke' Gottwald, Rami Yacoub and Alecia 'P!nk' Moore
Produced by Max Martin and Lukasz 'Dr. Luke' Gottwald
Recorded at Conway Recording Studios, Hollywood
Duration: 3:34
Released as a single in August 2006
Music video directed by Dave Meyers
Chart Position: USA: 9; Canada: 24; UK: 10; Australia: 5; Germany: 4

'U + Ur Hand,' P!nk's first collaboration with Max Martin and Dr. Luke, was initially considered for the first single from *I'm Not Dead*, with P!nk shooting music videos for both it and 'Stupid Girls' in December 2005. A clip of the song leaked in the summer of 2005, as it was one of five songs played to test audiences to gauge their reaction.

With 'Stupid Girls' being selected as the album's lead single, 'U + Ur Hand' was eventually released as the album's third single, after 'Who Knew,' causing controversy in the USA due to its overt reference to masturbation. In the album's electronic press kit, P!nk said: 'I did it with Max Martin and Dr. Luke. And it is pretty much about masturbation. Basically, we girls get a little fed up. I go to clubs because I like to dance. I don't want to be bothered. "Leave me alone, I don't want you to buy me a drink. I'll take the six bucks, but I'll get my own drink. Just leave me alone, want to dance by myself."'

Talking to *The Irish News* about working with Max Martin, P!nk said: 'I think you have to be open-minded about these things. I don't sell my records out of a car boot. The labels now go on about "what researches well" and all that stuff. I certainly wasn't going to do a Britney-style song, but Max Martin is an ex-punk rocker. He produced the song 'U + Ur Hand' on the album and the label loved it and wanted it as the single.'

In a behind-the-scenes look at shooting the video, P!nk said that she would often hear men whom women had rejected in a club say to each other, 'Looks like it's just me and my hand tonight,' inspiring the chorus lyrics.

The song's melody and production drew comparisons to '4ever,' released in August 2005 as the debut single from Australian twins, The Veronicas. '4ever' was also co-written and produced by Max Martin and Dr. Luke.

Set in a club and directed by Dave Meyers, P!nk told MTV: 'I didn't want it to be typical. Not another club video. That's not going to happen, until we can do it all suspended in the air on hovercrafts. It just won't be interesting. It's high-fashion, glam, vampirey, tough, sexy. It was four hours of makeup and one hour of shooting for every different look in the video. I'll never do it again, so enjoy it! Because it sucked!'

The video premiered in July 2006, featuring P!nk in six distinct looks, some heavily inspired by the late New Zealand artist, Martin 'Marty' Emonds, known for his bold comic art style, including 'Rocker Biker Girl', 'Baby Red Knuckles' and 'Suck on Hard Candy'. Emond's estate considered suing P!nk, Dave Meyers and Sony BMG, but decided against it, citing concerns over the financial feasibility of legal action.

P!nk was due to promote the song with a performance on *American Idol*; however, Fox refused to approve the song's lyrics, suggesting it be changed to 'U + Ur Heart.' P!nk's publicist said: 'We felt there was no way around what the song is about.' Talking on *The Kyle and Jackie O Show* in Australia about the suggested change, P!nk joked: 'I'm like, "What does that even mean, how do you have sex with your heart?"' Instead, she performed 'Who Knew' on the show.

Despite these controversies, 'U + Ur Hand' became a global hit for P!nk, reaching #1 on the USA Pop Airplay chart, returning her to the top 10 of the USA Billboard Hot 100, and being certified Platinum. In Australia, it reached #5 and was certified 3x Platinum.

'Runaway'

Written by Billy Mann and Alecia 'P!nk' Moore
Produced by Billy Mann and Josh Abraham
Recorded at Pulse Studios, Los Angeles and The Steakhouse, Los Angeles
Duration: 4:23

'Runaway' reflects on P!nk's childhood, describing her packing her bags to leave home and imagining the opportunities that might await her, such as singing in Paris, becoming a dancer in New Orleans, choosing a new family, and changing her name.

In an interview with *The Sydney Morning Herald*, P!nk said her mother questioned her about the lyrics, having been unaware of how P!nk felt. She said:

'It's been especially hard for them hearing me write about things they never knew about. My mum's like, "Were you really that angry? Was I really that in denial? Was I really that bad a parent?"'

'The One That Got Away'

Written by Billy Mann and Alecia 'P!nk' Moore
Produced by Billy Mann
Recorded at House of Blues Studios, West Hollywood
Duration: 4:42

'The One That Got Away' is another collaboration with Billy Mann, which P!nk highlighted as one of the songs from *I'm Not Dead* that she was most excited to play live on tour. An acoustic song, she told MTV: 'It's the classic "is this the one? Or is the grass really greener?" song.'

Speaking to audiences during the tour, Pink said that she wrote the song whilst 'extremely intoxicated' and added: 'I've realised as I play that song more and more that it's actually a stalker song. I didn't know when I wrote it, but I'm a stalker. So are you. That's why you like it. We understand each other!'

'I Got Money Now'

Written by Mike Elizondo and Alecia 'P!nk' Moore
Produced by Mike Elizondo
Recorded at Phantom Studios, Los Angeles
Duration: 3:55

'I Got Money Now' is a melancholic track co-written and produced by Mike Elizondo, who worked extensively with Dr. Dre to write and produce songs for Eminem, Mary J. Blige, and Eve.

In the introspective lyrics, P!nk explores the stereotype that money brings happiness, questioning whether working so hard at the expense of seeing friends and family is worth it.

'Conversations with My 13 Year Old Self'

Written by Billy Mann and Alecia 'P!nk' Moore
Produced by Billy Mann
Recorded at The Magic Shop, New York City
Duration: 3:50

'Conversations with My 13 Year Old Self' is a deeply personal song with P!nk addressing, and offering comfort to, her younger self.

In an interview with MTV, P!nk said: 'When I was 13, I was angry, bitter, and goofy. I'm very much a "cover up the pain and laugh" type. But that's how I was when I was thirteen. I was angry, lonely, confused, and experimental and just searching for a way out. It was therapeutic to write the song, it was therapeutic to just think about it. To go back and think about me, 26 now, to think about me 13 years ago. I needed a hug. It was an amazing thing to do because in my head I said, 'Okay who was she, what was her deal and what did she need and what could I have given her?' Little 13-year-old Alecia... really she would fight me and tell me to go fuck myself and she doesn't need me, but if I grabbed her and hugged her, she would melt and go and cry for days.'

Hidden Track

'I Have Seen the Rain' featuring James T. Moore

Written by James T. Moore and Alecia 'P!nk' Moore
Produced by Alecia 'P!nk' Moore
Recorded at The Studio, Philadelphia
Duration: 3:29

'I Have Seen the Rain' is a heartfelt, acoustic ballad based on an original song written by P!nk's father, James T. Moore. In addition to co-writing the finished version, he also duets with P!nk on the track, which tells the story of a soldier's return from war. The song, recorded by Billy Mann, is an unlisted bonus track at the very end of all CD editions of *I'm Not Dead*, except the Platinum Edition re-release. It is also listed on the album's 2018 and 2019 12" vinyl releases, with the song's lyrics and credits being printed for the first time.

Opening with a spoken-word introduction, P!nk says: 'This next song is called 'I Have Seen the Rain,' and it was written by my Daddy, Mr. Jim Moore. He wrote it back in Vietnam about 40 years ago. And I grew up singing it with him at different Vietnam veteran functions. That's how I learned how to harmonise and how to love an acoustic guitar. And the way that we recorded it, that was my dad's first time in a recording studio, and he always said that singers don't really have to work too hard - he changed his mind that day. When we did it live, him and I live in the vocal booth together, him playing and singing, and me harmonising - one take, straight through - that was really, really a good time. It was really special to be able to record a song with my dad. The first song I ever learned. We hope you like it and dedicate it to all the veterans out there.'

In an interview with *The Independent*, P!nk expanded on her father's experiences serving in Vietnam, saying that he refused to talk about his time serving until he turned 40. She said: 'It was when he started this Vietnam

Veterans Chapter 210 of Bucks County. He sought out all of the veterans that he knew who were in the county and asked them to join this thing where they would get together and have fundraisers for homeless people and senior citizens. And they would get together and they would talk. It was like group therapy. He had a group in the Air Force, and then went to Vietnam, and then life happened. And I thought what a blessing it would be to share my experience with my dad because he is most of the reason I am here, able to do music. And we just went into the studio, and he was so nervous and humble, which was huge for a girl to see. It was one of the most amazing experiences. It was a point where you go, "I've made it", and this is really special.'

P!nk added to MTV that her father was surprised when she announced that she had arranged for them to record the song. She said: 'He didn't believe I would just rent a studio and put him in there with a guitar and make him sing. He was so nervous, it was the most adorable experience for a father and daughter to share. He's just such a folk singer. I just love it.'

James T. Moore joined P!nk on stage to perform 'I Have Seen the Rain' at her *P!nk: Flash Mob* concert in April 2006, organised by MTV and VH1.

Bonus Tracks

'Fingers'

Written by Billy Mann and Alecia 'P!nk' Moore
Produced by Billy Mann
Co-Produced by Christopher Rojas
Recorded at The Magic Shop, New York City and Turtle Sound, New York City
Duration: 3:44

A bonus track on all international editions of *I'm Not Dead*, 'Fingers' (incorrectly listed as 'Fingerz' on the back cover), sees P!nk describe her recording a video of herself masturbating whilst her partner is asleep. She included the song on the setlist of the *I'm Not Dead* tour.

Talking about 'Fingers' in an interview with *The Independent*, P!nk said: 'Everything to me is a visual. My favourite songwriters are those who can paint a picture with their words. Maybe I don't do it as dramatically or deeply or as poignantly. But I like to paint a picture.'

'Centerfold'

Written by Greg Kurstin, Cathy Dennis and Alecia 'P!nk' Moore
Produced by Greg Kurstin
Recorded at Echo Studios, Los Angeles
Duration: 3:20

'Centerfold' was co-written by P!nk with Greg Kurstin, and British singer-songwriter Cathy Dennis. In addition to achieving three top ten singles on the USA Billboard Hot 100 in the early 1990s, Dennis found global success as a songwriter in 2001 with Kylie Minogue's hit 'Can't Get You Out of My Head,' followed by 'Toxic' by Britney Spears in 2003. Although this early collaboration became a bonus track, Kurstin later wrote extensively with P!nk for *The Truth About Love*, including its lead single, 'Blow Me (One Last Kiss).'

In the 'Centerfold' lyrics, P!nk taunts a controlling ex-boyfriend who has broken her heart, likening herself to a 'pretty little paper doll' and 'the angel in the centerfold', referencing the double-page posters printed in the middle of magazines such as *Playboy.*

'Centerfold' was included as a bonus track on the UK and Japanese editions of *I'm Not Dead* and appeared on later Europe-wide re-pressings. It also appears on the DVD side of the DualDisc edition of the album in both 5.1 surround sound and 'enhanced PCM stereo.'

'Heartbreaker'

Written by Greg Wells, Kara DioGuardi and Alecia 'P!nk' Moore
Produced by Greg Wells and Kara DioGuardi
Recorded at Rocket Carousel Studios, Los Angeles
Duration: 3:08

P!nk collaborated with the then up-and-coming Canadian songwriter and producer Greg Wells on songs for *I'm Not Dead*, around the same time he was working with Lindsay Lohan, The Veronicas, and Nick Lachey. He later reunited with P!nk on songs for *Funhouse* and went on to co-produce *The Greatest Showman—Reimagined.*

Kara DioGuardi co-wrote and co-produced 'Heartbreaker,' following her work on Kelly Clarkson's second album, *Breakaway*, and Ashlee Simpson's first two albums.

'Heartbreaker' is a powerful rock anthem in which P!nk questions the authenticity of her relationship and the longevity of her marriage, singing, 'There's a ring around my finger, but will you change your mind?'

The song was released on the commercial CD single of 'Stupid Girls' and later included as a bonus track on the 2007 CD/DVD re-releases.

'Disconnected'

Written by Butch Walker and Alecia 'P!nk' Moore
Produced by Butch Walker

Recorded at House of Blues Studios, Los Angeles and Chateau Marmont, Los Angeles
Duration: 3:57

'Disconnected' is a mid-tempo number written by P!nk and Butch Walker, with P!nk singing about her feelings of isolation and struggle to make meaningful connections amidst the noise of societal pressures. The song was released as the B-side to 'Who Knew.'

'Crash and Burn' featuring Gentleman

Written by Billy Mann and Alecia 'P!nk' Moore
Produced by Billy Mann
Co-Produced by MachoPsycho (Niklas 'Nikey' Olovson and Robin Lynch)
Recorded at Magic Shop, New York City; Fizhead Music, Gothenburg, Sweden and Turlic Sound, New York City
Duration: 4:25
Gentleman appears courtesy of Four Music Productions GmbH

'Crash and Burn' is a carefree, reggae-influenced mid-tempo song, produced by Billy Mann with MachoPsycho, featuring German reggae musician Tilmann Otto, better known as Gentleman. The song was released as the B-side to 'U + Ur Hand.'

In the lyrics, P!nk imagines a utopian world where she lives her life on an aeroplane, listing perks such as free drinks all day, masks when she feels under pressure, sunshine outside, having her phone switched off, and being free from political divides, greed, and propaganda.

Gentleman contributes an uplifting reggae rap, saying, "No matter see the world, no grown up, you are worried about tomorrow, life will not toil, get yourself together, drop your sorrow.'

'Words'

Written by Billy Mann and Alecia 'P!nk' Moore
Produced by Billy Mann
Recorded at House of Blues Studios, Los Angeles
Duration: 3:06

'Words' is a country-influenced acoustic, co-written and produced by Billy Mann. The song was released as the B-side to 'Nobody Knows.' Throughout the song, P!nk plays with puns involving letters, concluding, 'words are just words, they get in my way.'

The released version of the song was mixed by Tom Lord-Alge and is credited on streaming platforms as the 'alternative version.' The original version remains unavailable to the public.

Other Songs

'Tears in Heaven'—Various artists (Elton John, Velvet Revolver, P!nk, Gavin Rossdale, Gwen Stefani, Josh Groban, Phil Collins, Andre Bocelli, Katie Melua, Steven Tyler, Ringo Starr, Mary J. Blige, Rod Stewart, Robert Downey Jnr., and Ozzy and Kelly Osbourne)

Written by Eric Clapton and Will Jennings
Produced by Mark Hudson and Sharon Osborne
Duration: 4:30
Released as a single on 18 October 2005

In January 2005, Sharon Osbourne organised a special recording of the Eric Clapton single, 'Tears in Heaven,' to raise funds for Save the Children in the wake of both the Asian earthquake and tsunami. Save the Children is an international humanitarian charity that carries out vital work with children affected by emergencies, abuse, neglect and exploitation throughout the world.

Osbourne said she was particularly moved by the crisis, writing in the press release for the single: 'The whole of my family were supposed to go to Thailand three days after the disaster happened. This is why I personally feel so connected to the tragedy. It just goes to prove how uncontrollable nature is and the tragedy it can bring. My heart goes out to every person affected by this tragedy and that is why I am putting this together in the hope of raising more funds to help these people rebuild their lives, especially the children. Everyone has come together for this project and offered their time and full commitment without question.'

'Tears In Heaven' was co-written by Eric Clapton about the death of his four-year-old son Conor, who tragically died in 1991 by falling from the window of the star's New York apartment.

Recording for the song took place across multiple studios throughout 2005; Elton John and Andrea Bocelli recorded at Whitfield Street Studios in London, UK, while Gwen Stefani, Rod Stewart and the Osbournes recorded at The Village in Los Angeles. P!nk recorded her vocals in New York, Mary J. Blige recorded in Ozzy Osbourne's home in Malibu in April 2005, and Steven Tyler recorded his parts in Boston.

The song was completed and released in October 2005, with funds also contributing to the response to Hurricane Katrina. Osbourne said: 'The magnitude of these natural disasters surpasses anything we've seen in our lifetime. With this single and other relief efforts, our intent is to keep these tragedies at the forefront of everyone's minds. We must not forget and do all we can to help these people rebuild their lives. Music fans who purchase this single will aid the relief efforts and own a historic recording for which these talented artists graciously donated their time.'

'Tears in Heaven' was available to download exclusively from 7digital.com, which waived its fees through Sony BMG, with the record company paying for all recording and production costs and donating its royalties.

'One Step Closer to You'—Michael Franti and Spearhead

Written by Michael Franti
Produced by Michael Franti
Duration: 4:41

Reggae act Michael Franti and Spearhead released their fifth album, *Yell Fire!*, in July 2006, inspired by Franti's trip to the Middle East, where he visited Iraq, Israel, and the Palestinian territories. He enlisted P!nk and Wilburn 'Squidly' Cole to provide backing vocals for 'One Step Closer to You,' a reggae-tinged mid-tempo.

'Song Without a Chorus'—Butch Walker

Written by Butch Walker
Produced by Butch Walker and the Let's-Go-Out-Tonites
Recorded at Ruby Red Studios, Santa Monica
Duration: 2:36

'Song Without a Chorus' is taken from the third album by Butch Walker, who began working with P!nk during sessions for *I'm Not Dead.* The album, entitled *The Rise and Fall of Butch Walker and the Let's-Go-Out-Tonites*, was released in July 2006 and features uncredited vocals from P!nk on 'Song Without a Chorus.'

Butch Walker and P!nk performed the song together live on 30 March 2007 at his concert at the Theatre of Living Arts in Philadelphia.

'Rock and Roll Heaven's Gate'—Indigo Girls featuring P!nk

Written by Amy Ray
Produced by Mitchell Froom
Recorded at Mitchell Froom's Studio, Santa Monica
Duration: 3:14
Music video directed by Kendra Hillman, Tricia Cooke and Carrie Schrader

Indigo Girls began recording their tenth studio album, *Despite Our Differences*, in 2006. Having been asked to work with P!nk on 'Dear Mr. President,' they asked her to return the favour by appearing on 'Rock and Roll Heaven's Gate.' The song, written by Amy Ray, one half of Indigo Girls, opens with the lyrics, "It didn't happen for you, no one wants to hear the truth coming from three political queers.'

P!nk recorded her vocals for the song in May 2006, appearing in a behind-the-scenes 'in the studio' vlog on the Indigo Girls' YouTube channel. In an interview, Ray said: 'P!nk is an awesome person. She's just a really great human being and such a talented artist. When you're in the studio with her and you hear her sing without a band or effects -there's nothing else going on except her voice - it's just amazing. Her voice is tremendous. I had a song that I wanted her to sing on, so we invited her to the studio. She came and met with us at our studio when we were working in Santa Monica. She was totally slamming and we appreciate her generosity.'

Despite Our Differences was released in September 2006, their first and only album to be released through Hollywood Records. An animated music video for the song was released in July 2007, although it was not officially released as a single.

'I Am Not My Hair'—India.Arie featuring P!nk

Written by Drew Ramsey, Shannon Sanders and India Arie Simpson
Produced by Drew Ramsey, Shannon Sanders and India Arie Simpson
Recorded at India's Song, Atlanta; Southside Sound, Los Angeles, and Larrabee Studios, Los Angeles
Duration: 3:45

Soul singer-songwriter India.Arie released her third album, *Testimony: Vol.1, Life and Relationship*, in June 2006, with 'I Am Not My Hair' being the official lead single from the project. Arie said the concept for the song was conceived when she saw P!nk change the colour of her hair from pink to blonde, while the last verse was written after she saw Melissa Etheridge perform bald at the 47th Grammy Awards in 2005, while undergoing chemotherapy for breast cancer.

Lifetime Television approached Arie's record label for clearance to use the song as the theme to their new movie, *Why I Wore Lipstick to My Mastectomy*, based on the 2004 memoir by Geralyn Lucas, and starring Sarah Chalke from the sitcom *Scrubs*. Arie revealed that the original version of the song was a duet with P!nk, and that record label politics had prevented it from being the album version.

In an interview with *Billboard*, Arie said: 'We both had something to say with this song, and we wanted to work together. This duet should have been the original version on my album, but it fell through the cracks.'

The duet version of 'I Am Not My Hair' was released to digital stores across the USA on 17 October 2006. In addition to being used in the film, the song soundtracked an extensive advertising campaign promoting breast cancer screening and awareness.

'Waiting All Day for Sunday Night'

Written by Joan Jett and Desmond Child
Duration: 1:32

In August 2006, NBC approached P!nk to record a new theme tune for their *Sunday Night Football* programme. Reworking Joan Jett's 1988 single 'I Hate Myself for Loving You' with new lyrics, the show's producer, Fred Gaudelli, said: 'We chose P!nk as the signature voice because she is a tremendous talent with a crossover appeal that makes her relevant to all segments of our audience. A football fan knows the anticipation of waiting all day for the big game. When you hear this song on Sunday nights, you'll know the big game is about to kick off.'

P!nk added: 'This is something so different for me, it's like hearing yourself on the radio for the first time. I'm such a huge football fan that it's a great time.' P!nk's recording of the song was retired in 2007 when Faith Hill took over, evolving the track each year until 2013, when *American Idol* winner Carrie Underwood's version commenced.

Joan Jett said of the recordings: 'I'm not Kanye West and I'm not on the radio all the time, so it helps keep my band paid. I'm just glad I don't have to sing the new versions. I'd probably end up singing the football version onstage by accident!'

'Tell Me Something Good'

Written by Stevie Wonder
Produced by Butch Walker and John Powell
Recorded at Trackdown Scoring Studios, Sydney, Australia; 5 Cat Studio, Los Angeles; Sony Scoring Stage, Los Angeles; One Union Recording, San Francisco; Skywalker Sound TODD-AO Sound ADR, Santa Monica; Fox ADR, Los Angeles; Record Plant, Los Angeles and Abbey Road Studios, London, England
Duration: 3:10

In early 2006, P!nk was invited to record a cover of 'Tell Me Something Good' for the *Happy Feet* soundtrack. Written by Stevie Wonder, the song was produced by her friend and frequent collaborator Butch Walker, alongside movie composer John Powell.

Originally recorded and released in 1974 by American folk band Rufus, with Chaka Khan on lead vocals, 'Tell Me Something Good' became a top 3 hit on the USA Billboard Hot 100. It went on to win Best R&B Vocal Performance by a Duo, Group or Chorus at the 17th Grammy Awards in 1975.

P!nk's recording of the song was released on the *Happy Feet* soundtrack in October 2006 and is the first song heard in the movie. It marks her first association with the franchise, later making her voice acting debut in 2011's *Happy Feet Two*, and contributing an original song, 'Bridge of Light,' to the movie's soundtrack.

Unreleased Songs

'To Love Me Now'

Written by Mike Elizondo and Alecia 'P!nk' Moore
Produced by Mike Elizondo
Duration: 2:38

Registered on ASCAP as being recorded during sessions for *I'm Not Dead*, 'To Love Me Now' was also co-written and produced by Mike Elizondo. Over a squelchy R&B beat, P!nk sings, 'Don't stress me out, don't talk about no promises, your privilege is to love me now', before live drums and guitar replace the beat for the last verse and chorus.

The demo of the song leaked online in 2010.

Live Performances

'Dancing with Myself'

Written by Billy Idol and Tony James
Duration: 3:10

'Dancing with Myself' was recorded by punk rock band Gen X and first released in the UK in October 1980. Billy Idol, who co-wrote the song, re-recorded and re-released it the following year. The song was inspired by Idol's 1974 visit to Japan, where he watched people 'dancing to their own reflections in the mirror and not really with each other.'

On 30 September 2005, P!nk performed 'Dancing with Myself' at the South Street Seaport Museum in New York during a special benefit concert to raise funds for the Breast Cancer Research Foundation. Supported by Target, the event raised over $50,000 USD for the charity.

'Get Up, Stand Up'

Written by Bob Marley and Peter Tosh
Duration: 3:10

'Get Up, Stand Up' is a protest anthem for human rights, originally released on *Burnin'*, the sixth studio album from The Wailers, released in 1973. The 2011 film entitled *Bob Marley: Making of a Legend*, featuring archival footage from his former girlfriend and collaborator, Esther Anderson, reveals the song was inspired by a visit Marley made to Haiti, where he was overcome by the poverty he witnessed. 'Get Up, Stand Up' was the last song Marley performed live before his death in 1981, and has gone on to become one of his most well-known hits.

P!nk covered the song at her September 2005 benefit concert to raise funds for the Breast Cancer Research Foundation.

'Redemption Song'

Written by Bob Marley
Duration: 3:00

'Redemption Song' is the final song on *Uprising*, the last album by Bob Marley and the Wailers to be released during Marley's lifetime. An acoustic ballad played on guitar, the song was released as a single in October 1980, just months before his death in May 1981. The lyrics were inspired by a speech given by Jamaican political activist Marcus Garvey in October 1937, where he said, 'We are going to emancipate ourselves from mental slavery because whilst others might free the body, none but ourselves can free the mind.'

P!nk included a cover of 'Redemption Song' on her *I'm Not Dead* tour, playing it on guitar after 'Family Portrait.' In an interview with UK mobile network, Orange, she said: 'This is the only song I've ever been able to play on guitar and I remember it being mine and my best friend's favourite song when we were younger. We used to listen to it on snow days and plan to run away. Bob Marley is a hero of mine, more and more as I get older. How can you not love his music? Now that I am able to understand that his music was actually very political and preached about love and government, I've come to respect him in a whole new way.'

'Blister in the Sun'

Written by Gordon Gano

P!nk performed a cover of 'Blister in the Sun' by the rock band Violent Femmes on 8 July 2006 at Summerfest, an eleven-day music festival in Milwaukee, Wisconsin. 'Blister in the Sun' is the first song on their self-titled debut album, released in 1983, and was originally written with a female vocalist in mind.

Songwriter Gordon Gano, the lead singer and guitarist of Violent Femmes, is from Milwaukee, and P!nk covered 'Blister in the Sun' to celebrate performing in their hometown. She performed her full *I'm Not Dead* tour setlist, inserting the cover before 'What's Up?' by 4 Non Blondes. Struggling to remember the lyrics to the second verse, P!nk encouraged the crowd to join in, creating a memorable singalong.

Songwriting Credits

'Whatever Happened to the Heroes?'—Joss Stone

Written by Billy Mann, Christopher Rojas and Alecia 'P!nk' Moore
Produced by Beau Dozier
Duration: 3:57

British soul singer Joss Stone recorded 'Whatever Happened to the Heroes?' for the end credits to the 2003 Marvel movie, *The Fantastic Four*.

Billy Mann, who co-wrote the song with P!nk, and Christopher Rojas, confirmed on Instagram that the song was written specifically for the movie.

'Closet Full of Love'—Puffy

Written by Butch Walker, Kara DioGuardi and Alecia 'P!nk' Moore
Produced by Butch Walker
Duration: 3:00

'Closet Full of Love' was recorded by Japanese duo, Puffy, who released the song on their 2007 album, *Honeycreeper*.

Catalogue Registrations

'Don't Leave Me Today'

Written by Mike Elizondo and Alecia 'P!nk' Moore

'Betcha Didn't Know'

Written by Butch Walker and Alecia 'P!nk' Moore

'Hate That I Don't'

Written by Butch Walker and Alecia 'P!nk' Moore

'Flaws'

Written by Andrew Frampton, Steve Kipner, Wayne Wilkins and Alecia 'P!nk' Moore'

'Personal'

Written by Michael Franti and Alecia 'P!nk' Moore

'You Can't Go Home'

Written by Billy Mann, Marvin 'Molecules' Leonard and Alecia 'P!nk' Moore

6

Funhouse (2007–2008)

Released:	24 October 2008 (Europe) 25 October 2008 (Australia) 27 October 2008 (UK) 28 October 2008 (USA) 23 October 2009 (Europe and Australia—Tour Edition CD/DVD)
Chart Position:	USA: 2 Canada: 3 UK: 1 Australia: 1 Germany: 2

The success of *I'm Not Dead* led to P!nk touring extensively in 2006 and 2007, beginning in the USA and Canada before continuing to Europe, Australia, New Zealand, the UAE, and South Africa. After the tour concluded in September 2007, P!nk returned home for a few months to spend time with her husband, Carey Hart. However, rumours circulated that the couple was on the verge of separating, which they confirmed in February 2008.

P!nk posted on her website: 'Thank you for all of your support and love, it means a lot to me right now. The most important thing for you all to know, is that Carey and I love each other so, so much. This break up is not about cheating, anger, or fighting. I know it sounds like cliché bullshit, but we are best friends, and we will continue to be. All I know at this point, is that I want to make the best album I can, and Carey wants to do the best possible job he can with everything he has going on. He is a good man, so please support him as well. One never knows the future, but mine and Carey's just might involve beach babies and sunshine one day. Just not right now. Thanks for the concern and caring.'

P!nk channelled her emotions into songwriting, recording over thirty songs for what would eventually become *Funhouse*. She told *Canoe* Canada: 'Creating songs is my favourite part, but I've had consistent agony and joy in all of the records. I'm always defensive and a survival-oriented person. I think when I'm writing songs it's my chance to be vulnerable. I'm useless when I'm happy. I find a lot of other artists, painters, filmmakers, writers... I hear that a lot. I don't find myself alone in that, that happiness is useless as an emotion.'

With songwriting sessions initially taking a 'really dark' tone, P!nk sarcastically joked she wanted to call the album *Heartbreak is a Motherfucker*. However, she began to find optimism, telling *AllMusic*: 'I started having a little more fun, which is so much more positive, definitely... when I said I would have named it *Heartbreak is a Motherfucker* that was like my sarcasm as well, I thought that was funny, but it wasn't. So now you're seeing how not funny I am. It started out really dark. People were worried about me. And then it just got to be really, really fun and I started having a really good time.'

For the album, P!nk collaborated with a mix of producers, starting with Butch Walker, before heading to New York to work with Billy Mann. From there, she went to Sweden to write with Max Martin and then to London to write with Eg White. On writing abroad, she said: 'It was really good to get out of my house and get away from my life. No distractions. No phones.'

RCA Records UK's Managing Director, Craig Logan, helped A&R the record with P!nk, telling *Music Week* magazine: 'She always tends to start writing with people she has worked with previously. She always has a lot of strong ideas and things she wants to say, so those first collaborations are important. She really drives the songs but there's no set way of doing things. Sometimes it will start with an acoustic guitar, a real blank page; sometimes it will start with a track idea and other times it will start with a lyric. Each of the different writers brings something slightly new to the party.'

One writer P!nk notably chose not to work with on *Funhouse* is Dr. Luke, making her one of the first artists to decline to work with him. In 2014, singer Kesha Sebert filed a lawsuit against the producer, stating that he had sexually abused her, leading to a prolonged legal battle. When *The New York Times* asked P!nk about the matter in 2017, she responded: 'I don't know what happened. But I know that regardless of whether or not Dr. Luke did that, this is his karma and he earned it because he's not a good person. I have told him that to his face and I do not work with him. He doesn't do good business, he's not a kind person, he doesn't do the right thing when given ample opportunities to do so, and I don't really feel that bad for him.'

The album was completed in July, with its lead single, 'So What,' released in August. P!nk named the record *Funhouse*, explaining in the press release: 'I look at life like a carnival. Clowns are supposed to be happy, but they are really scary. Carnivals are supposed to be fun, but really, they are kind of creepy. But we go, and we buy cotton candy, and we force our laughter, and we get on rides, and we strap ourselves in, and we do it. And that's like life to me, and love. Love is supposed to be fun, but it can sometimes be really scary. And the funhouse mirrors that make you look so distorted that you don't recognise yourself, and you ask yourself, "How did I get here? How do I get out of here?" But you think that you want to do it again. That is the same as love and life. It's a metaphor for being in love and for life.'

The album was hugely successful, going on to sell over 4 million copies worldwide, and spawning two tours—the *Funhouse* tour and the *Funhouse Summer Carnival* tour, marking the first time P!nk had headlined a full arena tour across the USA and Canada.

Reflecting on *Funhouse* in a 2019 interview with *Variety* magazine, P!nk said: 'It was my divorce record. Carey and I had split and I was on my own and just a little bit wild. I remember, I hadn't spoken to Carey for, like, 8 months and it was really painful for me. I went to Sweden to work with Max Martin and when I wrote "Please Don't Leave Me", I tried calling Carey and he wouldn't answer my calls. I was so fucking lonely. And I made one of my best records from heartbreak... that album was very successful. Maybe a lot of people were going through a divorce at that moment.'

Album Tracks

'So What'

Written by Max Martin, Johan 'Shellback' Schuster and Alecia 'P!nk' Moore
Produced by Max Martin
Recorded at Maratone Studios, Stockholm, Sweden and House of Blues Studio, Los Angeles
Duration: 3:35
Released as a single in August 2008
Music video directed by Dave Meyers
Chart Position: USA: 1; Canada: 1; UK: 1; Australia: 1; Germany: 1

'So What' was the first single to be released from *Funhouse*, co-written and produced by Max Martin and Shellback. A defiant breakup anthem, written in the wake of her separation from husband, Carey Hart, the song has gone onto become arguably the biggest hit of P!nk's career, closing all of her tours since, with a now-iconic flight over the audience.

P!nk said the beat Martin played her in the studio sparked the song's conception. She said: 'I heard this beat from Max Martin and Johan, it's such a fun beat, and I was actually kidding when I said, "I guess I just lost my husband, I don't know where he went." It was really funny, so I said let's keep it and we kind of just went from there and it just got more and more wrong. The more lines we wrote, the stronger it was. And we kept it because I don't really care... I don't think about the consequences when I write songs and now I'm regretting every second of it... no I'm not!"

'So What' was one of the first songs Shellback had worked on with Max Martin, telling *Café* magazine that Deep Purple inspired the song. He went home and finished a demo track, including lyrics such as, 'So what, I am a rock star,' which were changed for the final song. He said: 'Max suggested hip-hop drums... before that the beat was more like "Seven Nation Army" by The White Stripes and it transformed the song into becoming P!nk.'

The song's lyrics feature a reference to Jessica Simpson, in the line, 'The waiter just took my table and gave it to Jessica Simp', which was misinterpreted as insulting, particularly as P!nk had parodied Simpson in the 'Stupid Girls' music video. She clarified to *AOL Music*: 'Everyone thinks I'm trashing Jessica Simpson, but I'm actually not at all. I'm actually saying that she's cooler than me cause the waiter keeps taking my table and giving it to her. It was a syllable thing with that. It would have been that or "the pilot just took my private jet and gave it to Haylie Duff", but that wasn't as cool, so it ended up being Jessica Simpson.'

The music video saw P!nk work again with long-time collaborator Dave Meyers, featuring Carey Hart in the video. In the *Funhouse* album press release, she explained this diffused some of the criticisms of the song's lyrics, saying: 'At first I was kind of irked because everyone was like, "Well, wait. I thought the split was amicable and now she's talking shit about him?! What the fuck? It's hypocritical." But once everyone saw the video and saw that Carey was in it, it shut everybody up, which was lovely. Carey hadn't heard the song before he did the video. That's how much he trusts and loves me. He pretty much just rolls his eyes, throws his hands up in the air, and hugs me. He gets it. He gets me. It's nice.'

On her website, she spoke about how fun it was to shoot the video, saying: 'If you ever get a chance to drive a lawnmower down Sunset Blvd, I highly suggest it. Thanks for making my day. I'm really, really, really excited. This video was too much fun... glad you likey and don't worry – Carey likey too. We are insane.'

P!nk reflected on the music video a few years later, telling *Entertainment Weekly*: 'Carey was my ex when we did the video. I didn't want to do it unless I could have him in the video, in fairness to him because I was calling him a tool. And also, I didn't want to come off like some man-eating bitch, because I loved him. And he came through. I had to drink a beer at 7am, I was so nervous the day of the shoot - I hadn't seen him in six months. I looked good that day! I made sure of it.'

'So What' was an instant success, becoming her first #1 single on the USA Billboard Hot 100 and reaching #1 in the UK, Australia and Canada. It was also a huge hit across Europe, reaching #1 on the European Hot 100, becoming the sixteenth biggest hit of 2008 on the chart. In 2009, it was nominated for Best Female Pop Vocal Performance at the 51st Grammy Awards, losing to Adele's 'Chasing Pavements.'

'Sober'

Written by Nate 'Danja' Hills, Marcella Araica, Kara DioGuardi and Alecia 'P!nk' Moore

Produced by Nate 'Danja' Hills, Tony Kanal and Jimmy Harry

Recorded at Sha Recording, Malibu; 3:20 Studios, Los Feliz and Henson Recording Studios, Hollywood

Duration: 4:11
Released as a single in November 2008
Music video directed by Jonas Åkerlund
Chart Position: USA: 15; Canada: 8; UK: 9; Australia: 6; Germany: 3

'Sober' is P!nk's first collaboration with Nate 'Danja' Hills, who worked extensively on both Nelly Furtado's 2006 album, *Loose*, and Britney Spears' 2007 album, *Blackout*, with additional production from Tony Kanal of No Doubt, and Jimmy Harry.

The song started during writing sessions with Danja and Kara DioGuardi, with P!nk saying in the *Funhouse* press release that the concept arose while drinking with friends. She said: 'Ironically I drank a lot… I wrote a song called "Sober", which actually, seriously is a dark, kind of sad song about the vices that we choose. I had this idea in my head, "How do I feel this good sober?" So I brought that idea to Danja and Kara DioGuardi, and we wrote this song. It's a pretty telling song. Then me and Tony Kanal and Jimmy Harry finished it, production-wise. We threw some strings on it and made it a little bit darker and a little bit more rocky. It's just a really, really personal beautiful song.'

She expanded further on VH1 *Storytellers*, saying: 'I was getting a divorce and I was drinking a lot… So everyone was at my house, all these new friends all of sudden, and I looked around and there's that moment when you're drinking where you just hate everyone that's at your house and I was thinking, "How do I feel this good sober?" Cause I'd love… that's the other side of drinking. Why do we drink, you know? To be free of pain, to be free of shyness, it's like that liquid courage. So how do I find this again without this vice? I'm not going to meet a cute anybody drunk all the time, and I'm on the market. So, I went to the studio the next day, and I thought, "Cool. I want to get drunk and write a song about sobriety." So that's what I did.'

During her UK press tour for the album in October, P!nk announced that 'Sober' would be the second single from *Funhouse*, days after filming the music video in Stockholm, Sweden with acclaimed director Jonas Åkerlund. The video, a dark piece featuring two versions of P!nk, starring Swedish model Petrah as her doppelganger, premiered on YouTube on 5 December 2008.

P!nk performed 'Sober' at the American Music Awards to officially launch the single, ahead of a duet performance of 'Angel' with Sarah McLachlan. The single reached #15 on the USA Billboard Hot 100 and was nominated for Best Female Pop Vocal Performance in 2010 at the 52nd Grammy Awards. It also reached #1 on Billboard's Adult Top 40 radio airplay chart, making her the first artist to achieve three consecutive chart-toppers.

'I Don't Believe You'

Written by Max Martin and Alecia 'P!nk' Moore
Produced by Max Martin

Recorded at Maratone Studios, Stockholm, Sweden; House of Blues Studios, Los Angeles and Decibel Studios, Stockholm, Sweden
Duration: 4:35 (Radio Edit: 3:50)
Released as a single in October 2009
Music video directed by Sophie Muller
Chart Position: Canada: 66; UK: 62; Australia: 23; Germany: 17

A heartbreaking ballad, 'I Don't Believe You' was written with Max Martin in Sweden, with P!nk confessing emotional truths about the breakdown of her relationship. It was released as the album's fifth single internationally and sixth in Australia.

In the album's press release, P!nk said: 'The first thing that comes to my mind with 'I Don't Believe You' is me standing in the vocal booth listening... actually in the control room, listening to this song, tears running down my face, just like "Fuck, really?" It's the vulnerable and weak side of me that I don't let out very often. And it's... yeah it's that song. And I love it, I love it. I love it. It's very near and dear to me.'

Talking to *The Los Angeles Times* in 2012, P!nk reflected on the song, saying: 'This is the song Carey and I cried to. It's the most heartbreaking song I've ever written. I've never been there before. I've never been in that much pain before as I was that night. That was tough, that was the darkest.'

After reuniting with her husband during the *Funhouse* tour, she told *The Daily Telegraph* in Australia: 'When I sing "I Don't Believe You", I know that would be a lot harder to do, had Carey and I not got back together. After I recorded it for the first time, I remember sitting in Stockholm listening to the song, sobbing, tears streaming down my face. I can still go to that place, but every day is a different day and we're working through it.'

Talking on *Oprah*, P!nk said: 'I was pretty sure I was perfect before the breakup. I spent six years trying to change someone else, and I think that that was a great distraction for me to not have to really look at myself and see what I had to change in me. My dad said, "If you can think of 20 things that you want in a person, then make sure you have all of those", and I didn't. So, it was very humbling for me. I'm not perfect. I think you learn more about yourself in the context of a relationship than you can outside of it. A lot of people like to just start over to come to the same problem.'

She added to *Vulture* in 2017: 'It's the first time I've ever given my power away. It's very vulnerable saying, "I don't believe that you don't want me anymore." It's a very vulnerable thing for an alpha dog to sing. I had to swallow my pride. I did that a lot; that's how our marriage got back together. We both swallowed our pride. It's a good thing to do.'

A music video for the song was shot in September 2009 in Los Angeles, directed by Sophie Muller, featuring P!nk wearing her actual wedding dress. Filmed in black and white, the emotional video sees P!nk searching for her husband on what appears to be their wedding day, before crying and singing to herself in the mirror.

'I Don't Believe You' reached #23 in Australia, where it was certified Platinum, and reached the top 20 in Germany. It also reached #17 on the USA Billboard 'Bubbling Under Hot 100' Singles chart. In 2012, a Mandarin translation of the song entitled 'Ke Neng Ni Hai Ai Wo' was released on the debut album from Aaron Yan, formerly of Taiwanese Mandopop boy band Fahrenheit.

'One Foot Wrong'

Written by Francis 'Eg' White and Alecia 'P!nk' Moore
Produced by Francis 'Eg' White
Recorded at Modern Dirt Laboratories, London, UK
Duration: 3:25

P!nk wrote and recorded 'One Foot Wrong' in London with Eg White, who had achieved international recognition following his work on Adele's *19*. Craig Logan, RCA Records UK Managing Director, helped A&R Funhouse and arranged the session, telling *Music Week* magazine: 'I told her she will either love it or hate it and she said, "Is this guy's name really Eg White? I have to work with him!" It was a big love fest. They really hit it off.' He added that the mastered song that appears on the album is, apart from some subtle additions, the original demo they recorded.

Talking about 'One Foot Wrong,' P!nk said the song is about an acid trip, saying: 'I used to be into a lot of crazy shit. Acid's the most awful drug ever. Don't take it. But, that song is also about losing control and how easy it is to lose the plot in life and teeter on the edge.'

She added on AOL Music: 'I wrote that song pretty much for myself. I don't have any fear to show that I am a person who is making mistakes. I am who I am. But that's really all of the responsibility I am taking. I don't feel obligated to anything.'

'Please Don't Leave Me'

Written by Max Martin and Alecia 'P!nk' Moore
Produced by Max Martin
Recorded at Maratone Studios, Stockholm, Sweden and Decibel Studios, Stockholm, Sweden
Duration: 3:51
Released as a single in January 2009
Music video directed by Dave Meyers
Chart Position: USA: 17; Canada: 8; UK: 12; Australia: 11; Germany: 8

'Please Don't Leave Me,' written with Max Martin in Sweden, was the third single to be released from *Funhouse*. The painfully honest, self-aware mid-tempo song features P!nk admitting truths about herself, acknowledging that what she says is not always what she means, as she sings, 'I always say how I don't need you, but it's always gonna come right back to this, please don't leave me.'

In an interview with AOL Music, P!nk said: '"Please Don't Leave Me" is funny to me. As I was writing it, I was thinking about my mother. We have a tendency to be really, really nasty and obnoxious, but we're lovable, so it's kind of like "screw you, but come back, go away, come back, I'm an asshole, love me anyway." That's kind of that song. It's a cliché to say we hurt the ones we love the most, but I think that we feel safe enough to really be ourselves and sometimes ourselves is not a pretty picture.' In the album's press release, P!nk added: 'I'm trying to be better. We're all a work in progress.'

A music video for the song was shot in late 2008, directed by Dave Meyers, and co-starring actor Eric Lively as her love interest, premiering on YouTube at the end of January 2009. A dark comedy influenced by horror movies, the video references *Misery*, *Cujo*, *The Shining* and *What Ever Happened to Baby Jane?* It was considered too violent for daytime play on music video channels, leading to a censored version being circulated, which edits some of the bloodier scenes, as well as removing a scene of domestic violence.

P!nk shot a second music video for the track, which was used as the backdrop to her performances of the song on her *Funhouse Summer Carnival* tour. The video is one of three, alongside 'Funhouse' and 'Leave Me Alone (I'm Lonely),' directed by Canadian filmmaker Cole Walliser, who is best known for inventing the GLAMBot camera. All three, known as the 'Funhouse Freakshow' videos, appear on the *Greatest Hits... So Far!!!* DVD.

Released as a single in early 2009, 'Please Don't Leave Me' was P!nk's first single to be released in the UK without a physical CD single release, reaching #12 on download sales alone. It has been certified 3x Platinum in Australia, where it peaked at #11, and reached #17 on the European Hot 100 singles chart.

'Bad Influence'

Written by Billy Mann, Butch Walker, MachoPsycho (Niklas 'Nikey' Olovson and Robin Lynch) and Alecia 'P!nk' Moore
Produced by Billy Mann, Butch Walker and MachoPsycho (Niklas 'Nikey' Olovson and Robin Lynch)
Recorded at Electric Studios, New York City and Malibuddha Studios, Malibu
Duration: 3:36
Released as a single in May 2009
Music video directed by Dave Meyers
Chart Position: Australia: 6; Germany: 26

Co-written by Butch Walker and Billy Mann, alongside Swedish production duo, MachoPsycho, 'Bad Influence' was released as the fourth single from *Funhouse* in Australia and the sixth single in Germany, Austria and Switzerland. The unapologetic anthem sees P!nk comparing herself to an unpredictable wind-up toy, as she admits, 'I can't help it, I like to party.' In the album's press release, she said: 'I'm with the Hindus on that one. Pleasure for pleasure's sake is not a guilty sin.'

In April 2009, the song was licensed by Australian mobile network Optus for use in an advert promoting both their services and P!nk's *Funhouse* tour, which hit Australia in late May. Sony Music Australia took the opportunity to release the song commercially as a single, with it reaching #6 on the singles chart.

Volkswagen also licensed the song for use in a commercial promoting the VW Polo, premiering in July 2009, but being shown throughout the year and into 2010. With P!nk's *Funhouse Tour – Live in Australia* CD/DVD set being released in October 2009, and the unexpected success of 'Glitter in the Air' in the USA and Canada extending the album's campaign, Sony Music Germany also chose to release 'Bad Influence' as a single. Available commercially in April 2010, the song peaked at #1 on the German radio airplay charts, reaching #26 on the singles chart, as well as charting at #20 in Austria and #44 in Switzerland.

'FUNHOUSE'

Written by Tony Kanal, Jimmy Harry and Alecia 'P!nk' Moore
Produced by Tony Kanal and Jimmy Harry
Recorded at 3:20 Studios, Los Feliz and Henson Recording Studios, Hollywood
Duration: 3:25
Released as a single in August 2009
Music video directed by Dave Meyers
Chart Position: USA: 44; Canada: 21; UK: 29; Australia: 6; Germany: 16

The album's title track, 'Funhouse,' was its fourth single worldwide and fifth in Australia, where 'Bad Influence' had been released earlier. The song, which P!nk wrote with Jimmy Harry and No Doubt's Tony Kanal, uses the metaphor of a funhouse turning into a nightmare to describe the breakdown of her relationship.

Describing the song, P!nk said: 'It's about when the box you're in doesn't fit anymore... burn that fucker down and start a new one. This was the first song I did with Tony Kanal of No Doubt and his writing partner Jimmy Harry. I fell in love with working with them. We wrote fun fucking songs together.'

P!nk reflected on the song in a later interview, telling *The Los Angeles Times* in 2012: 'That was dark. I hadn't been at my house in a really long time since Carey and I had broken up. I had to go there one night and I had to crawl through the doggy door because I didn't have a key. Just walking through the halls, it was like a museum. It was just crazy. I went to the studio the next day and told Tony Kanal from No Doubt, and he was like, "That's a song".'

A music video for the song, directed by Dave Meyers, premiered on 4Music in the UK on 20 June 2009, featuring P!nk walking around the remains of a fire-damaged house, encountering evil clowns that are referenced in the song's lyrics. As she navigates through a pet door, she sees Tony Kanal playing the piano, before leaving on a motorbike. A second video for the song was also shot as part of the 'Funhouse Freakshow' trilogy, used on the *Funhouse Summer Carnival* tour.

'Funhouse' was another commercial success for P!nk, peaking at #1 on the airplay charts in Australia, where it became her sixteenth top ten hit on the singles chart. It also reached the top 30 in the UK, Canada and Germany.

'Crystal Ball'

Written by Billy Mann and Alecia 'P!nk' Moore
Produced by Billy Mann
Recorded at Electric Lady, New York City
Duration: 3:26

'Crystal Ball' is a poignant ballad about learning to make peace with life's uncertainties and unpredictability. P!nk references her marriage to Carey Hart, as she sings, 'Sometimes you think everything is wrapped inside a diamond ring, love just needs a witness, and a little forgiveness.'

P!nk said the song is the one she is most proud of on the album, writing in the press release: 'I am proud of the songwriting, melody, and vocals on that song. I recorded it in one take and we didn't mix it. It just went straight to master. It was all about a vibe and not about perfection or being polished. I just love that song and I loved recording it. Me and Billy got in a room and lit some candles, had some wine, and threw up a guitar mic and two vocal mics and just went with it.'

In the *Funhouse* electronic press kit, P!nk compared the recording of 'Crystal Ball' to 'The One That Got Away' from *I'm Not Dead*, saying: 'There was no production, no pretention, no perfectionism - nothing, just a vibe… an energy captured and that's that song. You know, it's pretty obvious what it means, but just I don't want to know the future. I think that the best part is not knowing and "The One That Got Away" was one of those songs from the last record, where we've had a little bit maybe too much to drink or not enough… or we're kind of right in that yummy middle ground and then Billy gets so pissed at me because I always use the demos. I don't mix a lot of those songs… a lot of the songs on the record don't get mixed. Some of them don't even get mastered. I don't want them touched and then he's like, "Let me re-sing my parts!" "Absolutely not!" He gets so mad at me. On "The One That Got Away" and "Crystal Ball", if you listen close enough, he's singing the wrong words. We're not even singing the same song, but it's so beautiful cause it's an energy. It's nothing else but raw love recorded.'

P!nk also told *Canoe* Canada that 'Crystal Ball' is one of her father's favourites on the album. She said: 'Billy Mann is like my spiritual brother, there are no niceties with us. I just walk into a room and say, "You'll never guess what happened to me?" Then it's, "I got this book that will make you want to kill yourself!" We go deep right away. The day me and Carey split up, my dad came to hang out with me in New York and I played him "Crystal Ball." My dad gets really excited about music, and he had the headphones on. He was shouting,

"Honey, this song is going to be a fucking hit! I love it! It's like a country fucking hit, honey!" I'm like, "Dad, I'm right here, I can hear you." So that's cute, I like the thought of exciting him.'

'Mean'

Written by Butch Walker and Alecia 'P!nk' Moore
Produced by Butch Walker
Recorded at The Chateau Marmont, West Hollywood; The Document Room, Malibu and Malibuddha Studios, Malibu
Duration: 4:17

'Mean' was written by P!nk and Butch Walker, originally starting life before she separated from her husband whilst on a vacation. Combining Aerosmith arena-rock with country influences, P!nk questions, 'How did we get so mean? How do we just move on? How do you feel in the morning when it comes and everything's undone?'

In the *Funhouse* press release, she said: 'Everything starts out so yummy. Where did we lose the plot? How is it that you once were holding the door for me and now I'm slamming it in your face?'

Expanding on how 'Mean' was created, P!nk said: 'Fuck it, I'm just going to tell the truth, we can decide later if we want to go there... one of the last trips that me and Carey and took was me and Carey, Butch and Nora, his wife, and our really good friends Steve and Jade Astephen. We were like the six musketeers; we would always travel together. And this was one of our last trips, it was for Butch's birthday. We all went to Ojai, brought a guitar, and had a picnic. And I took Butch over, I hadn't started working on my record yet. We were all so close that everyone knew Carey and I were unravelling, even Carey and I did, and it was okay. It was sad and weird, and beautiful, because we all knew it was one of our last trips as a six. I took Butch over to the side away from them and said, "I want to write a song called 'How Did We Get So Mean?'" and we started writing it right there at the picnic in front of everyone, and it was awkward, beautiful, and amazing. There was still so much love at that picnic, so much honesty, and really good cheese! And then Butch was the first person I worked with after Carey and I decided to split. I sat there and cried through the rest of the song with Butch and we worked through it, and we recorded it with me singing into a laptop, crying, sad. I think everyone can relate to that song. My dad even cried when he listened to that song.'

'It's All Your Fault'

Written by Max Martin, Johan 'Shellback' Schuster and Alecia 'P!nk' Moore
Produced by Max Martin
Recorded at Maratone Studios, Stockholm, Sweden and Decibel Studios, Stockholm, Sweden
Duration: 3:52

'It's All Your Fault' captures P!nk's pain and regret following her relationship breakdown, working through blame and remorse. In the chorus she sings, 'It's all your fault, you called me beautiful,' later adding 'I wish you could feel as bad as I do, I have lost my mind.'

The song, written with Max Martin and Shellback, is also hopeful for reconciliation, as she admits, 'I'm trying to figure out what else to say to make you turn around and come back this way.'

'Ave Mary A'

Written by Billy Mann, Alecia 'P!nk' Moore and Pete Wallace
Produced by Billy Mann and Al Clay
Co-Produced by Pete Wallace
Recorded at Electric Lady, New York City and Westside Pacific Music, Pacific Palisades
Duration: 3:16

Prior to the release of *Funhouse*, P!nk told *AllMusic* Italy that she intentionally avoided political topics on the album. She explained: 'I purposely did not write anything political because "Dear Mr. President" wasn't a planned, staged attack. It was Martin Luther King Day and I was pissed off and I felt like I needed to ask these questions and then I felt like if I tried to do it again, it wouldn't be organic and it would be expected and I don't like putting myself in a box that way.'

'Ave Mary A' comes close, as P!nk offers social commentary with a title that intentionally echoes the Catholic prayer, 'Ave Maria,' Latin for 'Hail Mary.' Co-written by P!nk and Billy Mann, the song highlights issues like society's quickness to hate, referencing suicide bombers, school shootings, and a dependence on medication. The chorus acts as a prayer, with P!nk pleading, 'Help me let go of the chaos around me, the devil that hounds me, I need you to tell me "Child, be still".'

In the *Funhouse* electronic press kit, P!nk commented: 'It's just a song about how fucked up the world's become, and how I think we've all lost the plot a bit.'

'Glitter in the Air'

Written by Billy Mann and Alecia 'P!nk' Moore
Produced by Billy Mann
Recorded at The Magic Shop, New York City
Duration: 3:47 (5:12—Live at the 52nd Grammy Awards)
Released as a single in January 2010
Music video directed by Dave Meyers
Chart Position: USA: 18; Canada: 13

One of P!nk's most delicate and emotional songs, 'Glitter in the Air' is a reflective ballad about taking risks in love and life, posing a series of thought-provoking questions to the listener. In the *Funhouse* press interview, P!nk said: 'I still don't have some of the answers to the questions I pose on this record. I'm still figuring it all out. I hope that anyone that listens to that song can answer "yes" to every one of those questions because if they can, they've had a yummy, yummy night.'

P!nk performed the song live at the 52nd Grammy Awards in 2010, becoming an iconic career high for her in the USA. During the unforgettable performance, P!nk sang live after being lifted from a tank of water, executing a perfectly choreographed ballet routine with trapeze artists, spreading water as she twirled on aerial silks.

The performance received critical acclaim, with P!nk telling Oprah Winfrey on her show: 'I almost try to make sure I breathe a little more than normal so people know that my mic's live. I was like, "Well, why can't I do it and sing?" Everyone's pretty much done everything else there is to do. When I walked out and I was nervous, my voice was shaking. Then when I get in the silks, I'm no longer thinking… my mind turns off and my voice turns on. It feels like after 10 years people still don't know what I do. "Glitter in the Air" is very spiritual and it's very sensual and it's very sophisticated and visually beautiful, so I just wanted to really show up. I didn't fall; I didn't mess up the words. That was a good night for me.'

In 2019, P!nk reminisced about the performance during an interview with *Billboard* magazine, saying: 'They let me do a song that wasn't a single, that no one ever heard before. They let me fly 100 feet in the air, with no harness, with water. It was so much fun.'

Immediately after the broadcast, RCA Records issued 'Glitter in the Air' to radio across the USA and Canada, while a special *Live at the 52nd Grammy Awards* download single was released the following day, containing both the audio and video of her performance. A further download EP was released in June, containing the album version of the song and the live recording from her *Funhouse Tour—Live in Australia* CD/DVD.

John Fleckenstein, Chief Operating Officer at RCA Records, reflected on the performance in a 2023 *Music Week* magazine interview. He said: 'I think most of America remembers it as this "A-ha!" moment. The impact that performance had on America, really, was that moment of like, 'Oh, yeah, this next chapter of Alecia is going to be gigantic."'

'Glitter in the Air' became the sixth and final single from *Funhouse* in the USA and Canada, reaching #18 on the Billboard Hot 100 in the USA and #13 on the Canadian singles chart.

Bonus Tracks

'This Is How It Goes Down' featuring Travis McCoy

Written by Butch Walker, Alecia 'P!nk' Moore and Travis McCoy
Produced by Butch Walker
Additional Production by Al Clay

Recorded at The Chateau Marmont, West Hollywood; The Document Room, Malibu; Malibuddha Studios, Malibu and Westside Pacific Music, Pacific Palisades
Duration: 3:18
Travis McCoy appears courtesy of Fueled by Ramen LLC

'This Is How It Goes Down' was co-written by American rapper Travis McCoy from punk-rap group, Gym Class Heroes, who also feature on the track. The song was included as a bonus track on all international editions of *Funhouse* outside of the USA and Canada.

In the lyrics, P!nk sings about her partner having an affair, using double entendres such as, 'Does she make it hard? Hard to speak,' adding, 'Darling, she won't ever be me.' Travis McCoy's rap continues in the same vein, admitting, 'I should've been more cautious, and clever, whatever, you'll never find a dude with a better head game - and you can take that both ways.'

'Boring'

Written by Max Martin, Johan 'Shellback' Schuster and Alecia 'P!nk' Moore
Produced by Max Martin
Recorded at Decibel Studios, Stockholm, Sweden and House of Blues Studios, Los Angeles
Duration: 3:14

'Boring' was written with Max Martin and Shellback and appears as an exclusive bonus track on editions of *Funhouse* in the UK and Japan.

In the flirtatious, humorous lyrics, P!nk asserts how unimpressed she is with the stereotypical qualities men expect her to want, such as 'fast car', 'money', 'hot friends' and 'rock band'.

'Why Did I Ever Like You?'

Written by Greg Wells and Alecia 'P!nk' Moore
Produced by Greg Wells
Recorded at Rocket Carousel Studio, Los Angeles
Duration: 3:25

Having collaborated with Greg Wells during sessions for *I'm Not Dead*, P!nk reunited with him for *Funhouse*. As with 'Heartbreaker,' one of their songs became a bonus track, with 'Why Did I Ever Like You?' featured exclusively for those who purchased the album on iTunes.

In the song's lyrics, written after her separation from Carey Hart, P!nk sharply declares that she would still hate him, even if she lost everything in an earthquake, comparing her attraction to him to an illusion or magic trick.

'Push You Away'

Written by Butch Walker and Alecia 'P!nk' Moore
Produced by Butch Walker
Recorded at The Chateau Marmont, West Hollywood; The Document Room, Malibu and Malibuddha Studios, Malibu
Duration: 3:02

'Push You Away' was co-written and produced by Butch Walker, featured as a bonus track on both the tour edition of *Funhouse* and the *Funhouse: Live in Australia* CD/DVD. In the regretful lyrics, P!nk reflects on ending her relationship with Carey Hart, referencing her hit single 'Leave Me Alone (I'm Lonely)' singing, 'I wish you'd never listen to me!'

'Could've Had Everything'

Written by Francis 'Eg' White and Alecia 'P!nk' Moore
Produced by Francis 'Eg' White
Recorded at Modern Dirt Laboratories, London, UK
Duration: 3:09

The introspective 'Could've Had Everything' was written and recorded whilst P!nk was working with Eg White in London, UK. In the song, P!nk contemplates whether she has self-sabotaged or defiantly made the right choices, singing, 'I could've had everything, this perfect life I'm in, screwing myself over.'

'Could've Had Everything' was released as the B-side to 'So What.'

'When We're Through'

Written by Butch Walker and Alecia 'P!nk' Moore
Produced by Butch Walker
Recorded at Chateau Marmont, Los Angeles; The Document Room, Malibu and Malibuddha Studios, Malibu
Duration: 4:22

'When We're Through' was written with Butch Walker and released internationally as the B-side to 'Sober.' The song is a stream of consciousness, inspired by 'Me and Bobby McGee,' made famous by one of P!nk's heroes, Janis Joplin, who died aged 27.

The lyrics reference Joplin and her influence on P!nk, as she sings: 'Janis sings to me just like she's sitting by my side and I wonder just how many times she sat like me and cried - I've made it past the age of 27 so there's no use in dying.'

Other Songs

'Sing'—Annie Lennox featuring Various Artists

Written by Annie Lennox
Produced by Glen Ballard
Duration: 4:21
Released as a single on 1 December 2007 (UK)

British singer-songwriter and half of Eurythmics, Annie Lennox, released her fourth studio album *Songs of Mass Destruction* in October 2007, featuring the song 'Sing,' which became the second single from the album. 'Sing' was intended to raise awareness of HIV/AIDS in Africa, with a note from Lennox on the front cover saying, 'Several years ago I personally witnessed Nelson Mandela, standing in front of his former prison cell on Robben Island, addressing the world's media. His message was that the pandemic of HIV/AIDS in Africa was in fact, a genocide. Since that time, I resolved to do as much as I can to bring attention to the HIV/AIDS crisis.'

Lennox told *BBC News*: 'Because the incidence of HIV/AIDS is on the rise for women, especially in the pandemic across the whole of the African continent, I thought perhaps I could be of benefit by writing a song and empowering those women who do not have an international voice.'

She personally invited renowned and successful female artists to join her on the song. Twenty-three artists responded, including Madonna, P!nk, Anastacia, Shakira, Celine Dion, Dido, Sarah McLachlan, Faith Hill, Gladys Knight and Angélique Kidjo. P!nk recorded her vocals for the song in Zurich, Germany.

In January 2007, P!nk told *The Herald Sun* in Australia how excited she was about the collaboration, saying: 'I'm not talking about it, I don't know what she wants to say about it yet. I'll let her let the cat out of the bag. But it's very exciting. I love her. I've remixed "Get the Party Started" with Eurythmics' "Sweet Dreams (Are Made of This)" and it's my favourite song to perform.'

'Sing,' which incorporates elements of 'Jikelele' by The Generics, an activist group that helped defy patent laws to bring anti-viral medication into South Africa, was released as a single in the UK on World AIDS Day 2007. Remixes of the song by Dean Coleman, Harry 'Choo Choo' Romero, and Moto Blanco were circulated to clubs in the USA, causing the song to hit #18 on the Billboard Dance Club Songs chart.

'Here Comes the...'—Butch Walker featuring Alecia Moore

Written by Butch Walker
Produced by Butch Walker
Duration: 4:09

Butch Walker released 'Here Comes the...' on his album *Sycamore Meadows* in November 2008, featuring backing vocals from P!nk (credited as Alecia Moore). The song was released as a single in Australia and New Zealand in January 2010, with the album following there in March.

A music video was shot for the song, directed by Roy LaManna and Lucia Holm; however, P!nk does not appear in the video.

'We've Got Scurvy'

Written by Eban Schletter and Steven Banks
Produced by Butch Walker
Duration: 0:52

In February 2009, Nickelodeon released a tie-in album to celebrate the tenth anniversary of the hit animated series, *SpongeBob SquarePants*, entitled *SpongeBob's Greatest Hits*. In July, the album was reissued with three bonus tracks, including the sea shanty, 'We've Got Scurvy,' performed by P!nk.

The song appears in the season six episode, 'Truth or Square', which aired in November 2009, where P!nk and her band appear to perform in Patchy the Pirate's 'TV Extravaganza.' A music video for the song was also shot at the time; it premiered in July 2009 in the VH1 documentary, *Square Roots: The Story of SpongeBob SquarePants*.

In an interview with *The Los Angeles Times* in 2023, P!nk was asked about her worst single. After initially choosing 'True Love', she said: 'I did put out that *SpongeBob* thing. "We've Got Scurvy"? I wish I never did that. That was a real mistake.'

'Imagine' Intro—Herbie Hancock featuring P!nk and Seal

Written by John Lennon
Produced by Larry Klein and Herbie Hancock
Recorded at Ocean Way Recording, Hollywood
Duration: 7:18

American jazz pianist Herbie Hancock released his forty-first studio album, *The Imagine Project,* in June 2010, featuring cover versions of well-known inspirational anthems. P!nk and Seal provide vocals for the first part of 'Imagine' on the album, which, while credited separately in the album release credits, is attached as part of the track on both physical and digital formats. The remainder of 'Imagine' features India.Arie, Jeff Beck, Konono No. 1 and Oumou Sangaré.

P!nk spoke about the song in a 2007 interview with UK mobile network, Orange, saying: 'It just encompasses everything. Musically it's beautiful and I love John Lennon and everything he and the Beatles stood for. I don't think there's a songwriter alive who doesn't wish they'd wrote this song. The lyrics are amazing. It's perfect; it's how we want the world to be. I wanted to grow up in a world like the one he described.'

Both P!nk and Seal were included when the song was awarded Best Pop Collaboration with Vocals in 2011 at the 53rd Grammy Awards.

'Don't Give Up'—Herbie Hancock featuring P!nk and John Legend

Written by Peter Gabriel
Produced by Larry Klein and Herbie Hancock
Recorded at Abbey Road Studios, London, UK; Ocean Way Recording, Hollywood; Market Street, Santa Monica and Garage Sale Studios, Los Angeles
Duration: 7:27

'Don't Give Up' was originally released in 1986 as a duet between British performers, Peter Gabriel, who wrote and co-produced the song, and Kate Bush. Reflecting on the song in 2019, Gabriel said: 'I'd seen a TV programme about the effect of unemployment on family life, so that played into my own problems at that time. I think a combination of that and domestic difficulties. A lot of people like that song, a lot of people say to me that it came at a very good time in their life. It's fantastic that, a great feeling.'

The song reached #9 on the UK singles chart and has since been covered by artists including Willie Nelson and Sinéad O'Connor in 1992, and Alicia Keys and Bono in 2005. Hancock told *Blast* magazine: 'I knew who John Legend was and I had met him a few times. I had never met P!nk before. It was great working with all of them because I told everybody what the purpose was. Because, really, the record was driven by the purpose of making the record, which is "peace to global collaboration". "Don't Give Up" came out better than I had expected. P!nk sounds beautiful on it.'

'Won't Back Down'—Eminem featuring P!nk

Written by 'DJ Khalil' Abdul-Rahman, Erik Alcock, Columbus 'Rahki' Smith and Marshall 'Eminem' Mathers,
Produced by 'DJ Khalil' Abdul-Rahman
Recorded at Effigy Studios, Ferndale
Duration: 4:25
Chart Position: USA: 62; Canada: 65; UK: 82; Australia: 87

'Won't Back Down' was the first collaboration between Eminem and P!nk, appearing on his seventh studio album *Recovery*, released on 21 June 2010 in the UK and USA. Although not a single, airplay and digital sales saw the song chart in P!nk's three biggest territories, selling over a million copies in the USA, where it was certified Platinum. It was also certified Gold in Australia and Silver in the UK, leading Eminem to include it on his 2022 greatest hits compilation, *Curtain Call* 2.

While promoting the album, Eminem told *Rap-Up*: 'I laid my parts first and kinda heard P!nk on the record. I felt like she would smash it, so I gave her a call and she was with it, so we did it. I've always respected what she does.'

Live Performances

'Sweet Child O' Mine'—Steel Panther and P!nk

Written by William 'Axl Rose' Bruce Rose, Saul 'Slash' Hudson, Michael 'Duff' McKagan, Steven Adler and Jeffrey 'Izzy Stradlin' Isbell
Duration: 4:10

In March 2008 at Key Club Hollywood, P!nk joined the glam metal band, Steel Panther, on stage to perform a cover of 'Sweet Child O' Mine,' the 1988 single from Guns N' Roses. The song, released on the debut Guns N' Roses album, *Appetite for Destruction*, became their only #1 on the USA Billboard Hot 100.

After the performance, Steel Panther's Satchel said, 'We're now called Pink Panther', before joking to P!nk, 'You're like ten times better than Ashlee Simpson.'

'Killing Me Softly with His Song'

Written by Charles Fox and Norman Gimbel
Duration: 4:27

'Killing Me Softly with His Song' was originally written and recorded in 1971, with a 1973 version by Roberta Flack becoming a #1 hit on the USA Billboard Hot 100. The song became a hit for the second time in 1996, when Fugees recorded a new version of the song, titled 'Killing Me Softly,' which reached #1 in over twenty countries.

According to the official credits, Norman Gimbel wrote the song's lyrics, and Charles Fox composed the music and melody, primarily on the piano. However, this has been disputed by Lori Lieberman, a singer-songwriter who was signed to a management deal with the pair at the age of 19. Gimbel, who was married, was having a secret romantic affair with Lieberman, and she later revealed that both men refused to credit her for her involvement in writing the song.

Lieberman recalled that she was inspired to write the song after seeing Don McLean perform 'Empty Chairs' at the Troubadour in Los Angeles. She composed the song as 'Killing Me Softly with his Blues', with Gimbel adding some finishing touches and suggesting the change from 'Blues' to 'Song'. Talking to *NextTribe* in 2019, Lieberman recalled: 'I never asked for a penny, for anything, I just wanted the correct story to be told.'

P!nk performed a cover of the song during promotional concerts for *Funhouse*, including at Café de Paris in London, and the Metro in Sydney.

'Crazy'

Written by Brian 'Danger Mouse' Burton and Thomas 'CeeLo Green' Callaway
Includes elements of 'Last Man Standing' written and performed by Gianfranco Reverberi and Gianpiero Reverberi
Duration: 5:20

Singer-songwriter CeeLo Green and producer Danger Mouse collaborated under the name Gnarls Barkley, releasing their debut single, 'Crazy,' in March 2006. It became a global hit, becoming one of the biggest singles of the year in the USA and UK, where it peaked at #1.

As a result of the song's success, P!nk included a cover of 'Crazy' whilst promoting *Funhouse* in 2008, performing it during the album's promotional concerts in October and November. 'Crazy' was also included as the main set closer on the *Funhouse* tour and appeared on the *Funhouse Tour: Live in Australia* CD/DVD set.

'Angel'—Sarah McLachlan and P!nk

Written by Sarah McLachlan
Duration: 4:00

'Angel' was written in 1997 by Canadian singer-songwriter Sarah McLachlan for her fourth studio album, *Surfacing*. Although McLachlan wrote the song in response to the death of Jonathan Melvoin, the Smashing Pumpkins' keyboardist, who died of a heroin overdose, its sombre lyrics and ethereal melody have resonated in other ways. In addition to receiving significant airplay as a song of mourning after the 11 September 2001 attacks in New York City, it has also been used in fundraising advertisements for the American Society for the Prevention of Cruelty to Animals (ASPCA).

P!nk performed 'Sober' at the 2008 American Music Awards in November, promoting *Funhouse*, and later joined Sarah McLachlan for a duet of 'Angel.' McLachlan told *Entertainment Weekly* that she first met P!nk at Ellen DeGeneres' fiftieth birthday party. She said: 'P!nk told me about seeing Prince play "Angel" at Coachella, and how she sang every word at the top of her lungs. I thought, "Hmm... I think I know who might be able to sing it with me." I love her voice - she's got a great rock 'n' roll grit that's also really soulful.'

'I Touch Myself'

Written by Tom Kelly, Billy Steinberg, Christine Amphlett and Mark McEntee
Duration: 4:11

During P!nk's *Funhouse* tour, she performed a cover of 'I Touch Myself,' originally released by the Australian group, Divinyls, in 1990. The song appeared in the setlist after 'Don't Let Me Get Me' and before 'Please Don't Leave Me,' and was included on the *Funhouse Tour: Live in Australia* CD/DVD set. P!nk told *The Daily Telegraph* Australia: 'I have to have a sexy bit in there somewhere! I'm carrying on from "Fingers" and "Oh My God" - you know, stripper poles and naked ladies.'

Billy Steinberg and Tom Kelly, the songwriting duo behind Madonna's 'Like A Virgin' and 'Eternal Flame' by the Bangles, had the initial concept for the song before they met Christine Amphlett from Divinyls. She was attracted to the song, with its double entendre referring to the 'touch' of female masturbation and self-love, as well as being a source of emotional reassurance. 'I Touch Myself' became a huge commercial success, reaching the top ten in the UK and USA, and #1 in Australia. Amphlett passed away in 2013 of breast cancer, aged just 53.

'Babe I'm Gonna Leave You'

Written by Anne Bredon
Duration: 6:13

'Babe I'm Gonna Leave You' is a haunting folk-blues track written by American songwriter Anne Bredon in the late 1950s. The song was first released by Joan Baez in 1962, with later covers following, including a 1969 recording by Led Zeppelin, which has since become the song's definitive version.

P!nk included a cover of the song on her *Funhouse* tour, performing it after 'Trouble' in the setlist, with a recording of the song appearing on the *Funhouse Tour: Live in Australia* CD/DVD set. She also performed it during her 2017 festival dates, in a few of her outdoor summer shows in 2022 and 2023, and at the January 2025 FireAid benefit concert in Los Angeles.

'Bohemian Rhapsody'

Written by Freddie Mercury
Duration: 5:51

P!nk continued to express her love for British band Queen during her *Funhouse* tour, including a cover of 'Bohemian Rhapsody' in the setlist following 'Sober.' The song is featured on the *Funhouse Tour: Live in Australia* CD/DVD set.

An epic rock opera, 'Bohemian Rhapsody' is widely regarded as one of Queen's most iconic songs. Since its release in 1975, it has been certified Diamond in the USA and 5x Platinum in the UK. P!nk also included the song in select performances during her outdoor summer shows in 2022.

Talking to Alice 97.3 in 2012, she joked her backing singers hated her for including it. She said: 'I have my background singers, and they hate me. I'm like, "You take that, you take that part." We did "Bohemian Rhapsody" on the last run, full version. My background singer, Stacy, was like, "Really? What did I do? I got that part?" I was like, "Yep!"'

'My Generation'/ 'Basket Case'/'Roxanne' Medley featuring Butch Walker

'My Generation' Written by Pete Townshend
'Basket Case' Written by Billie Joe Armstrong, Mike Dirnt and Frank 'Tré Cool' Wright III
'Roxanne' Written by Gordon 'Sting' Sumner
Duration: 7:42

With collaborator and friend Butch Walker supporting her on the *Funhouse Summer Carnival* tour in 2010, P!nk invited him to join her for a medley of three iconic songs— The Who's 'My Generation', Green Day's 'Basket Case' and 'Roxanne' by the Police.

'My Generation' was written by Pete Townshend of English rock band The Who, released in October 1965, becoming their biggest hit in the UK. Although it only reached #74 on the USA Billboard Hot 100, it was inducted into the Grammy Hall of Fame in 1999, in recognition of its 'lasting qualitative or historical significance.'

'Basket Case' is one of the biggest hits recorded by American pop-punk band Green Day, becoming the second single to be taken from their third studio album, *Dookie*, in August 1994. It reached #7 on the UK singles chart and was nominated for Best Rock Vocal Performance by a Duo or Group at the 37th Grammy Awards in 1995.

'Roxanne' was written by Sting and released by his band, the Police, in 1978 as the lead single from their debut album, *Outlandos d'Amour*. The song did not chart in the UK upon initial release but reached #12 following a re-release in April 1979, as a result of it charting at #32 on the USA Billboard Hot 100.

'Free Fallin'

Written by Tom Petty, Jeff Lynne
Duration: 4:05

P!nk performed a cover of 'Free Fallin'' during her *Funhouse Summer Carnival* tour date in Landgraf in the Netherlands on 30 May 2010, which formed part of their annual Pinkpop festival. P!nk entered an inflatable bumper ball during the performance and travelled over the audience.

'Free Fallin'' was co-written and recorded by Tom Petty for his 1989 debut album, *Full Moon Fever*. It became his highest-charting single when it was released in early 1990, peaking at #11 in the Netherlands on the Dutch Top 40 Tipparade chart and #7 on the USA Billboard Hot 100.

Songwriting Credits

'Outside of You'—Hilary Duff

Written by Raine Maida, Chantal Kreviazuk and Alecia 'P!nk' Moore
Produced by Chico Bennett, Richard Vission and Raine Maida
Duration: 3:44

'Outside of You' was written for *I'm Not Dead* by P!nk and Canadian husband-and-wife team, Raine Maida and Chantal Kreviazuk, who worked with Avril Lavigne on her second album, *Under My Skin*. Hilary Duff recorded the song for her March 2007 album, *Dignity*.

In an interview with *The Torontoist*, Maida said: 'With the songwriting-for-hire thing, we try to write with people who come in with some sort of idea. I'm really not about just writing a song for the sake of selling it to someone. The Hilary song was actually something we wrote with P!nk but it didn't get up on her record. Hilary loved the song and did it, so we didn't really write with her, but P!nk is an amazing writer and I have such a respect for her. That side of the business is interesting. We do it as something to work that side of the brain.'

A clip of P!nk's demo recording of the song leaked online in 2021.

'So In Love'—Suzie McNeil

Written by Marti Frederiksen and Alecia 'P!nk' Moore
Produced by Marti Frederiksen
Duration: 4:04

Canadian singer-songwriter Suzie McNeil was one of the backing vocalists on P!nk's *I'm Not Dead* tour in 2006, before starring in the Toronto production of Queen's *We Will Rock You* musical in 2007. She released her debut album, *Broken and Beautiful*, in April that year, produced by Marti Frederiksen, who previously collaborated with P!nk on *M!ssundaztood* album track, 'Misery.'

'So In Love,' the album's fourth song, was co-written by P!nk during those sessions. P!nk's original demo recording of the song is currently unavailable to the public.

'I Will'—Natalia

Written by Marti Frederiksen and Alecia 'P!nk' Moore
Produced by Ingo Politz, Bernd Wendlandt and André 'Brix' Buchmann
Recorded at Valcon Studio I, Berlin, Germany
Duration: 3:30

Belgian singer Natalia, who rose to fame after finishing second in the 2003 Flemish series of *Idool*, released her third studio album, *Everything and More*, in May 2007.

Natalia is one of the biggest selling acts in Belgian history and had met P!nk before recording 'I Will,' a song that was written during the *M!ssundaztood* sessions with Marti Frederiksen. In July 2007, they reunited backstage at P!nk's gig at the Sleuyter Arena in Ostend, where Natalia presented her with a platinum disc for *I'm Not Dead.* During the meeting, P!nk expressed how pleased she was with Natalia's rendition of 'I Will.'

'No One Else'—Alison Iraheta

Written by Greg Wells, Kara DioGuardi and Alecia 'P!nk' Moore
Produced by Greg Wells
Duration: 4:00

'No One Else' was co-written and recorded by P!nk for potential inclusion on *I'm Not Dead*, in the same sessions as B-side, 'Heartbreaker.' Although unused, the song was played for *American Idol* season 8 contestant Alison Iraheta, who recorded it for her 2009 debut album, *Just Like You*.

In an interview with *MassLive*, Iraheta said: 'My favourite is "No One Else", the one that P!nk and Kara wrote... it's just something that I really related to. I related to all of the songs but definitely that one the most. It's such a heartfelt song. You could pretty much dedicate that to anyone.'

The song was later translated into Spanish in 2011 and recorded by Mallorcan performer Chenoa for her EP, *Como un Fantasma*, as 'Simplemente Tú.'

P!nk's demo of 'No One Else' is currently unavailable to the public.

Catalogue Registrations

'Happy Face'

Written by Billy Mann, Alecia 'P!nk' Moore and Pete Wallace

'I Don't Love You Anymore'

Written by Billy Mann and Alecia 'P!nk' Moore

7

Greatest Hits... So Far!!! (1999–2010)

Released:	12 November 2010 (Europe and Australia) 15 November 2010 (UK) 16 November 2010 (USA)
Chart Position:	USA: 5 Canada: 4 UK: 5 Australia: 1 Germany: 3

Greatest Hits... So Far!!! is a compilation of singles from across P!nk's first five studio albums—*Can't Take Me Home*, *M!ssundaztood*, *Try This*, *I'm Not Dead* and *Funhouse*—alongside three new recordings. While P!nk was contractually obliged to release the album, her life had changed since she released *Funhouse*. After reuniting with her husband, Carey Hart, she was planning to start a family, with this compilation marking the end of a chapter of her life.

Talking to *Redbook* magazine, she confirmed how they reconciled, explaining how Carey had asked her to fly to Las Vegas to perform at his club on New Year's Eve. She said: 'After sound check I told him that he needed to come to my room. I had made him a photo album of all the cards he had ever given me, of all the photos of our entire relationship. I spent months on this album. On the last page, I pasted a photo of me from a really bad movie I made years ago (2007's *Catacombs*) with my neck slit and blood everywhere. Next to it, I wrote, "This is me without you." On the next page, there was a picture of a baby. And I wrote, "The rest is unwritten." The divorce papers that we never signed were behind that page. I was like, "The rest is up to you." And I did all of this in his favourite bra and panties.'

In interviews to promote the compilation, P!nk confirmed her conflicted feelings about releasing a greatest hits collection. Speaking to *The Los Angeles*

Times, she said: 'I was not inspired at all for this album. I always figured you need to be 60 or better, to have a little more past, to put one of these out. I fought it for years. That and dolls, to me, just don't need to happen. Record companies, I found out, can put out compilations without your permission. I wanted it done my way, so I jumped on board. Then, the less sceptical I felt about it, I started to feel a little proud. I decided, all right.'

She added to *Billboard* magazine: "I'm happier now than I was when it was first being talked about. I had been putting it off for years, although that sounds pretty funny. I don't feel old enough, I guess. At the end of the day, when I get out of my own way, which is what I had to do, it's something to really be proud of, because when I was a little girl, all I wanted to do was make one hit record. To be able to put out an album full of them is pretty damn special.'

Having agreed to authorise and participate in the compilation, P!nk had sessions with Max Martin and Shellback in September 2010 to write and record some new songs, resulting in 'Raise Your Glass' and 'Fucking Perfect.' She was already pregnant with her first child during these sessions, confirming rumours during her appearance on *The Ellen DeGeneres Show* in November. She said: 'I didn't want to talk about it because I was just really nervous and I have had a miscarriage before. I worked for it... it was not an 'oops'.'

Greatest Hits... So Far!!! was released on both standard edition CD and deluxe edition CD and DVD formats, with the DVD featuring many of P!nk's music videos to date. The tracklist was changed for different territories to best reflect the singles that had most recognition or success in that region. The standard USA and Canada release features sixteen songs, omitting both earlier and less successful singles such as 'Most Girls,' 'You Make Me Sick,' 'Feel Good Time,' 'God is a DJ,' 'Funhouse,' and 'I Don't Believe You,' as well as previously unreleased song, 'Heartbreak Down,' which was co-written and produced by Butch Walker. However, 'Dear Mr. President,' although not released as a single in those countries, had become so recognisable that it was included. 'Funhouse' and 'I Don't Believe You' were also included on the deluxe CD/DVD edition.

Internationally, the standard edition featured nineteen songs, removing 'Glitter in the Air' but adding 'You Make Me Sick,' 'Bad Influence,' 'Funhouse' and 'Heartbreak Down.' The deluxe edition CD/DVD adds a further two songs—P!nk's original recording of 'Whataya Want from Me' (recorded by Adam Lambert)' and 'I Don't Believe You.' The DVD was also released as a standalone music video album in some countries, including Australia.

The album was re-released in Japan in October 2019 following 'So What' being selected as the theme song for the sixth season of the hit Japanese drama, *Doctor-X: Surgeon Michiko Daimon*. Entitled *Greatest Hits... So Far 2019*!!!, it features twenty tracks; the original nineteen-track edition with a revised running order, opening with 'So What,' and adding the Bimbo Jones Radio Mix of the song as a bonus track.

Greatest Hits... So Far!!! was a commercial success for P!nk, debuting at #14 on the USA Billboard Top 200 before climbing to #5. It also reached the top 5 in Canada, Germany, Switzerland and Austria. In Australia, it debuted at #1, becoming the country's biggest-selling album of the year. It has since been certified 11x Platinum, with the standalone DVD also certified 2x Platinum. In the UK, the album peaked at #5 but has remained a staple of the album chart, selling over 1.2 million copies as of 2025.

Album Tracks

'Raise Your Glass'

Written by Max Martin, Johan 'Shellback' Schuster and Alecia 'P!nk' Moore
Produced by Max Martin and Johan 'Shellback' Schuster
Recorded at Woodshed Recording, Malibu
Duration: 3:23
Released as a single in October 2010
Music video directed by Dave Meyers
Chart Position: USA: 1; Canada: 2; UK: 13; Australia: 1; Germany: 5

'Raise Your Glass' was the first single released from *Greatest Hits... So Far!!!*, an anthem that P!nk wrote with Max Martin and Shellback to thank fans for their support. In an interview with MTV in October 2010, she said: 'I don't know if it's going to be huge, but it is new. I did three new songs. It was good timing. I had been on the road for two years and I hadn't written anything and I wanted to write a song about underdogs.' She added: 'To me it's about being an underdog and celebrating imperfections and celebrating the fact that we're dirty little freaks.'

In her 2012 interview for *The Truth About Love*, P!nk added that husband Carey Hart, inspired the song. She recalled: 'Carey dropped me off at the studio on the day that I wrote it and I was like, "I don't know", because I was pregnant and huge and I just wanted to go eat cheesecake. And I said, "I don't have anything to say". He's like, "Well, you know, this is the greatest hits. It's a thank you to your fans. So write a thank you to your fans." And so I wrote "Raise Your Glass".'

While recording the song, P!nk encouraged Carey to join her in the studio to record backing vocals. She said: 'He overcame his shyness to be able to do that and it was painful. It was adorable. He was adorable. But he was really nervous to do it by himself so we all had to do it with him.'

The music video for the song was filmed in early October and directed by Dave Meyers, featuring a same-sex wedding. Talking about the video to MTV, P!nk said: 'I threw my best friend's wedding in my backyard. She is gay and she married her wife, and it was absolutely beautiful. At the end of it her mum said, "Why can't this be legal?" and started crying. It was just the most heartbreaking thing I've ever seen, so that's why I'm doing it in my video.'

'Raise Your Glass' became P!nk's third #1 on the USA Billboard Hot 100, peaking in its eighth week on the chart and reached #1 in Australia. The song is featured in the Broadway and West End hit *Moulin Rouge: The Musical*, as part of a medley with 'Shut Up and Dance' by Walk the Moon. The show, which opened in New York in June 2019 and in London in July 2022, is based on the movie and includes the version of 'Lady Marmalade' that featured P!nk.

'Fuckin' Perfect'

Written by Max Martin, Johan 'Shellback' Schuster and Alecia 'P!nk' Moore
Produced by Max Martin and Johan 'Shellback' Schuster
Recorded at Woodshed Recording, Malibu
Duration: 3:33
Released as a single in January 2011
Music video directed by Dave Meyers
Chart Position: USA: 2; Canada: 2; UK: 10; Australia: 10; Germany: 7

The second new track on *Greatest Hits... So Far!!!*, 'Fuckin' Perfect' is an empowering anthem about self-worth. The censored version of the song was renamed to 'F**kin' Perfect' with a clean version entitled 'Perfect' created for radio.

In her press interview for *The Truth About Love*, P!nk said: 'With "Perfect", Carey was going through kind of a rough time and I started out writing it about him because I just don't think he knows how awesome he is and no one tells him. I sure as hell don't. Or I don't enough. And so, it started out being about him and then it was sort of about me... and then it was about my fans and then it was about my baby and my belly.'

Dave Meyers collaborated with P!nk on the controversial video, filmed while P!nk was pregnant in December 2010. It stars actress Tina Majorino as an artist who overcomes personal struggles to become successful, including controversial scenes of self-harm. Majorino said in 2019: 'The music video is, to this day, one of the brightest highlights of my career so far. P!nk asking me to be a part of her incredible and endlessly brilliant and inspiring legacy will forever be an honour I cherish.'

Explaining the intention behind the video, P!nk released a statement on her official website, saying: 'I'm sure my newest video for "F**kin' Perfect" will be much like some of my other videos, which basically means I expect it will ruffle some feathers. My favourite books, art pieces, films, and music, always have something jarring about them. I want art to make me think. In order to do that, it may piss me off or make me uncomfortable. That promotes awareness and change, or at least some discussion. That is my intention. You can't move mountains by whispering at them. Cutting, and suicide, two very different symptoms of the same problem, are gaining on us (the problem being alienation and depression; the symptoms, cutting and suicide). I personally don't know a single person who doesn't know at least two of these victims personally. A lot of us have seen certain starlets showing off their latest scars on a red carpet somewhere, usually right before they head back to their favourite rehab. It's a problem, and it's something we should talk about. We can choose to ignore the problem, and therefore ignore this video, but that won't make it go away. I don't support or encourage suicide or cutting. I support the kids out there that feel so desperate/numb/powerless, that feel unseen and unheard and can't see another way. I want them to know I'm aware. I have been there. I see them. Sometimes that's all it takes.'

She added: 'Making this video was a very emotional experience for me, as was writing this song. I have a life inside of me, and I want her or him to know that I will accept him or her with open and loving and welcoming arms. And though I will prepare this little munchkin for a sometimes cruel world, I will also equip this kid to see all the beauty in it as well. There are good people in this world that are open-minded and loving. There are those that accept us with all of our flaws. I do that with my fans/friends, and I will do that with my child, whoever they decide to be.'

'Fuckin' Perfect' became P!nk's eleventh top 10 hit on the USA Billboard Hot 100 singles chart, eventually peaking at #2. It reached the top 10 in the UK, Australia and Germany, where it topped the airplay charts, becoming her eighth consecutive single to reach the top. In 2012, 'Fuckin' Perfect' was nominated for Best Pop Solo Performance at the 54th Grammy Awards, which Adele's 'Someone Like You' won. The song also appears in the Max Martin jukebox musical, *& Juliet*, which opened in the UK in 2019 before transferring to Broadway in 2022.

Bonus Tracks

'Heartbreak Down'

Written by Butch Walker and Alecia 'P!nk' Moore
Produced by Butch Walker
Recorded at RubyRed Studios, California
Duration: 3:18

'Heartbreak Down' is the third original song written specifically for *Greatest Hits… So Far!!!* produced and co-written by Butch Walker, with P!nk talking about a one-night stand that has developed into a toxic relationship.

The song was exclusively available in the USA and Canada as part of the album download on Apple iTunes and appears on the standard album internationally.

'Whataya Want from Me'

Written by Max Martin, Johan 'Shellback' Schuster and Alecia 'P!nk' Moore
Produced by Max Martin and Johan 'Shellback' Schuster
Recorded at Maratone Studios, Stockholm, Sweden and House of Blues Studios, Los Angeles
Duration: 3:46

'Whataya Want from Me' was written during P!nk's sessions in Sweden for *Funhouse* but didn't make the final album tracklist. A year after the album was released, *American Idol* runner-up Adam Lambert announced that the song would be the second single from his debut album ahead of its release in November 2009.

In a 2012 interview with *The Los Angeles Times*, P!nk said: 'Adam Lambert killed this song. That was fun. I always liked this song, I just didn't want it on the record. *Funhouse* was very much about my problem with Carey and I didn't want to dilute it with my problems with other people.'

P!nk's recording of 'Whataya Want from Me' was included on the UK, Europe, and Australia Deluxe CD/DVD editions of *Greatest Hits... So Far!!!* Alongside 'Fuckin' Perfect,' the song is the second song co-written by P!nk feature in the Max Martin jukebox musical, *& Juliet*.

Other Songs

'We Are the World 25 for Haiti'—Artists for Haiti

Written by Michael Jackson and Lionel Richie
Produced by Quincy Jones, Lionel Richie, Wyclef Jean, Nadir 'RedOne' Khayat and Humberto Gattica
Co-Produced by Rickey Minor, Mervyn Warren and Patti Austin
Recorded at Henson Recording Studios, Los Angeles
Duration: 6:57 (Short Version: 3:25)
Released as a single in February 2010
Music video directed by Paul Haggis
Chart Position: USA: 2; UK: 50; Australia: 18

The concept of artists uniting to record a charity single gained massive success in 1984 when Bob Geldof organised a group of musicians to record 'Do They Know It's Christmas?' under the collective Band Aid Trust, raising funds for the famine in Ethiopia. This inspired American musician and activist Harry Belafonte to create an American equivalent, enlisting Michael Jackson and Lionel Richie to write 'We Are the World' the following year. The song sold over 20 million physical copies, reaching #1 worldwide. Following the catastrophic earthquake in Haiti in January 2010, over eighty artists, including P!nk, re-recorded the song, re-titled 'We Are the World 25 for Haiti.'

The song was recorded on 1 February 2010 with Quincy Jones, who worked on the original, collaborating with Haitian-American musician Wyclef Jean. A 25th anniversary re-recording of the song had been discussed in late 2009, but Jones and Lionel Richie, who co-wrote the song, were lukewarm to the idea. However, the urgency of fundraising for Haiti changed their minds, with Visa covering the costs of bringing the song together.

P!nk sings a solo on the song, performing the lines, 'There's a choice we're making, we're saving our own lives.'

'We Are the World 25 for Haiti' premiered at the Winter Olympics less than two weeks after it was recorded and sold over 250,000 downloads in just three days.

8

The Truth About Love (2011–2012)

Released:	14 September 2012 (Europe and Australia) 17 September 2012 (UK) 18 September 2012 (USA and Canada) 30 November 2012 (Europe and Australia—Fan Edition)
Chart Position:	USA: 1 Canada: 1 UK: 2 Australia: 1 Germany: 1

The Truth About Love is P!nk's first album since becoming a mother, with studio sessions starting in late 2011 when her daughter Willow Sage Hart was under 7 months old. Within months of organising a strict schedule that prioritised time with her daughter while allowing her time to work, she had written over forty songs for the album.

P!nk spoke about the album's recording sessions in its press launch video, saying: 'I went to the studio in January. Willow was 7 months old, and up until then, I was a full-time mama. I don't know what headspace I was in; I mean, I'm still nursing. She's 14 months now, so I'm still with her every couple of hours. I've never left her for more than 5 hours; I'm completely smitten and so obsessed with her. So the headspace I was in was, "How do I do this? Is this even possible? Do I want to do this? Of course, I want to do this, but how do I do this? I don't want to screw up my kid. I don't want to be a rock star cliché parent. How do I do both, and how do I do both excellently?" I'm a Virgo, a perfectionist, and an overthinker. I don't know how I wrote 40 songs. I have no idea, but it happened, and it worked, and I'm proud of it; she's happy, and we're all happy.'

The album is named after the song, 'The Truth About Love,' which P!nk wrote with Billy Mann in one of her early sessions whilst experimenting with returning to music. In addition to being her favourite on the album, she told *MTV News*: 'I realised it also sums up my whole adventure in this lifetime. I used to be really motivated to do really dangerous and stupid things for love, and I was really fearful of love. When I was a little girl, "love" meant fighting and bickering and losing your parents. But now love is also having a child and unconditional and beautiful and, with my husband, sexual. Musically, it's not a Sade record where you know what you're going to get when you put it on. It's a P!nk record; you have no idea what you're going to get. I don't know what I'm doing when I go in to record an album, so I think that's the theme: questions and experiences and running from - and running to – love.'

In P!nk's own words, the sound of *The Truth About Love* is 'a typical clusterfuck... that's kind of what I call it. I'm like a mystery bag, you put your hand in, you don't know what you're going to get. It's all over the place. No one will ever, ever trap me in a genre. I think that annoys; I think that's why people don't understand me. It's because they'll never be able to put me in a box. The only common thread is my voice. You're going to have rock and roll, you're going to have R&B. You're going to have a country ballad and a folk song and a pop, Max Martin, radio-friendly hit. So I think that's kind of the mystery bag, that's what's fun.'

Much of the album was conceived with Greg Kurstin, including the album's first two singles, 'Blow Me (One Last Kiss)' and 'Try,' which marks one of the first times P!nk accepted an outside submission for a single since her debut album. Talking to *Billboard* magazine, P!nk said: 'Greg Kurstin comes with these brilliant tracks, crazy tracks - these musical compositions. And he's so fucking brilliant that everything he plays you, you want to throw up in your mouth. "Blow Me (One Last Kiss)" was the first track he played me and I was like, "Stop." "You don't want to hear the rest?" "No." Next day, he played another one. "Stop." "You don't want to hear the rest?" "No." Day by day, by day. "Blow Me" was first, and then it was either "Walk of Shame" or "Try" last, because I didn't actually write "Try." Every day it was different because he's so good. And he's so witty and funny and awesome and lovely. I'm so lucky with the people I get to work with.'

At the end of November, the album was re-released outside of the USA and Canada in a special CD/DVD package, entitled the 'fan edition,' containing all twenty of the songs that had been released on various region-exclusive and platform-exclusive editions of the album. The DVD also featured the music videos for 'Blow Me (One Last Kiss)' and 'Try,' as well as four live performances from her Los Angeles concert.

In a 2019 interview with *Variety* magazine, P!nk reflected on recording *The Truth About Love*, saying: 'It was the first time that I would work in the studio during the day. I was about to breastfeed and I would put her down for a nap and then come back. It was very kind of daytime-y sober. I felt really present making the record, because normally we'd open a bottle of wine and shit-talk and record at 1 in the morning. It just wasn't that anymore.'

Album Tracks

'Are We All We Are'

Written by Butch Walker, John Hill, Emile Haynie and Alecia 'P!nk' Moore
Produced by Butch Walker, John Hill and Emile Haynie
Recorded at Earthstar Creation Center, California; Ruby Red Studios, Santa Monica and Sonora Recorders, Los Angeles
Duration: 3:37

'Are We All We Are' is a high-energy anthemic opening to *The Truth About Love*, containing a chant of, 'We've had enough, we've had it up to here, are we all we are?' inspired by American politics. Co-written with long-term collaborator Butch Walker, the song features co-production from John Hill, who worked extensively with Santigold and Shakira, and Emile Haynie, who worked on Lana Del Rey's *Born to Die* and *Paradise*.

In a track-by-track interview, P!nk said: 'I love a chant, I love a reason to yell and it just seems like the perfect tour opener. And it's just kind of "the 99%" song. It's the rest of us. My family is very working class and my brother is in the military, and I come from a military family. And I'm an American, and the politics are a little frustrating in this country.'

Although 'Are We All We Are' was not a commercial single, P!nk performed the song to promote the album, and it was sent to radio in parts of Europe, including the UK, at the end of 2013.

'Blow Me (One Last Kiss)'

Written by Greg Kurstin and Alecia 'P!nk' Moore
Produced by Greg Kurstin
Recorded at Echo Studios, Los Angeles and Earthstar Creation Center, California
Duration: 4:16
Released as a single in July 2012
Music video directed by Dave Meyers
Chart Position: USA: 5; Canada: 4; UK: 3; Australia: 1; Germany: 10

'Blow Me (One Last Kiss)' was the first single to be taken from *The Truth About Love*, premiering in July 2012. The song is a fiery breakup anthem with P!nk delivering sharp, tongue-in-cheek lyrics over an infectious pop beat, co-written and produced by Greg Kurstin.

Kurstin spoke to *Billboard* magazine about the process of writing the lyrics, saying: 'P!nk kept coming back to "Let's throw in the towel" and it was one of those things where I had to say, "Is that line really the song?" So then I came back with "Blow me one last kiss" and we got really excited. Most of the time with P!nk she's so strong writing lyrics I don't really interfere. I let her do her thing. That could've been the only time I did that.'

Talking to MTV ahead of the song's premiere, P!nk said: 'My new single is called "Blow Me." I believe the record company added the "(One Last Kiss)." The moment I heard it and it was finished, I thought, "This is the song at 2am, in New York, dancing, drunk, letting off steam." I could picture all my punk-rock friends dancing and singing along on the dance floor.'

In an interview with *USA Today* she explained that the song is about fear: 'It started with the lyric "white knuckles and sweaty palms from hanging on too tight." We're so afraid to lose something - people, jobs, love - that we end up squeezing the life out of it, sabotaging it and losing it anyway.'

P!nk said the song is also about her reconciliation with husband Carey Hart. She told *Entertainment Weekly*: 'Carey and I were getting back together, so I had to be a little bit nice. Those songs are really easy for me to write. It started out being about how we hold on so tight that we choke the life out of it. Everybody thinks, "Oh, another breakup song from P!nk." But it's about 50,000 different things and 10 different people.'

Dave Meyers directed the music video for the song, which was shot in Malibu and stars Sebastian De La Forza as P!nk's love interest. A pastiche of French black-and-white movies, the video is entitled 'Blow Me Un Dernier Baiser' (a rough translation of 'Blow Me One Last Kiss'). In a behind-the-scenes video clip, Meyers said: 'It's probably my 14th or 15th video with P!nk. We're out in Malibu State Park trying to do something a little different. The theme is a French countryside love story but there's a little bit of eccentrics in there. There's a flying bike at the end!'

The video premiered on 27 July 2012, with the only colour used being burgundy, appearing on two occasions: when P!nk throws a glass of red wine, and then later when she explodes a red heart-shaped balloon of red wine to sabotage a wedding before flying off. At the end of August, a 'colour' version of the music video was released, emulating the modern colourisation of black-and-white movies.

P!nk's first performance of 'Blow Me (One Last Kiss)' was at the 2012 MTV Video Music Awards, where she floated over the audience and her dancers, who were wearing giant red lips, referencing the single cover. The song became P!nk's sixth #1 single in Australia, being certified 5x Platinum, and reached the top 5 in the UK, USA and Canada. It peaked at #10 in Germany, where it was released on CD single with the B-side, 'The King is Dead but the Queen is Alive.'

'Try'

Written by Michael Busbee and Ben West
Produced by Greg Kurstin
Recorded at Earthstar Creation Center, California and Echo Studios, Los Angeles
Duration: 4:07
Released as a single in October 2012
Music video directed by Floria Sigismondi
Chart Position: USA: 9; Canada: 4; UK: 8; Australia: 6; Germany: 2

'Try,' the second single to be released from *The Truth About Love*, is an emotional anthem about showing resilience after a relationship breakdown. Originally a country song written and produced by the late Michael Busbee and Ben West under their alias, GoNorthToGoSouth, the duo saw hit potential in the song and asked their publishers to help it get to the right artist.

In a 2016 *Songwriter Universe* magazine interview, Busbee recalled: 'We wrote it, and I turned it into my publishing company. They loved it. Eventually, my manager and one of my publishers at the time pitched it to a friend of ours, Rani Hancock, who was at RCA at the time. Originally, we were going to try to get it on Kelly Clarkson. There was talk of Daughtry doing it. I actually recorded it with Adam Lambert, but it just wasn't the right fit. Eventually, I had to call Rani and go, "Hey, what are we doing with this song?" She's like, "Do you mind if I keep it a little bit longer and pitch it to P!nk?" It was one of the first outside songs she had recorded in a long time. She's an amazing artist, and for her to take an outside song - a lot of people aren't willing to do that stuff, but she was.'

The music video for 'Try' was shot in early August, co-starring Broadway performer Colt Prattes, with choreography from the Golden Boyz (RJ Durell and Nick Florez) and aerial work from Sebastien Stella. In a press release, P!nk said: 'Making this video was the most fun I've ever had in my entire career. I never wanted it to end. It's my favourite video ever.'

P!nk later recreated the video for her performance of 'Try' at the 2012 American Music Awards, helping the song climb into the top 20 of the USA Billboard Hot 100, where it peaked at #9.

In 2017, P!nk said on BBC Radio 1: 'This is the classic case of my mum's favourite song of every album being the one song I didn't write. I write my own material, but I'm smart enough to know that sometimes you have to get out of your own way. I grew up singing other people's songs. That was one I had to have and I'm so glad because that video is a video that needed to get made.'

'Just Give Me a Reason' featuring Nate Ruess

Written by Jeff Bhasker, Nate Ruess and Alecia 'P!nk' Moore
Produced by Jeff Bhasker
Recorded at Earthstar Creation Center, California
Duration: 4:03
Nate Ruess appears courtesy of Fueled by Ramen, LLC
Released as a single in February 2013
Music video directed by Diane Martel
Chart Position: USA: 1; Canada: 1; UK: 2; Australia: 1; Germany: 1

'Just Give Me a Reason' is a duet with Nate Ruess of the band Fun, exploring the complexities of a relationship on the brink of falling apart. Talking about the song's creation to Spotify, P!nk said the song came out of a songwriting session with Ruess and producer Jeff Bhasker, and that she knew it needed to be a duet.

P!nk told *Billboard* magazine: 'Nate wasn't sure that he wanted to be on a collaboration with a pop star. Their label is an independent label, they weren't sure. And I just kept telling them - well, I kind of tricked him into doing it... and he had to do it because he's my favourite voice right now, aside from probably Adele. I went back in and wrote the second verse and I sort of pitched the song. And he was like, "Yeah, I don't know how my band's going to feel about it." And I was like, "Yeah, I get it. I wouldn't want to be on a song with a pop star either. But you can't deny that it's a conversation - you just put the vocals down as the scratch vocal and I'll get Gotye to sing it." And I knew that was a huge dig. And he sang it, and I knew, no matter what he said, no one was going to sing it better. It just took many, many months of convincing.'

Reflecting on the initial inspiration for writing the song, P!nk added to Spotify that she was thinking about trivial arguments and small, sometimes misinterpreted actions that get taken out of perspective in a relationship. She said: 'I find that there's always one person in the relationship that's feeling a lot more than the other person. I feel like sometimes I'm like, "the way you passed me the butter this morning.... I kind of feel like we're going to be over in a month and we need to talk," and he's like, "I just passed you the fucking butter, what are you talking about?"'

Producer Jeff Bhasker told *Billboard* magazine that he was introduced to P!nk by RCA Records CEO Peter Edge, who thought they would work well together. He said: 'We just kind of did it in one day and got together and hammered it out. It just kind of magically came together, and almost in an improvisational way. I started playing some chords and Nate just started singing, and P!nk started typing down lyrics and we just kind of put the song together from there. It was an unusually collaborative and spontaneous song.'

A music video was shot for the song in November 2012, directed by Diane Martel, and featuring P!nk's husband, Carey Hart. In the video, P!nk and Nate Ruess sing to each other using vintage microphones, whilst in a dream sequence, P!nk is seen on a floating bed watching Nate on TV, accompanied by a teddy bear with illuminated eyes. P!nk is also shown on the bed with her husband in happier times, and in a choreographed underwater sequence, filmed in a swimming pool in Los Angeles. In 2013, the music video won Best Collaboration at the MTV Video Music Awards, marking her sixth overall award including two for 'Lady Marmalade' in 2001.

Released in early 2013 as the third single from *The Truth About Love*, 'Just Give Me a Reason' became P!nk's fourth #1 on the USA Billboard Hot 100 and reached #1 in over 12 other countries. It has become one of her signature songs, being certified 13x Platinum in Australia, 3x Platinum in the UK, and 2x Platinum in the USA. The song was nominated for Best Pop Duo/Group Performance and Song of the Year at the 56th Grammy Awards in 2014, where P!nk performed 'Try' before being joined by Nate for 'Just Give Me a Reason.' P!nk included the song as part of her hits medley at the 2019 BRIT Awards in the UK, joined by Bastille's Dan Smith.

An interpolation of the song is used in contemporary Christian singer Lauren Daigle's 2023 single, 'Thank God I Do,' produced by Mike Elizondo, who worked with P!nk on *I'm Not Dead.*

'True Love' featuring Lily Allen

Written by Greg Kurstin, Lily Allen and Alecia 'P!nk' Moore
Produced by Greg Kurstin
Recorded at Earthstar Creation Center, California; Modern World Studios, Tetbury, UK and Echo Studios, Los Angeles
Duration: 3:50
Lily Allen appears courtesy of Parlophone Records
Released as a single in July 2013
Music video directed by Sophie Muller
Chart Position: USA: 53; Canada: 20; UK: 16; Australia: 5; Germany: 43

'True Love' features British performer Lily Allen, credited on the album under her then-marital name, Lily Rose Cooper. The song was released as the fourth single from *The Truth About Love* in July 2013, when Lily had reverted to her maiden name.

Despite being a duet, P!nk and Lily Allen never met during the song's creation. Producer Greg Kurstin, who had worked with both artists, facilitated the collaboration, believing their styles would complement each other perfectly.

P!nk, a longtime admirer of Lily Allen's sharp and clever lyricism, shared her thoughts on working with her in an interview with *The Independent*. She said: 'I'm such a fan of Lily. I've loved every lyric she's ever written, especially the song "Fuck You." And I just thought she would be perfect for the song - she's funny and clever and witty and has a beautiful tone to her voice. I like her a lot, I kinda love her, and I've never met her! She's a mum, I'm a mum, I get it. But when Lily sings about getting shit-faced in a bar, I know it's for real. And I knew she'd write this fucking sarcastic thing like I did. And it's so cool what she wrote.'

In a later interview with *ELLE*, she added: 'We geek out over music together. She's like the over-the-ocean equivalent of a shit-talker like me.'

In August 2012, a five-month pregnant Lily flew to Los Angeles to perform 'True Love' with P!nk for her VH1 *Storytellers* special. Lily also makes a cameo in the pop-art-inspired music video, chopping vegetables for a giant blender. The video, directed by Sophie Muller, features P!nk's husband, Carey Hart, and their daughter, Willow, with scenes of P!nk performing.

During promotion for the single, P!nk revealed to ABC that her relationship with Hart inspired the song. She said: 'I've been in a relationship with this man for 10 years and I've figured out no one can push your buttons like your mother or your partner. I have a tattoo on my wrist that says "True Love" with Carey's name under it. I think lyrically, it's really funny and really honest, and people think I'm nuts anyway, so why not tell the truth?'

'True Love' was another hit for P!nk in Australia, reaching #5 on the singles chart. It peaked at #43 in Germany, where it was released on CD single, backed with a live recording of 'Slut Like You' from Los Angeles. In 2015, an ASCAP error saw the song incorrectly registered under titles including 'Entertainment Tonight' and 'I Want What You Got (I Got What You Want).'

In 2023, when *The Los Angeles Times* asked about her best and worst singles, P!nk said: 'Worst? I mean, there's been so many. Maybe "True Love." Because it's mean. Carey's got thick skin, but I owe him a love song.' However, she changed her answer, recalling releasing 'We've Got Scurvy,' from *SpongeBob's Greatest Hits*.

'How Come You're Not Here'

Written by Greg Kurstin and Alecia 'P!nk' Moore
Produced by Greg Kurstin
Recorded at Earthstar Creation Center, California and Echo Studio, Los Angeles
Duration: 3:12

'How Come You're Not Here' is another collaboration with Greg Kurstin, featuring P!nk delivering droll lyrics about waiting for someone who disappears in a relationship. As she questions, 'Are you hiding in the closet? Are you underneath the bed? Did you go for a long walk off a short pier? Should I worry you've been bitten or somebody got you high?' the song's production uses vocal effects to create a 1970s glam-rock sound.

In an interview with *The Advocate* magazine, P!nk said: 'First of all, the reason my voice sounds so cool in that song is absolutely 150% the distortion. We were just inspired to go rock-and-roll. Great rock-and-roll songs are either revolutionary or political, or about total heartbreak, or just shit-talking. So, I talked shit for four minutes!'

Talking about writing the song's sarcastic lyrics to *The Independent*, she said: 'It's about how I'm awesome, if not slightly psychotic. I had this picture in my head like Carey's trying to leave me. And to me, it's a game of hide and seek - cause why would he ever try to leave me? It's this whole cartoon delusional thing. You know, we had that breakup, and that second verse is my favourite second verse that I've ever written: "I heard some rumours about another girl, I heard she's cute, but she stores nuts like a squirrel... that's all cool, I'll wait right here till you get bored and she gets carded for beer." That kind of shit I have in my back pocket. It's so easy to go back there.'

'How Come You're Not Here' is the first of two songs on the album to feature percussion from P!nk's daughter, Willow. In an interview with MTV, P!nk said that Willow plays bells on the song, saying: 'There was a basket of shit, and she came over and pulled out the bells and started banging on them, and I was like, "Record it!"'

'Slut Like You'

Written by Max Martin, Johan 'Shellback' Schuster and Alecia 'P!nk' Moore
Produced by Max Martin and Johan 'Shellback' Schuster
Recorded at Conway Studios, Los Angeles and Earthstar Creation Center, California
Duration: 3:42

A cheeky, effervescent feminist pop song about reclaiming sexual power as a woman, 'Slut Like You' is the only collaboration with Max Martin and Shellback on *The Truth About Love*.

In her Spotify album commentary, P!nk said: 'I kept thinking, as I was writing the song, how mad mothers were going to be at me, but really it's my form of feminism. I've always had such a problem that men can sleep with ten women and "they're players" and then women can sleep with five and we're "sluts." I just think that's so unfair... as females we pay for our choices a lot more than men do. "Slut Like You" is my really unsophisticated way of taking the power back.'

'The Truth About Love'

Written by Billy Mann, David Schuler and Alecia 'P!nk' Moore
Produced by Billy Mann
Co-Produced by David Schuler
Recorded at Turtle Sound Studios, Weston and Earthstar Creation Center, California
Duration: 3:50

The album's title track sees P!nk reflecting on the complexities and contradictions of love, with her tongue-in-cheek humour.

In a press interview for the album, P!nk said: 'Billy Mann is also a very long-standing relationship of mine, musically and personally. He's like my brother from another mother. He is the most intense, loving person I've ever met in my life. I start the album with him because I feel safe with him - it's the no-shame zone. We dare to suck. And I can do that with him and he can do that with me. And it was all an experiment, really. I kept telling everyone this is just an experiment. I'm a mum; I have no idea what I have to say. I don't know if I can sing anymore or if I want to. When "The Truth About Love" happened, I was like, "maybe this isn't an experiment." And I kind of hit my groove. And then as we kept going and going and going, it was still my favourite song. My favourite part about the song is all the questions, and my favourite line is "sandwiches without the crust." And then I realised there was a theme to all of it. And it was, it's all just my many different sides of this exhausting search that I've been on for love.'

'Beam Me Up'

Written by Billy Mann, David Schuler and Alecia 'P!nk' Moore
Produced by Billy Mann
Co-Produced by David Schuler
Recorded at Turtle Sound Studios, Weston and Earthstar Creation Center, California
Duration: 4:27

An incredibly emotional ballad about loss and the desire for escape, 'Beam Me Up' is one of the most emotionally raw songs of P!nk's career, referencing the phrase from "Star Trek.'

In a press interview for the album, P!nk said: 'It deals with the loss of a loved one, the loss of a child. It's very, very, very, very, very personal and it's very close to my heart. I guess I'll just put it that way.' She added in a live web stream that the song was about a very close friend who lost a young child, and that it was the hardest song to write for the album.

Billy Mann, who co-wrote the song, told *Variety* magazine in 2017: 'I've gotten more fan mail from other parents who lost a child from that song than from most others. Photos of lyric tattoos, incredible stories. After the mass shooting of children in Sandy Hook, and the nation was stunned, iHeart Radio DJ Elvis Duran played "Beam Me Up" on his morning show each day to help people heal.'

Due to the song's heavy subject matter, P!nk did not include 'Beam Me Up' on *The Truth About Love* world tour setlist; however, she did perform it in Melbourne, Australia, dedicating it to a couple that had written to her about their own experience. She also performed the song at her October 2014 fundraiser, *The Power of Pink: An Acoustic Evening with P!nk & Friends*, raising funds for the Breast Cancer Prevention Clinic at the Margie Petersen Breast Centre.

'Walk of Shame'

Written by Greg Kurstin and Alecia 'P!nk' Moore
Produced by Greg Kurstin
Recorded at Earthstar Creation Center, California and Echo Studio, Los Angeles
Duration: 2:44

'Walk of Shame' is a light-hearted, playful song about owning mistakes with no regrets, co-written and produced by Greg Kurstin.

P!nk said her husband Carey, who is from Las Vegas, inspired the song: 'I remember him being in Vegas calling me from the diner in the Hard Rock because he had business in the Hard Rock at 8 o'clock in the morning and he would be narrating for me the continuous walk of shame he'd be seeing out of the casino because that's just constant in Vegas. Can you imagine being a like a diner employee in the mornings and the shit you get to see? The shame walk back to your cab and I just think it's funny because we've all done it and I just thought it would be a hilarious video. It's just that -there's nothing really that deep, it's just that regret the morning after.'

'Here Comes the Weekend' featuring Eminem

Written by 'DJ Khalil' Abdul-Rahman, Pranam 'Chin' Injeti, Erik Alcock, Liz Rodrigues, Alecia 'P!nk' Moore and Marshall 'Eminem' Mathers
Produced by 'DJ Khalil' Abdul-Rahman and Pranam 'Chin' Injeti
Recorded at Suite 203
Duration: 4:24
Eminem appears courtesy of Interscope Records

P!nk reunites with Eminem on 'Here Comes the Weekend," produced by DJ Khalil, following their duet on his 2010 record, *Recovery*. The song was intended to be the first single from *The Truth About Love*.

In her Spotify album commentary, P!nk said: 'Eminem found this song for us, and I did a song with him on his last record. The friendship swap was that he would do one on mine. I've always been a huge Eminem fan. I think he's a brilliant lyricist. He makes me laugh and I'm stoked that he's on my album!'

'Where Did the Beat Go?'

Written by Billy Mann, Tracklacers (Jon Keep and Steve Daly) and Alecia 'P!nk' Moore
Produced by Billy Mann
Co-Produced by Tracklacers (Jon Keep and Steve Daly)
Recorded at Turtle Sound Studios, Weston; New Track City, London, UK; New Tracy City, Los Angeles; Monster Island, Nashville and Earthstar Creation Center, California
Duration: 4:18

Another melancholic, introspective track, written with Billy Mann and the British team, Tracklacers, 'Where Did the Beat Go?' (often misidentified as 'Afterglow' because of its use in the song's chorus), is one of the few tracks from the standard edition of *The Truth About Love* that P!nk has never performed live.

In the album's press interview, P!nk said: 'It's about affairs. It's just about how easy it is to fantasise when not being loved, for I think both sides, everyone's like, "Oh, the male cheats," but I think women cheat more than men; we just don't get caught. Monogamy and long-term relationships are very interesting, just the psychology of it all. I remember Scarlett Johansson said, "Monogamy isn't natural" and she got so persecuted for saying that. It's just her opinion. A guy could say that, and no one would blink, but if a woman says that, she's a scarlet pariah, so I think it's an interesting topic to explore.'

'The Great Escape'

Written by Dan Wilson and Alecia 'P!nk' Moore
Produced by Dan Wilson
Recorded at Earthstar Creation Center, California; Ballroom West, Los Angeles and Mission Sound, New York City
Duration: 4:24

A slow, piano-driven ballad, 'The Great Escape' was co-written and produced by Semisonic's Dan Wilson, who worked with Adele on her global hit single, 'Someone Like You.'

In her Spotify album commentary, P!nk mentioned that while some have interpreted the song as being about suicide, she wrote it about feeling emotions rather than hiding from them. She explained: 'For me, it's about how I think the entire world is numbed down on something, whether it's antidepressants or anti-anxiety… it just seems like there's a pill for everything now… and I have very personal relationships that frustrate the hell out of me because they can't feel anything. I personally need my highs; I need my lows… I think a lot of people are now taught to be afraid of their emotions or to hide them or to swallow them down.'

Bonus Tracks

'The King is Dead but the Queen is Alive'

Written by Billy Mann, Butch Walker, MachoPsycho (Niklas 'Nikey' Olovson and Robin Lynch) and Alecia 'P!nk' Moore
Produced by Billy Mann, Butch Walker and MachoPsycho (Niklas 'Nikey' Olovson and Robin Lynch)
Recorded at Turtle Sound Studios, Weston; Fishead Music, Gothenburg, Sweden; Ruby Red Studios, Santa Monica; West Trad Studios, California and Earthstar Creation Center, California
Duration: 3:44

'The King is Dead but the Queen is Alive' is a collaboration between two of P!nk's longest-standing partners, Billy Mann and Butch Walker. The Swedish duo MachoPsycho, who contributed to songs on *I'm Not Dead* and *Funhouse*, also worked on the song. In the lyrics, P!nk compares the end of a toxic relationship to a Queen overthrowing a King in a monarchy by beheading him, referencing British King Henry VIII's six wives, two of whom were beheaded.

In addition to serving as the B-side for 'Blow Me (One Last Kiss),' the song was also included as the last song on 'fan edition' of *The Truth About Love*.

'My Signature Move'

Written by Butch Walker, Jake Sinclair and Alecia 'P!nk' Moore
Produced by Butch Walker
Recorded at Earthstar Creation Center, California and Ruby Red Studios, Santa Monica
Duration: 3:44

'My Signature Move' was co-written by P!nk and Butch Walker alongside Jake Sinclair, who collaborated with Walker on his 2010 studio album, *I Liked It Better When You Had No Heart.*

In the song, P!nk unapologetically acknowledges her tendency to self-sabotage, candidly calling out her confrontational nature and flair for creating drama, summarising and embracing her flaws as her 'signature move.'

'Is This Thing On?

Written by Butch Walker, Jake Sinclair and Alecia 'P!nk' Moore
Produced by Butch Walker
Recorded at Earthstar Creation Center, California and Ruby Red Studios, Santa Monica
Duration: 4:21

'Is This Thing On?' is another collaboration with Butch Walker and Jake Sinclair, released on the deluxe edition of *The Truth About Love*. In the lyrics, P!nk delves into the challenges of sustaining a long-term relationship, drawing on her marriage to Carey Hart. She reflects on how to keep it fresh and passionate without faking it. The title's question, commonly spoken into a microphone to test if it's working, serves as a metaphor for checking the emotional health of the relationship.

In 2017, *Billboard* magazine highlighted 'Is This Thing On?' in their list of P!nk's 'Top 10 Deep Cuts', highlighting her best songs that were not released as singles.

'Run'

Written by Butch Walker, Jake Sinclair and Alecia 'P!nk' Moore
Produced by Butch Walker
Recorded at Earthstar Creation Center, California and Ruby Red Studios, Santa Monica
Duration: 4:11

'Run' is a 1980s-inspired power ballad, written by P!nk for her daughter, Willow, offering her advice while reminding her that, no matter what, she can always run back to her. Although the song did not make *The Truth About Love*, it was released on the deluxe edition.

P!nk spoke about 'Run' during her 2012 episode of VH1's *Behind the Music*, saying she wrote it about her hopes for her daughter. 'I want Willow to wave her freak flag and I don't want to be authoritative and stomp on her spirit and make her fall in line. That's not what I want. I want her to be herself.'

The song features vocals from Boyce Buchanan, representing P!nk's daughter. In a webchat to promote *The Truth About Love*, P!nk was asked who provided the featured vocals. She said: 'A little girl! We found a really young girl - Butch did actually - to sing on that, and I actually wasn't there when she sang it because I can't handle it. I can't handle little girls anymore, I'm too emotional, and I would've been crying and she would've been uncomfortable. So I wasn't allowed to go to that.'

'Good Old Days'

Written by Billy Mann, David Schuler and Alecia 'P!nk' Moore
Produced by Billy Mann
Co-Produced by David Schuler
Recorded at Turtle Sound Studios, Weston and Earthstar Creation Center, California
Duration: 4:02

'Good Old Days,' written with Billy Mann and David Schuler, sees P!nk reflecting on the passage of time and embracing the present, especially when the future is uncertain. Singing, 'One, two, three, four, five years ago… I didn't see a belly with a child on the inside,' she recalls how she never imagined being pregnant. She continues, 'One, two, three, four, five years from now, I hope I'm still getting down, I hope I'm still around,' concluding, 'It's all good right now.'

'Chaos & Piss'

Written by Francis 'Eg' White and Alecia 'P!nk' Moore
Produced by Francis 'Eg' White
Recorded at Earthstar Creation Center, California and Modern Dirt Laboratories, London, UK
Duration: 3:59

P!nk worked with Eg White in his London studio on songs for *Funhouse*, but for *The Truth About Love*, they wrote together online, with P!nk staying in California. Although the results of their sessions did not make the main album, P!nk wrote in the credits: 'Eg White – the mad scientist, your spirit is inspiring and infectious – I adore you!"

'Chaos & Piss' is the only song from their work together to be officially released, available exclusively on the iTunes deluxe edition of the album. It was later included on the 'fan edition' of the album, alongside 'Timebomb' and 'The King is Dead but the Queen is Alive.'

The instrumental version of the song was featured during *The Truth About Love* tour as a dance interlude, played after P!nk left the stage following her performance of 'Sober.'

'TIMEBOMB'

Written by Greg Kurstin and Alecia 'P!nk' Moore
Produced by Greg Kurstin
Recorded at Earthstar Creation Center, California and Echo Studio, Los Angeles
Duration: 3:34

'Timebomb' was available exclusively as a bonus track for those who purchased *The Truth About Love* on Apple's iTunes. A further collaboration with Greg Kurstin, the song features P!nk comparing love to a boomerang—a traditional tool some Aboriginal Australians used for hunting, which spins about an axis and returns to the person who threw it—rather than a ticking timebomb.

'Timebomb' is the second song recorded for the album to feature P!nk's daughter Willow on percussion. Speaking to MTV in July 2012, P!nk said: 'She went up to the bass guitar during the recording of "Timebomb" and started plucking away. She's actually pretty good! She's better on bass than I am!'

Other Songs

'HAPPY FEET TWO OPENING MEDLEY'—P!NK, COMMON, BENJAMIN 'LIL P-NUT' FLORES JR. AND *HAPPY FEET TWO* CHORUS

Produced by John Powell and Wade Robson
Recorded at The Simon Leadley Scoring Stage, Sydney, Australia; Trackdown Scoring Studios, Sydney, Australia; Eastman Scoring Stage, Los Angeles; 5 Cat Studio, Los Angeles; Fantasy Studios, Berkeley and Woodshed Studio, Malibu
Duration: 4:06

'Rhythm Nation'
Written by James Harris III, Terry Lewis and Janet Jackson
'(Dance and Shout) Shake Your Body Down to the Ground'
Written by Michael Jackson and Randy Jackson
'Seymour Rap'
Written by Wade Robson
'Mama Said Knock You Out'
Written by James Todd Smith, Marlon Williams, George Clinton, Gregory Jacobs, James McCants, Leroy McCants, Walter Morrison and William Collins
Includes a sample of 'Trip to Your Heart' written by Sylvester Stewart

'SexyBack'
Written by Timothy 'Timbaland' Mosley, Nate 'Danja' Hills and Justin Timberlake
'Shake It Fast'
Written by Pharrell Williams, Chad Hugo and Michael Tyler
'Ain't Nobody'
Written by David 'Hawk' Wolinksi
'Do Your Thing'
Written by Simon Ratcliffe and Felix Buxton
Includes an interpolation of 'Fungii Mama' written by Richard 'Blue' Mitchell

A fan of the movie *Happy Feet*, for which she recorded a cover of 'Tell Me Something Good,' P!nk was approached to provide the voice of Gloria in its follow-up movie, *Happy Feet Two*. Brittany Murphy, who passed away in 2009, provided the voice in the original film.

George Miller, director of *Happy Feet Two*, said: 'P!nk was a natural for the role and has been really superb. She had sung in the opening of the first movie and wanted to be involved again because she's compassionate and a great animal lover.'

P!nk spoke about doing voiceover work for the first time, saying: 'I got to watch Brad Pitt and Matt Damon not only record some of their dialogue, but they also had to sing. They just went for it, and I thought, "Wow, I really have nothing to fear in there!"'

'Happy Feet Two Opening Medley' opens the movie, featuring some of the film's characters performing iconic hits. P!nk voices Gloria, Common voices Seymour, and Benjamin 'Lil P-Nut' Flores Jr. voices Atticus, with all three performing in the medley alongside the *Happy Feet Two* chorus. In addition to Janet Jackson's 'Rhythm Nation', the medley includes '(Dance and Shout) Shake Your Body Down to the Ground' performed by the Jackson 5, 'Mama Said Knock You Out' made famous by Five Finger Death Punch and Tech N9ne, Justin Timberlake's 'SexyBack', 'Shake It Fast' (the clean title for 'Shake Ya Ass') performed by Mystikal, 'Ain't Nobody' made famous by Rufus and Chaka Khan, and Basement Jaxx's 'Do Your Thing'.

'Bridge of Light' P!nk and *Happy Feet Two* Chorus

Written by Billy Mann and Alecia 'P!nk' Moore
Produced by Billy Mann
Recorded at The Simon Leadley Scoring Stage, Sydney, Australia; Trackdown Scoring Studios, Sydney, Australia; Eastman Scoring Stage, Los Angeles; 5 Cat Studio, Los Angeles; Fantasy Studios, Berkeley and Woodshed Studio, Malibu
Duration: 4:06

Released as a single in December 2011
Chart Position: Australia: 26; Germany: 8

In addition to cover versions, P!nk was approached to write a brand-new song for the soundtrack of *Happy Feet Two*. The result is 'Bridge of Light,' a gospel-influenced ballad written by P!nk and Billy Mann.

In a press interview to promote the movie, P!nk shared how the opportunity to write 'Bridge of Light' came about: 'When George first asked me to voice Gloria, I thought he was joking. I was so excited for the first film, and when I went and I was the first song, that was enough for me. I mean I get excited still! Then he asked me to write a song where Gloria can't get to her baby, and the only way she can get to him is through song. You've heard all of these songs that have already been written and the songs that they're thinking of for that part, but can you write one? And you're thinking, "Oh my God, hell no, I can't do this." And then I went into the studio with Billy Mann. We just thought, "We have to write the best song that we've ever written in our entire world, but let's not take it too seriously", and as soon as we stopped thinking about all of that and the pressure of it all. "How am I going to get to someone and comfort them?" And so you think of lullabies as a kid, and you think of the simplest, sweetest thing you can think of, and then you play the piano and write your song.'

'Bridge of Light' was released as a commercial single in Germany, Austria and Switzerland, reaching the top 10 in all three countries.

'Under Pressure'/'Rhythm Nation'—P!nk and *Happy Feet Two* Chorus

'Under Pressure'
Written by David Bowie, John Deacon, Brian May, Freddie Mercury and Roger Taylor
'Rhythm Nation'
Written by James Harris III, Terry Lewis and Janet Jackson

Produced by John Powell and David Hirschfelder
Recorded at The Simon Leadley Scoring Stage, Sydney, Australia; Trackdown Scoring Studios, Sydney, Australia; Eastman Scoring Stage, Los Angeles; 5 Cat Studio, Los Angeles; Fantasy Studios, Berkeley and Woodshed Studio, Malibu
Duration: 4:06

P!nk performed a medley of two iconic hits, Queen's 'Under Pressure' and Janet Jackson's 'Rhythm Nation', for the soundtrack to *Happy Feet Two*.

The song is performed during the film's climax, as the penguins, elephant seals, and other sea creatures dance on the Doomberg (a massive iceberg blocking the entrance and exit of their territory) to help free their trapped friends.

'Guns and Roses'—T.I. featuring P!nk

Written by Tyler 'T-Minus' Williams, Nikhil Seetharam, Clifford 'T.I.' Harris Jr., Jacob Kasher, Kelly Sheehan and Alecia 'P!nk' Moore
Produced by Tyler 'T-Minus' Williams
Duration: 4:28

P!nk appears on T.I.'s 2012 album, *Trouble Man; Heavy is the Head*, singing the chorus of 'Guns and Roses,' which includes the lyrics, 'We'd wake up on a bed of guns and roses, and we don't know which one to choose, when either way we're gonna lose.'

T.I. told *Billboard* magazine: 'We found that we had a few things in common. We clicked. She real people, she from the streets. I'm a real cat, I'm from the streets. We found ourselves in rooms where we were like, 'You know what? These people fake as hell in here. Let's get out of here."' He added to *Fuse*: 'I got a record with P!nk called "Guns and Roses", it's a dope joint.'

Unreleased Songs

'Exit Strategy'

Written by Dan Wilson and Alecia 'P!nk' Moore
Produced by Dan Wilson
Duration: 4:42

P!nk's love for Janis Joplin shines through on 'Exit Strategy,' a piano-driven blues track in which she asks, 'What's your exit strategy? Mine is simply gonna be get out, get gone, get free, save myself, now you tell me... everybody has a loaded gun, waiting for the other one to make one wrong move and then it's done.' The demo recording of the song leaked in 2022.

'Daughter'

Written by Alecia 'P!nk' Moore
Produced by Dan Wilson
Duration: 3:08

'Daughter' is another track that leaked online in 2022. Although the producer is unconfirmed, it is believed to be Dan Wilson, as it leaked alongside 'Exit Strategy.'

An emotional ballad sung to her father, P!nk sings: 'Why can't you ever say "I'm sorry"? Why can't you ever say that you're wrong? I know you got your demons and they made you the victim... but I'm the daughter who needs a father.'

Live Performances

'What Makes a Man'—City and Colour and P!nk

Written by Dallas Green
Duration: 3:56

Dallas Green, the Canadian singer-songwriter who releases music as City and Colour, met P!nk through a mutual friend, going on tour with her in June 2010 as one of the support acts for the UK leg of the *Funhouse Summer Carnival* tour. When he learned she would be attending his show at the Orpheum Theatre in Los Angeles on 3 November 2011, as part of his *Little Hell* tour, he invited her to join him on stage for a duet.

Green told NPR in 2014: 'I played a show in Los Angeles, and Alecia came to the show. And on her way to the show, I texted her and was like, "Hey, do you want to sing in a song with me?" And she was like, "OK." So she got to the show, and we just went over a version of one my songs in the bathroom. And then she came up and sang it with me live - and that moment was where we both sang together for the first time in front of people.'

P!nk joined City and Colour on the song 'What Makes a Man,' which Green has described as one of his favourite songs to sing live. The reaction to their duet, both from the audience and their own experience of performing together, eventually led to their 2014 album together, *rose ave*. They have performed the song together again, including at two fundraising concerts in September 2024.

'Silent Night'—Butch Walker and P!nk

Written by Franz Xaver Gruber and Joseph Mohr
Duration: 1:30

Christmas classic 'Silent Night' has been recorded more than 137,000 times, having originally been performed for the first time in 1818 in German. The song was translated into English in 1859 by John Freeman Young, a priest serving at Trinity Church, New York City.

P!nk joined Butch Walker for an acapella cover of 'Silent Night' at the Hotel Café, Los Angeles on 11 December 2011.

'Walkin' After Midnight'—Butch Walker and P!nk

Written by Alan Block and Don Hecht
Duration: 2:25

'Walkin' After Midnight' was written in 1954 for pop star Kay Starr, whose record label rejected the song. Lynn Howard recorded and released it in August 1956, before Patsy Cline recorded the song that November. Cline's recording of the song was released as a single in February 1957 and went onto reach #12 on the USA Billboard Hot 100 singles chart.

P!nk joined Butch Walker for an acoustic cover of 'Walkin' After Midnight' at the Hotel Café, Los Angeles on 11 December 2011.

'Just a Girl'

Written by Gwen Stefani and Tom Dumont
Duration: 5:03 ('Funhouse'/'Just a Girl' Medley)

'Just a Girl' was the first song Gwen Stefani of the ska-punk band No Doubt wrote the lyrics to alone, talking about her experiences of growing up as a woman, with sharp, sarcastic lyrics about society's perception of gender. It was released as the lead single from No Doubt's third studio album, *Tragic Kingdom*, in 1995, reaching #23 on the USA Billboard Hot 100 and #3 in Australia and the UK.

P!nk first performed 'Just a Girl' when she joined No Doubt on stage for their set at the iHeartRadio Music Festival in Las Vegas on 21 September 2012. She posted on Instagram afterwards: 'I just got off stage from the raddest surprise performance with No Doubt. She really is that cool.'

In 2018, P!nk included it on her *Beautiful Trauma* tour in 2018, incorporating 'Just a Girl' into a medley with 'Funhouse.' Gwen returned the honour, joining P!nk on stage to perform the song at the Staples Center in Los Angeles on 31 May 2018.

Although they didn't perform together, Gwen Stefani supported P!nk on her Summer Carnival 2023 tour dates in London, part of the British Summer Time festival in Hyde Park. Afterwards, P!nk wrote to her on Instagram: 'I have known you for a long time and I have looked up to you like a big sister. You're the coolest, kindest, and you always have the most swag in the room. Thank you for spending your weekend with me.'

'Girl on Fire'

Written by Alicia Keys, Salaam Remi and Jeff Bhasker
Contains a portion of 'The Big Beat' written and performed by Billy Squier
Duration: 3:28

'Girl on Fire' is the first single from Alicia Keys' fifth album of the same name, released in September 2012. Keys told *The New York Times* magazine: 'It came from this interview that I did, and the woman wrote something like, "She's like a girl on fire," and I was like, "I love that." And I remember thinking, "I'm writing a song called 'Girl on Fire' for sure." A girl on fire is loud and obnoxious and destructive and just, like, totally unrelenting and she's free, you know what I mean?'

P!nk performed a cover of 'Girl on Fire' at BBC Radio 1's Live Lounge in the UK, while promoting *The Truth About Love* in December. Before singing the song, she said, 'I love her, and we share the same first name!'

'Wicked Game'

Written by Chris Isaak
Duration: 4:58

'Wicked Game' was originally released in 1989 on Chris Isaak's third album, *Heart Shaped World*. P!nk included a cover of the song on *The Truth About Love* tour in 2012, performing it after 'Try.'

'Time After Time'

Written by Cyndi Lauper and Rob Hyman
Duration: 3:28

Considered a timeless classic, 'Time After Time' was a #1 hit on the USA Billboard Hot 100 in 1984 for Cyndi Lauper, taken from her debut album, *She's So Unusual*. Reflecting on the song to *American Songwriter* in 2022, Lauper said: 'It's really about testing love. If you love somebody, you're there, whatever happens, you're there. I think that is what grabbed people and the fact that there were real moments of humanity in it.'

Heralding Lauper as one of her influences, P!nk decided to play 'Time After Time' on *The Truth About Love* tour throughout its Australia leg, starting in Perth in June 2013. She later incorporated it into the setlist for the European leg of the *Beautiful Trauma* tour in 2019.

P!nk joined Cyndi to perform a duet of the song at her third annual *Cyndi Lauper and Friends: Home for the Holidays* benefit concert at the Beacon Theatre in New York on 7 December 2013, raising awareness and funds for homeless young LGBTQ+ people.

In addition, P!nk has also performed the song at two other fundraising events—in February 2015 at the unite4:humanity event at the Beverly Hilton Hotel and in October 2019 at the Teen Cancer America event in the Pacific Palisades.

'Fire and Rain'

Written by James Taylor
Duration: 2:55

'Fire and Rain' was written by singer-songwriter James Taylor and released in 1970 on his second studio album, *Sweet Baby James*. Taylor wrote the song while in rehab, reflecting on a friend who died by suicide while he was in London recording his debut album.

In April 2013, P!nk performed a cover of 'Fire and Rain' during *The Truth About Love* tour, telling the audience in Dublin, Ireland, that she used to sing the song with her dad, James T. Moore. She continued performing it after 'Who Knew' during dates in the UK, France and the Netherlands, until the first of three nights at The O2 Arena in London, after which she removed it from the setlist.

Songwriting Credits

'Hands on Me'—Chila Lynn

Written by Lester Mendez, Jamie Houston and Alecia 'P!nk' Moore
Produced by Max Miglin, Adrian Noher and Dagoberto A. González Jr.
Duration: 4:05

Written during some of the earliest sessions for *I'm Not Dead*, 'Hands on Me' was recorded and released in 2012 by Cuban singer-songwriter Chila Lynn on her debut album, *Real Woman*. Lynn's version has new production from Latin Grammy award-winning producer, Max Miglin.

'A Una Carta'—Chenoa

Written by Lester Mendez, Jamie Houston and Alecia 'P!nk' Moore
Produced by Nigel Walker
Duration: 4:10

During sessions with Lester Mendez, who has worked extensively with Shakira and worked on Jewel's pop crossover album, *0304*, P!nk wrote a song entitled 'Girlz Guide to Loserz.' Translated into Spanish in 2011, Mallorcan performer Chenoa recorded the song for her EP, *Como un Fantasma*.

'Simplemente Tú'—Chenoa

Written by Greg Wells, Kara DioGuardi and Alecia 'P!nk' Moore
Produced by Nigel Walker
Duration: 4:05
Released as a single in June 2012

'Simplemente Tú' started life as 'No One Else,' co-written and recorded by P!nk for potential inclusion on *I'm Not Dead*. It was recorded and released by Alison Iraheta on her 2009 debut album, *Just Like You*.

Translated into Spanish, it was recorded by Chenoa for her EP *Como un Fantasma* and was released as a single in Spain in June 2012.

'I Walk Alone'—Cher

Written by Billy Mann, Alecia 'P!nk' Moore and MachoPsycho (Niklas 'Nikey' Olovson and Robin Lynch)
Produced by Billy Mann and MachoPsycho (Niklas 'Nikey' Olovson and Robin Lynch)
Recorded at Eargasm Studios, Santa Monica; Turtle Sound Studios, Weston; Fishhead Music, Gothenburg, Sweden and Wally World, Davie
Duration: 3:23
Released as a single in January 2014

Cher's twenty-fifth studio album, *Closer to the Truth*, was released in September 2013, after nearly two years of writing and recording. Taking its title from a lyric in 'I Walk Alone,' one of two songs P!nk co-wrote on the album, Cher's mission for the album was to record songs that she liked.

Billy Mann submitted two songs for the album that he had written with P!nk, working with Cher to record both 'I Walk Alone' and 'Lie to Me.' P!nk told *The Herald Sun* in Australia: 'It's such an honour. I finally feel like a songwriter. And I'm such a fan.'

In an interview with Audacy, Cher said: 'P!nk wrote "I Walk Alone" and it kind of goes in and out of everything. I don't even know what it is, but the banjo in the beginning… I just thought, "Oh, I don't know if I like this, what is it? It's like some sort of Ozark music and I'm not sure if anyone's going to understand it!" But then it was so cool and the song is so weird and I thought, "You know it's perfect, it just makes total sense." P!nk's songs, I just loved from 5 seconds into them. She's such a great singer and she's a great songwriter. I mean she's like the total package. I understood them and when you hear them, you'll understand why I understood them and they're so personal, but they work for both of us.'

'I Walk Alone' was released as a single from *Closer to the Truth* in the UK, with a remix package following in April. P!nk's demo of the song leaked online in 2020, with her backing vocals being included on Cher's recording.

'Lie to Me'—Cher

Written by Billy Mann and Alecia 'P!nk' Moore
Produced by Billy Mann
Recorded at Eargasm Studios, Santa Monica; Turtle Sound Studios, Weston and Wally World, Davie
Duration: 3:19

P!nk and Billy Mann worked on a second country-tinged ballad for Cher's *Closer to the Truth* entitled 'Lie to Me.' Cher told Audacy: 'I think one of the best songs is "Lie to Me", which was also written by P!nk.'

In an interview with *Billboard* magazine, P!nk confirmed that she had written both songs for herself. She said: 'Cher recorded two of my songs, which is fucking huge for me, and such an honour. I still can't believe it. But I can, because I wrote those songs for myself - but then when I hear her sing them, I'm like, "Right. Yeah. Of course!"'

Cher later appeared as a God-like figure in P!nk's music video for 'All I Know So Far.'

'Here Comes the Lightning'—Big B

Written by James Perkins, Jake Sinclair, Butch Walker, Alecia 'P!nk' Moore and Bryan 'Big B' Mahoney
Produced by Butch Walker and Alecia 'P!nk' Moore
Duration: 2:52

'Here Comes the Lightning' appears on Big B's album, *Fool's Gold*, released in July 2013.

Big B said in an interview: 'I was lucky enough to work with Pink and Butch Walker on 'Here Comes the Lightning.' I had been friends with P!nk's husband, Carey Hart, for the past fifteen years, and I had become good friends with her as well. We had talked about making music together for a long time and for this record it finally happened. Butch had some music that went with the ideas that we had, and as soon as he played us the track, P!nk and I just both grabbed a pen and pad and starting writing to it. It turned out to be an awesome song, and we were fortunate enough to create a dope video to back it up.'

Catalogue Registrations

'Lost'

Written by Butch Walker and Alecia 'P!nk' Moore

'Go To Hell Your Way (I'll Go Mine)'

Written by Butch Walker, Alecia 'P!nk' Moore and Brandi Carlile

'Hypocrite'

Written by Butch Walker and Alecia 'P!nk' Moore

'Black Gold'

Written by Billy Mann and Alecia 'P!nk' Moore

'Bittersweet Delight'
Written by Billy Mann and Alecia 'P!nk' Moore

'Careful What You Wish For'
Written by Billy Mann and Alecia 'P!nk' Moore

'Healed'
Written by Billy Mann and Alecia 'P!nk' Moore

'Pieces'
Written by Billy Mann and Alecia 'P!nk' Moore

'Gimme Some Sugar'
Written by Billy Mann, David Schuler and Alecia 'P!nk' Moore

'So Clever'
Written by Francis 'Eg' White and Alecia 'P!nk' Moore

'So I'
Written by Francis 'Eg' White and Alecia 'P!nk' Moore

'Is That the Best You've Got?'
Written by Francis 'Eg' White and Alecia 'P!nk' Moore

'Me and My Friends'
Written by Dan Wilson and Alecia 'P!nk' Moore

'Gorilla'
Written by Dan Wilson and Alecia 'P!nk' Moore

9

rose ave. (2014)—You+Me

Released:	10 October 2014 (Europe and Australia)
	13 October 2014 (UK)
	14 October 2014 (USA and Canada)
Chart Position:	USA: 4
	Canada: 1
	UK: 10
	Australia: 2
	Germany: 6

Canadian singer-songwriter Dallas Green began releasing music as City and Colour in 2005. Having met P!nk through a mutual friend, he began touring after releasing his second album in February 2008, including as a support act on the UK leg of her *Funhouse Summer Carnival* tour in June 2010. Their friendship grew, and after performing a duet of 'What Makes a Man' at Green's November 2011 show in Los Angeles, became aware of their musical synergy.

While promoting *Greatest Hits... So Far!!!* in 2010, P!nk told *The Los Angeles Times* that she wanted to record an album that would be 'just absolutely, consciously, not trying to get played on the radio.' She elaborated to *Billboard* magazine: 'I always joke that my favourite artist from the '60s and '70s would have never gotten radio play today, Janis Joplin. You would probably have never heard "Summertime" on the radio. If it's not 3 and a half minutes long, it ain't getting played. I want to go and just write. I want to do my acoustic rock 'n' roll record, which I always wanted to do since I was a little girl.'

rose ave. might not be the album she originally envisioned, but it did allow her the freedom to write without focusing on creating radio hits. In a 2016 interview with *The Canadian Press*, Green recalled: 'Alecia and I had talked about it for a long time - not about making a record, but the idea of singing together and trying to write a song. When we had the time to do it, that really lit a fire of creativity because it was something different. The idea of collaborating with a female voice and a different writer was what I needed, I guess, to create a bunch of new songs.'

Plans for the album started in February 2014, after Green texted P!nk to ask if she wanted to hang out together while he was visiting Venice. Having secretly set up a studio so they could work together, she suggested that they visit and drop off his guitar. However, that night they wrote and recorded 'From a Closet in Norway (Oslo Blues).'

Talking to *Vulture* in 2014, P!nk said: 'It's rad that we're such good friends. I put a lot of pressure on myself when I walk into a songwriting thing. Like, "I'm gonna feel like such a dick, like a useless waste of skin." But this time, if it didn't work, I still got to hang out with my friend for a week. Dallas was having his own internal struggle about the whole thing. I told him, "Whatever, there's beer, there's wine, there's whiskey." We did eight songs that first week, then I had to go on tour; then we came back for two days. But if you count the amount of time we were actually working and not just at the bar, it was more like four days.'

rose ave. was named after the location of the studio where they wrote the album, credited to You+Me, rather than either of their existing artist names. P!nk explained to *The Associated Press* why she chose to be called Alecia Moore throughout the record's credits: 'This has nothing to do with P!nk. P!nk was my nickname as a kid but it's become this thing that I do. If you say the name "P!nk", you conjure up a woman hanging from a ceiling in a piece of cloth, screaming about her husband. This is just me and my friend Dallas. He doesn't call me P!nk.'

Although the duo considered secretly releasing *rose ave.* online with no name attached, because of their existing record company contracts it was released as a joint project between RCA Records and Dine Alone Records. P!nk told *The Guardian*: 'This is a passion thing. We're friends and we wanted to sing together. We handed our record companies an album and they were like, "What?" And we were like, "We don't know, that's your job."'

The album charted at #1 in Green's native Canada and reached the top 10 in the USA, UK, Germany, and Australia.

In a Facebook video in 2021, Green confirmed he had been working on new songs for You+Me. The following year, he posted a photo on Instagram in the studio with Moore, accompanied by musician Matt Kelly, and producer Simon Gooding. You+Me reunited in September 2024 to perform at One805LIVE! to raise money for first responders in Santa Barbara County, California, and at the Epidermolysis Bullosa Medical Research Foundation's annual fundraiser, #Rock4EB.

P!nk confirmed during the latter concert that they had recorded more music as You+Me, with Green confirming that they had worked on a second album. Talking to *Rolling Stone* magazine in late 2024, Green said: 'It's going to come out at some point. We've been recording it over a bunch of years. But I wrote some songs recently that we finished recording this year and those are at the top of my mind right now. She announced it on stage and I was like, "Oh, you're talking about this? I'm gonna talk about it!" I would hope that it comes out sooner than later but there's a lot going on; she's just finished the feat of doing back-to-back stadium tours and I'm just about to finish two and a half years of touring myself.'

Album Tracks

'Capsized'

Written by Alecia 'P!nk' Moore and Dallas Green
Produced by Alecia 'P!nk' Moore and Dallas Green
Recorded at Earthstar Creation Center, California
Duration: 3:35

'Capsized' opens *rose ave.*, with You+Me exploring the feeling of being emotionally overwhelmed in a relationship, as they metaphorically struggle to keep afloat. P!nk plays the thunder spring on the song.

In the duo's *rose ave.* promotional interview video, Green says to P!nk: 'It's super cool, it's moody. I was watching you sing "Somewhere Over the Rainbow" somewhere on TV, in my house in Toronto, and I came up with the intro guitar part and ran into the bathroom and recorded it on my phone… and then I flew to your house and showed that to you, and you were like, "Well, I got this idea, like these two ships" and then, "Bam – we have a song." It's so simple, but it's so heavy.'

'From a Closet in Norway (Oslo Blues)'

Written by Alecia 'P!nk' Moore and Dallas Green
Produced by Alecia 'P!nk' Moore and Dallas Green
Recorded at Earthstar Creation Center, California
Duration: 3:16

'From a Closet in Norway (Oslo Blues)' is a tender ballad about 'good days and bad days, and how sometimes, the bad days make you completely forget about how good the good days are,' according to Green. The song was the first to be written and recorded by You+Me, with its title reflecting the fact that Green wrote the original riff of the song in a closet in Oslo, Norway.

P!nk added in their interview video, 'The highs are so high that the lows are killing me. That was another thing from the Oscars too, which is funny. I was watching Cate Blanchett's speech, and she was. is always incredible. And she was talking about how many women made movies that year, and how those movies made money, and how the Earth is round, now guys, right? And so the chorus was, "if the Earth is round now, why can't we have everything?" Inspired by Cate Blanchett, I'd like her to know.'

'Gently'

Written by Alecia 'P!nk' Moore and Dallas Green
Produced by Alecia 'P!nk' Moore and Dallas Green
Recorded at Earthstar Creation Center, California
Duration: 3:32

'Gently' was inspired by an article Green read about performers' fears of their fame and popularity fading and whether he shared those same anxieties. The song was the second song they worked on together. He explained: 'I just kind of said to myself, "I wouldn't mind going gently." If that's the way it's supposed to be, then that's the way it's supposed to be. I guess I don't ever want to force myself.'

He added, in conversation with P!nk: 'It was one of the first ones we did together, and I sat and played and sang that one all the way through. And then I watched you go into the booth and just create that whole harmony part for the whole song. And I remember you were getting mad at yourself. You were like, "I'm gonna get it. I'm gonna get it." And I'm like, "Alecia, I've been singing that song for like, a year, and this is your fourth time singing it, and it's ripping my face off." It was just really blending well and it made me feel like we could actually, really get something going.'

'Love Gone Wrong'

Written by Alecia 'P!nk' Moore and Dallas Green
Produced by Alecia 'P!nk' Moore and Dallas Green
Recorded at Earthstar Creation Center, California
Duration: 4:21

'Love Gone Wrong' tells the story of a couple parting ways, each sharing their side of the story but ultimately agreeing on the finality of their split in the chorus. Although other songs on *rose ave.* were completed before 'Love Gone Wrong,' it was the first song to be considered for the project. While P!nk was on tour, Green sent her a text with the riff and part of the song, prompting her to stop in her tracks and realise that their collaboration would be a success.

She recalled: 'I was in Chicago, and I listened to it on the treadmill, and I was like, "Holy shit." I looked around. Everyone was looking at me, carry on. And that's when I knew that it was gonna be okay. Before we even stepped foot in that studio to drop your guitars off. It's that old soul that I think Dallas and I were in another life, probably when we went to church together. And it's just an easy song to hear, an easy song to sing, easy song to be with.'

'You and Me'

Written by Alecia 'P!nk' Moore and Dallas Green
Produced by Alecia 'P!nk' Moore and Dallas Green

Recorded at Earthstar Creation Center, California
Duration: 3:12
Chart Position: Canada: 48; Germany: 91

'You and Me' was one of the final songs recorded for the album, featuring You+Me harmonising throughout. Although singles from the album were not released to radio, 'You and Me' offered the first glimpse into *rose ave.* with an official lyric video released on YouTube on 8 September 2014, a month before the album's release. They also performed the song on *The Ellen DeGeneres Show* on 13 October and *The Jimmy Kimmel Show* a few days later. As a result of the promotion, it charted at #48 on the Billboard Canadian Hot 100 singles chart.

The lyrics convey a deep connection between soulmates, with lines like, "You can be flawed enough but perfect for a person, someone who will be there for you when you start to fall apart, guiding your direction when you're riding through the dark.'

In the album's promotional interview, P!nk reflected: 'It reminded me of Peter, Paul and Mary when I first heard it, and that's why I instantly fell in love. Because this record, for me, is how I grew up, with my dad playing guitar and singing and harmonising and writing stories. There's just such a simple beauty in it.'

'Unbeliever'

Written by Alecia 'P!nk' Moore and Dallas Green
Produced by Alecia 'P!nk' Moore and Dallas Green
Recorded at Earthstar Creation Center, California
Duration: 3:41

'Unbeliever' is one of the lighter moments on *rose ave.* with You+Me singing about 'hanging on' for someone who counts on you. The duo performed the song live on *The Jimmy Kimmel Show* to promote the album on 16 October 2014.

Green admitted in their press interview that he had originally intended for the song to be slower, saying: 'Alecia had something to do in the morning, so I went to the studio early, and I tried to have things kind of built and ready for her. So when she'd come in, I'd be like, "I got you something." And I remember I recorded this really slow, sad version of the song, which is what I usually do. And Alecia walks in, so I go, "What do you think?" She goes, "I don't love it... can it be happier?" I changed the key up a little bit, sped it up. And now it's just one of my favourites.'

P!nk added: As we were recording it, he kept getting slower and slower and trying to go back to the sad way. I'm like, "No!"'

'Second Guess'

Written by Alecia 'P!nk' Moore and Dallas Green
Produced by Alecia 'P!nk' Moore and Dallas Green

Recorded at Earthstar Creation Center, California
Duration: 3:27

'Second Guess' is about having hope and knowing things will get better, even when it feels impossible to get there.

In their press commentary on the album, Green says: 'For me, every song is a little bit different... it's the way that we finish each other's sentences on this one and then sort of meet in the middle for the chorus, and the round in the bridge.'

'Break the Cycle'

Written by Alecia 'P!nk' Moore and Dallas Green
Produced by Alecia 'P!nk' Moore and Dallas Green
Recorded at Earthstar Creation Center, California
Duration: 4:05

'Break the Cycle' is a very personal song to P!nk, written about her mother. She recalls: 'We were at the bar talking, and I really wanted to write a song about my mom, and it maybe didn't turn out to be quite the love song I thought it would be, but it's very honest. It's about patterns and habits and love and trying to do better. It's about trying to understand someone else. You can let a person know that you know what they're going through, or what they went through. It's a gift you give that person.'

In their album interview, Green recalls to her: 'The rhythm that I came up with for the first guitar part was already super weird, and the vocal line that you came up with on top of that for the verse... I was like, when you started singing that, "Where did you get that from?" It was great. That one to me was very different, an out of nowhere song. I did not expect that one at all, and it's so good.'

'Open Door'

Written by Alecia 'P!nk' Moore and Dallas Green
Produced by Alecia 'P!nk' Moore and Dallas Green
Recorded at Earthstar Creation Center, California
Duration: 3:41

'Open Door' is a letter to Green's parents, reflecting on his career as a travelling musician and the sacrifices made to live life on the road.

In the album press commentary, he said: 'It's a special one for me, because it's about my mum and dad. I guess that's essentially where the idea for me came from was, I do this thing just like Alecia does, where I don't necessarily get to see... you sacrifice a lot of relationships to try and do something that you feel is the right thing, or what you're supposed to be doing. And I have always just only known how to tell people how I feel by singing it to them. And so that's kind of where that one comes from for me.'

'No Ordinary Love'

Written by Sade Adu and Stuart Matthewman
Produced by Alecia 'P!nk' Moore and Dallas Green
Recorded at Earthstar Creation Center, California
Duration: 4:09

Trustfall—Tour Deluxe Edition (2023) Live
Arranged by Paul Mirkovich
Duration: 3:42

The lead single from British soul group Sade's 1992 album *Love Deluxe*, 'No Ordinary Love,' won the award for Best R&B Performance by a Duo or Group with Vocals at the 25th Grammy Awards in 1993. In an interview with *Details* magazine, the band's frontperson, Sade Adu, said the song is about 'love that isn't supposed to work. Reason says that love is not supposed to work, but faith makes it happen. Sort of like re-finding something that you've lost, just because you're sure of it.'

You+Me recorded a cover of 'No Ordinary Love' for *rose ave.*, turning the song into a duet, with Green on lead. He said: 'If I had to pick one song to sing for the rest of my life, it would be that song, because she was one of my mother's favourites, and she's one of my favourites. And I just love that song so much.' P!nk added: 'Me too, I love everything about her.'

A solo version of the song was included on P!nk's *Summer Carnival* 2023 tour, with a live recording of it appearing on the Tour Deluxe Edition of *Trustfall*.

10

Beautiful Trauma (2014–2017)

Released:	13 October 2017
Chart Position:	USA: 1
	Canada: 1
	UK: 1
	Australia: 1
	Germany: 2

Beautiful Trauma, P!nk's first solo album in nearly five years, was over three years in the making. Following the global success of *The Truth About Love* and its 140-date world tour, she consciously decided to take a break from music to focus on her family and personal life.

P!nk said this break influenced the songs she wrote for *Beautiful Trauma*, and the album it became. Talking to *USA Today*, she said: 'The difference between this record and a lot of other records was I was living a normal life while writing. Normally, since I was 19, I've gone: "Make a record, promo, go on tour. Make a record, promo, go on tour." It's been this cycle. This is the first time I've been like, "Take my daughter to preschool. Go on a date with my husband." It's real life that's been on my mind.'

During the hiatus, P!nk also expanded her family, welcoming her second child, Jameson Moon Hart, on 26 December 2016. This delayed the release of *Beautiful Trauma* by a few months, enabling her to continue recording. She also sadly experienced a miscarriage before Jameson's birth. In an interview with *The New York Times*, she said: 'I've had several, but this one snuck up on me. The funniest part of all of it was my record company was super excited because I was pregnant. They were like, "Oh, this means we're getting to the goal." So when they found out I had a miscarriage, they were like, "Ah, we're so sorry." They're a bunch of men in suits - they have no idea what to do. And I could just see their wheels turning: "So, yeah - you're going to try again?" And I'm like, "Yeah, I'm going to try again."'

The sessions for *Beautiful Trauma* began with P!nk's long-term collaborators, including Billy Mann. However, she found the first year of writing challenging, as she had to rediscover her voice. She told *The Los Angeles Times*: 'I spent a year just writing slow, sad songs, thinking I was Adele.' Both personal and global events influenced the album's content—her miscarriage, her father James's cancer diagnosis, and her feelings about Donald Trump's election as President of the United States of America in 2016.

These events led to the creation of the album's title track, 'Beautiful Trauma,' which P!nk wrote with Jack Antonoff. Antonoff was previously part of the band Fun alongside her previous collaborator, Nate Ruess, and had gone on to work with Sara Bareilles and Taylor Swift.

Talking to NPR, she said: 'I think life is really traumatic, and it feels - even though it makes me sound like my parents to say this - like it's getting more so. But I also think that there's really beautiful people in the world, and there's more good than bad, and there's love to be made and joy to be had. I try to hold on to the beautiful part. But, you know, my dad always says something to me: "I wish you enough." And what he means by that is, I wish you enough rain to be able to enjoy the sunshine. And I wish you enough hard times to be able to enjoy the easy bits. And that's beautiful trauma to me.'

Apple Music commissioned an exclusive half-hour documentary entitled *On the Record: P!nk – Beautiful Trauma* to promote the album. In the documentary, P!nk said: 'I guess in some ways, each record, I meet at least one new threshold for myself. And I think this time it was, I think vocally, I've never been in a better place. On a couple of these records, I nailed it.'

Whilst *Beautiful Trauma* was described by Roger Davies, P!nk's manager, as 'a continuation of the previous records,' it expanded her range of collaborators to include Johnny McDaid, Steve Mac, Julia Michaels, Mattman & Robin, and Tobias Jesso Jr. The album's promotional campaign kicked off with her being presented with the Michael Jackson Video Vanguard award at the 2017 MTV Video Music Awards in August, where she included 'What About Us' as part of a hits medley. P!nk also visited Europe to promote the album, appearing on *The X Factor* in the UK, *Quotidien* in France and *The Voice of Germany*.

Beautiful Trauma was another success for P!nk, charting at #1 in the USA, UK, and Australia, selling over 5 million copies worldwide. In support of the album, she embarked on her seventh tour, performing in arenas and stadiums across North America, Europe, Australia and New Zealand, and Brazil. The tour became the tenth highest-grossing tour of all time according to figures reported to Billboard Boxscore, with over 3 million people having attended.

Reflecting on the album in *Entertainment Weekly*, P!nk said: 'There was no other goal than to not have an album full of slow, sad songs, because that's all I had for a while. We're always very involved with real people with real struggles and are constantly watching the news and taking it all in. But at the same time, we live on a farm, so I've been a soccer mom for four years, taking my daughter to preschool, doing bake sales, lemonade stands, kindergarten, and all that sort of stuff! Each album is a snapshot of where you are at that time, if you're being honest.'

Album Tracks

'Beautiful Trauma'

Written by Jack Antonoff and Alecia 'P!nk' Moore
Produced by Jack Antonoff
Recorded at Earthstar Creation Center, California; The Village, Los Angeles and Rough Customer Studio, New York City
Duration: 4:10
Released as a single in September 2017
Music video directed by The GoldenBoyz (Nick Florez and RJ Durell)
Chart Position: USA: 78; Canada: 51; UK: 25; Australia: 25; Germany: 80

'Beautiful Trauma,' P!nk's first collaboration with Jack Antonoff, opens the album as its title track, setting the tone for the rest of the record. The song includes a reference to a personal story about slashing her husband's car tyres in 2004: 'We were on fire, I slashed your tyres.' On *The Tonight Show with Jimmy Fallon*, she explained: 'I had 13 stitches in my hand from trying to slash his tyres and I learned from that. I got through the first tyre. The second one was where I lost steam and hit the metal part and not rubber.'

Ahead of the song's release, P!nk posted on Twitter: 'I wrote the song with a very awesome person and named the album after it because life is fucking traumatic. But it's also incredibly beautiful, too. There's a lot of beauty still and beautiful souls. Enjoy.'

In an interview about the album in *Vulture* magazine, she talked about her relationship and the origins of the song. She said: 'Jack and I got together, and he is a loveable human being, and we were just sort of trading funny relationship stories. You know, long-term relationships are a lot of work. It's fucking hard, especially when you have kids. I've seen a lot of our friends go through terrible divorces, and I don't want that. I went through that as a kid; Carey did many times. I like to fight for things I believe in. Life is fucking traumatic. Like, my dad just beat cancer. Chemo was traumatic. Having your dad dying of cancer is traumatic. Turning on the news is traumatic. Mother Nature is fucking traumatic. Everywhere you look, it's really that word. But at the same time, there are so many rad, good people in the world. There are so many people who aren't racist, who aren't douchebags. You go to Haiti, it's the poorest country in the world, and people are dancing, sharing food, cooking, and loving. There's just love to be made still. I think beauty and trauma go - that's just what life is. If you can surround yourself with the right people and find your village, then you'll be good.'

'Beautiful Trauma' was released as the first promotional single from the album in late September, two weeks before the album's launch. However, following

P!nk's dislike of the music video she had shot for 'Revenge,' it became the album's official second single in November. Two music videos were released for the song, both directed and choreographed by The GoldenBoyz. The first, a 'Dance Video,' was released in October 2017, featuring model Larsen Thompson.

The second music video, starring P!nk and Channing Tatum, premiered the following month, starring the couple as Fred and Ginger Hart, wearing kitsch 1950s-style vivid, bright-coloured clothes. The video takes an unexpected twist when it's revealed that the secret to their happy marriage is sexual exploration, with P!nk as dominatrix, and the swapping of gender roles, with them both cross-dressing.

P!nk promoted the song with a performance on *Saturday Night Live* during the album's release week. In November, with the song confirmed as the second single, she performed it at the 2017 American Music Awards, walking the side of the JW Marriott Hotel in Los Angeles while suspended from a high wire.

'Revenge' featuring Eminem

Written by Max Martin, Johan 'Shellback' Schuster, Alecia 'P!nk' Moore and Marshall 'Eminem' Mathers
Produced by Max Martin and Johan 'Shellback' Schuster
Recorded at MXM Studios, Los Angeles; Conway Recording Studios, Los Angeles and MXM Studios, Stockholm, Sweden
Duration: 3:47
Eminem appears courtesy of Aftermath Records
Music video directed by Georgia Hudson
Chart Position: Canada: 63; UK: 33; Australia: 21; Germany: 84

'Revenge' showcases P!nk at her most playful, as she and Eminem take a tongue-in-cheek approach to the idea of getting even in a relationship. Talking to *The Los Angeles Times*, P!nk said: 'We wrote the song, Johan, Max and I, and I wanted a rap Grammy. So, I drank a lot of wine and I wrote a rap, and I was mediocrely impressed by my rap skills. Then I went home and drank more wine, because that always sounds like a good idea, and I emailed Eminem and I said, "I've loved you since you gave me your autograph in 2001 at the MTV Awards, and I'm gonna be a rapper now and you're gonna rap with me." And he wrote back and said "OK."'

In an interview with *Billboard*, P!nk revealed that the song is her mother's favourite song on the album. Asked about criticisms of Eminem's lyrics by *The Guardian*, she added: 'The reason I love Eminem is, number one, I think he's a lyrical genius, I think he's one of the best that ever did it. I think he's funny as shit. I don't think he believes in any of the shit he says. Otherwise, why would he respect a woman like me? Which he does. And I think he's one of those people that likes to take the piss out of all the shit we hold so precious and so dear. I think all of us get a little too serious at times and that's why I think it is hilarious that he says, "You're a whore, you're a whore, this is war."' She joked to *The New York Times* that she told her daughter that Eminem says 'horse' rather than 'whore' in the song.

The song's lyrics reference two very different examples of revenge. It opens with P!nk singing, 'Like Leo in *The Revenant*,' referring to the 2015 film in which Leonardo DiCaprio's character seeks revenge for his son's murder. The lyrics then shift to 'Abel in that Bible bit,' referencing the story of Cain and Abel from Genesis, where Cain kills Abel out of jealousy and anger.

An elaborate music video for the song was filmed in September 2017, featuring Eminem lookalikes and directed by Georgia Hudson. However, P!nk later told *The Sun*: 'We shot it and it was terrible. It's never coming out. It just didn't work and it was the wrong timing for it. I looked like hell, it was awful. Thank God Eminem wasn't in it. If he was in it, I would have been mortified. We had Eminem lookalikes. 'Beautiful Trauma' is better.' An unfinished version of the video leaked online in 2019.

'Whatever You Want'

Written by Max Martin, Johan 'Shellback' Schuster and Alecia 'P!nk' Moore
Produced by Max Martin and Johan 'Shellback' Schuster
Recorded at MXM Studios, Los Angeles and MXM Studios, Stockholm, Sweden
Duration: 4:01
Released as a single in June 2018
Music video directed by Brad Comfort
Chart Position: Australia: 44

'Whatever You Want' was released as the second promotional single from *Beautiful Trauma*, following the album's title track, becoming available for sale on digital download sites one week before the album's release. A collaboration with Max Martin and Shellback, the heartfelt pop-rock anthem is about fighting for love and commitment, with P!nk singing: 'I feel like our ship's going down tonight, but it's always darkest before the light and that's enough for me to try.'

The Los Angeles Times asked P!nk about writing 'Whatever You Want' with Martin, commenting that it is 'not the type of pop banger he's known for.' She responded: 'I wasn't feeling that way most of the time in the last four years.'

During her Apple Music exclusive documentary, she added: 'I've been working with Max and Johan for a long time. We can get pretty serious. "Whatever You Want" was just basically, "What do you want to write about?" I said, "Carey?" We have felt like our ship is going down so many times. Sometimes in a really real way, and sometimes we have crashed, and we have split. But we always come back. I think that true love is always coming back to the table, and "Whatever You Want" is sort of about that.'

A music video for the song was released exclusively on Apple Music on 1 March 2018, featuring behind-the-scenes footage from P!nk's *Beautiful Trauma* world tour, and clips from her performances at the Super Bowl LII and the 2017 MTV Video Music Awards. A remix EP featuring remixes from Faux Tales, FTampa and Embody was released on digital download sites worldwide later in the year.

'What About Us'

Written by Johnny McDaid, Steve Mac and Alecia 'P!nk' Moore
Produced by Steve Mac
Recorded at The Village Studios, Los Angeles and Rokstone Studios, London, UK
Duration: 4:30 (Radio Edit: 3:55)
Released as a single in August 2017
Music video directed by Georgia Hudson
Chart Position: USA: 13; Canada: 6; UK: 3; Australia: 1; Germany: 3

'What About Us' is P!nk's first collaboration with Irish singer-songwriter Johnny McDaid, a member of the band Snow Patrol, and British songwriter-producer Steve Mac. Both men had previously worked with Ed Sheeran, including on 'Shape of You,' a global hit at the start of 2017. A powerful, emotional battle cry set to an electronic pop instrumental, 'What About Us' is a political protest song that sees P!nk confront disillusionment in the wake of the 2016 Presidential election.

Talking about the song, and comparisons to 'Dear Mr. President' to *Vulture* magazine, P!nk said: 'Honestly, a lot of people have said, "When are you gonna make 'Dear Mr. President 2'?" And I'm not. Because there are no words. I wouldn't know what to say. I feel like "What About Us" is one of the more sophisticated songs that I've written because it was a little more poetic and inclusive. I think it's a beautiful song. It feels good in my body, number one. And it says everything I needed to say: "What about us?" I knew the video would paint that picture as well.'

She added to BBC Radio 1: 'I'm feeling a little ashamed right now of America and its leaders. And I think the American dream is still alive because there's still a lot of beautiful people in the country that have beautiful hearts and beautiful minds. I just think the American dream has changed from what it used to be. It used to be "go to college, get a job, have a family, 2.1 children." I don't know how that works exactly? But I think now the American dream is different. I think you write your own now. I think you can do whatever you can figure out in your brain. I'm super into that, actually. I would just like to see us have some peace, some inclusion and some kindness.'

Before performing the song on *Good Morning America*, P!nk said: 'I don't like to tell people what songs are about just because it's whatever it is for you. Like for one of my girlfriends, for her, it's about love. For me, it's about how government has failed us. And it can be about all of it, really.'

For the music video, P!nk collaborated with director Georgia Hudson. The video opens with excerpts of political speeches and highlights individuals from marginalised groups who had become political targets under Trump's administration, including immigrants, same-sex couples, and minorities. Chants of 'We are going to reject hate! We are going to reject racism!' and 'Now is the time to protect our community' are also heard in the video.

Hudson told *PromoNews*: 'P!nk is a real artist, I actually quite love her. She had told me about this dream she had, and we worked it in to the choreography, for the final desert dance. When she saw it, she was moved to tears, she was there with us, involved, I respect her.'

'What About Us' became another #1 single for P!nk in Australia, being certified 8x Platinum, and reached the top 3 in the UK, where it is 2x Platinum. A remix package, featuring new versions of the song from Cash Cash, Madison Mars, Pink Pandy, Barry Harris and Tiësto was also commissioned and released later in the year.

'But We Lost It'

Written by Greg Kurstin and Alecia 'P!nk' Moore
Produced by Greg Kurstin
Recorded at Earthstar Creation Center, California
Duration: 3:27

A heartfelt ballad about the fragility of love, 'But We Lost It,' co-written and produced by Greg Kurstin, sees P!nk reflecting on a relationship that has fallen apart, comparing emotional healing to that of a broken bone.

In an interview with *Vulture* magazine in 2023, P!nk revealed she was surprised to find the song was a favourite of one of her daughter's friends. She said: 'I was actually with Willow and all her little girlfriends the other night. We were doing karaoke and they pulled out some deep cuts. They shocked me. 'But We Lost It,' from *Beautiful Trauma*, was her friend's favourite song. I was like, "What? How did you even hear that song? You're 14. Why do you even understand what I'm saying? Who hurt you?" They're all so random.'

To date, P!nk has not performed the song live in full; however, her pianist, Jason Chapman, played a clip of it during the 'guess the song' segment of her concert at a handful of *Summer Carnival* tour dates in 2023 and 2024.

'Barbies'

Written by Ross Golan, The Struts (Jakob Jerlström and Ludwig Söderberg), Julia Michaels and Alecia 'P!nk' Moore
Produced by The Struts (Jakob Jerlström and Ludwig Söderberg)
Recorded at Wolf Cousins Studios, Stockholm, Sweden and MXM Studios, Los Angeles
Duration: 3:44

'Barbies' is a nostalgic song, longing for the simplicity and innocence of childhood, co-written by Julia Michaels. Michaels, a solo artist in her own right, co-wrote hits for Selena Gomez and Britney Spears and worked extensively with Gwen Stefani on her 2016 album, *This Is What the Truth Feels Like*.

In her Apple Music documentary, P!nk said: 'I love Julia. She's so talented. That song makes my heart hurt. I mean, it's just, it's beautiful. The melody, the sentiment. I'm turning 38 in a couple of days, and I still feel like a 17-year-old boy. Or like an

8-year-old girl at times. And it's really hard for me to believe that I'm a grown-up and that I'm supposed to be responsible for my kids now. And I am. I've gone way too far responsible. But I think we all feel like that when the pressure's mounting up and we have these responsibilities and the weight of the world, it feels like, is on your shoulders. And you just want to go back to playing in your room.'

'Where We Go'

Written by Greg Kurstin and Alecia 'P!nk' Moore
Produced by Greg Kurstin
Recorded at Earthstar Creation Center, California
Duration: 4:27

Greg Kurstin co-wrote and produced the anthemic 'Where We Go.' In the song's existential lyrics, P!nk reflects on the fleeting nature of relationships and life itself while confronting uncertainty and inevitability head-on. As of 2019, 'Where We Go' was P!nk's fifth most popular non-single in the UK, with over 5.78million streams.

'For Now'

Written by Max Martin, Mattias 'Mattman' Larsson, Robin Fredriksson, Julia Michaels and Alecia 'P!nk' Moore
Produced by Mattias 'Mattman' Larsson and Robin Fredriksson
Recorded at Wolf Cousins Studios, Stockholm, Sweden and MXM Studios, Los Angeles
Duration: 3:36

'For Now' is P!nk's first collaboration with Swedish producers Mattman and Robin, who are part of Max Martin's Wolf Cousins production house. In addition to producing 'Run Away With Me' by Carly Rae Jepsen, they have worked extensively with songwriter Julia Michaels on songs for other artists such as Selena Gomez and Britney Spears. The song's lyrics reflect on the early part of a relationship that has caused pain, with P!nk asking to 'freeze frame, pause, rewind, stop and get back to the older familiar thoughts.'

'Secrets'

Written by Max Martin, Johan 'Shellback' Schuster, Oscar Holter and Alecia 'P!nk' Moore
Produced by Max Martin, Johan 'Shellback' Schuster and Oscar Holter
Recorded at MXM Studios, Stockholm, Sweden; Wolf Cousins Studios, Stockholm, Sweden and Conway Studios, Los Angeles
Duration: 3:29

Released as a single in August 2018
Music video directed by Alecia 'P!nk' Moore and Larn Poland

Swedish songwriter and producer Oscar Holter, who worked on 'Just Like Fire,' joined P!nk, Max Martin and Shellback to write 'Secrets.' Upbeat, with influences of deep house, the song's lyrics talk about the hidden parts of ourselves we're afraid to show as P!nk repeats, 'Everybody's got a secret.'

A music video for 'Secrets' was filmed in Perth, Australia, featuring six of her dancers performing in a warehouse that was part of the Fringe World Festival. The song was sent to Hot Adult Contemporary Radio in the USA, and a remix EP was released worldwide on digital download sites, featuring new versions from Syn Cole, Until Dawn, Rescue Rangerz and DJ Suri and Chris Daniel.

'Better Life'

Written by Jack Antonoff, Alecia 'P!nk' Moore and Sam Dew
Produced by Jack Antonoff
Recorded at Earthstar Creation Center, California; The Village, Los Angeles and Rough Customer Studio, New York City
Duration: 3:20

'Better Life' is a soulful, doo-wop-inspired R&B song, produced by Jack Antonoff, featuring his Bleachers bandmate, Evan Smith, on saxophone. In the song's lyrics, P!nk admits to feeling paranoid about her partner liking photos of others on social media and acknowledges her jealousy, questioning if the spark is gone from their relationship.

In a press interview, P!nk explained: 'That song was inspired by a conversation I was having with a friend of mine who is going through a divorce. We were talking about social media and how we only sort of post the good stuff, so we tend to start believing everybody else's life is better than ours, and it's all bullshit... I was going to start an Instagram page which was all the bad stuff that no one actually posts. Like what you look like when you wake up in the morning or in the middle of an argument or when your baby won't go to sleep.'

'I Am Here'

Written by Billy Mann, Christian Medice and Alecia 'P!nk' Moore
Produced by Billy Mann and Christian Medice
Recorded at Earthstar Creation Center, California; Turtle Sound Studios, Weston and Houser Audio, Philadelphia
Duration: 4:06

'I Am Here' is a rousing, self-affirming song about living authentically and making the most of life despite its ups and downs. The song, co-written and co-produced by Billy Mann and Christian Medice, was one of the first songs written for *Beautiful Trauma*. Conceived in early 2016, before P!nk was pregnant with her second child, Jameson, it was recorded in July 2017 at Houser Audio in Aston, featuring thirty members of the Bill Jolly Choir.

Reflecting on the song on Instagram in 2024, Billy Mann wrote: 'We knew from the beginning phase of writing and recording in Los Angeles that we would wind up where this photo took place: back 'home' in Philly singing with a local gospel choir. The decision to take 'I Am Here' gospel was made at the very start and then we had to walk backwards from a predetermined outcome and deliver all the steps that got Alecia the end result she wanted. This song to many can feel like a prayer; I guess depending on where they are in their lives. We don't know what fate has in store for any of us in this world. I often remind my own kids to remember to be in the moment. Celebrate the journey taken that brought us to right now. I have to remind myself, too. I am here.'

'Wild Hearts Can't Be Broken'

Written by Michael Busbee and Alecia 'P!nk' Moore
Produced by Michael Busbee
Recorded at Woodshed Recording, Malibu and Azteca Market, Glassell Park
Duration: 3:21

A stripped-down, emotional ballad, 'Wild Hearts Can't Be Broken' was co-written and produced by the late Busbee, who wrote 'Try.' A song about standing firm in the face of adversity, P!nk said in an interview with *The Financial Times* that the song is a 'feminist chant.'

Footage from the songwriting session is featured in P!nk's Apple Music documentary, where she confirmed that the song was originally written for the *Suffragette* movie. She said: 'Well, Busbee and I started writing the song for a movie about the suffragette movement, which is women's right to vote. You have to fight for what's rightly yours, which is rights and respect and love and kindness and compassion, and you have to be willing to die for it. These women were.'

'You Get My Love'

Written by Tobias Jesso Jr. and Alecia 'P!nk' Moore
Produced by Tobias Jesso Jr. and Alecia 'P!nk' Moore
Recorded at Earthstar Creation Center, California
Duration: 5:11

The album closer, 'You Get My Love,' was written and produced by P!nk with Canadian musician, Tobias Jesso Jr., best known for his work with Sia and Adele. The tender, piano-driven ballad highlights P!nk's vulnerable side as she expresses that, despite her mistakes, her love remains steadfast and dependable.

Above: Having arrived in the UK to promote 'There You Go' in May 2000, P!nk took part in a photoshoot to be syndicated in teen magazines across Europe, with her soon-to-be-iconic pink hair. (*Photo by Robert Hoetink / Dreamstime.com*)

Right: With *Can't Take Me Home* establishing her in the R&B/soul genre, P!nk co-hosted the sixth annual Soul Train Lady of Soul Awards, held at the Santa Monica Civic Auditorium on 2 September 2000. (*Photo by s_bukley / Depositphotos*)

P!nk attended her first Grammy Awards afterparty on 21 February 2001, held at the Conga Room on Wilshire Boulevard, Los Angeles. (*Photo by s_bukley / Depositphotos*)

P!nk brought her dog Fucker with her to the 2001 MTV Movie Awards, held at the Shrine Auditorium, Los Angeles, on 2 June 2001. (*Photo by s_bukley / Depositphotos*)

Right: Just weeks after their performance of 'Lady Marmalade' at the 2001 MTV Movie Awards, P!nk, Christina Aguilera, Mya and Lil' Kim reunited at KIIS-FM's Wango Tango event at Dodger Stadium, Los Angeles, on 16 June 2001. (*Photo by s_bukley / Depositphotos*)

Below: P!nk returned with her second album, the critically acclaimed *M!ssundaztood*, in December 2001, featuring collaborations with Linda Perry, Dallas Austin and Scott Storch. To celebrate its release, she held an album signing for fans at Virgin Megastore, Hollywood. (*Photo by s_bukley / Depositphotos*)

P!nk met her husband and muse Carey Hart in 2001, making one of her first official appearances with him as her boyfriend at the 2002 ESPN Action Sports and Music Awards at Universal Studios, Hollywood, on 13 April 2002. (*Photo by s_bukley / Depositphotos*)

P!nk attended MTV's *mtv:ICON*, honouring Aerosmith, held at Sony Studios, Culver City, on 14 April 2002. She performed a cover of their 1989 single 'Janie's Got a Gun', which was also included on the setlist of her *Party* tour. (*Photo by s_bukley / Depositphotos*)

Having recorded 'Feel Good Time', the lead single from the *Charlie's Angels: Full Throttle* soundtrack, P!nk attended the film's world premiere at the Chinese Theatre, Hollywood, on 18 June 2003, bringing Linda Perry as her guest. (*Photo by s_bukley / Depositphotos*)

With the *Try This* tour complete, P!nk attended NEXT, the Second Semi-Annual Fashion Wire Daily event, at Mondrian Hotel's SkyBar in West Hollywood on 25 October 2004. (*Photo by PopularImages / Depositphotos*)

InTouch Weekly magazine organised a celebration for photographer Chris Ameruoso and his book *Pets and Their Stars Unleashed*, which took place at the Cabana Club, Hollywood, on 21 September 2005. Raising funds for the Linda Blair WorldHeart Foundation, which supports and rehabilitates neglected and abandoned animals, P!nk attended with her bulldog, Elvis. She said: 'I'm here to support the cause. Any charity for animals, I'm there.' (*Photo by s_bukley / Depositphotos*)

P!nk won Best Pop Video for 'Stupid Girls' at the 2006 MTV Video Music Awards, held at Radio City Music Hall, Rockefeller Center, New York, on 31 August 2006. (*Photo by Kristin Callahan, Everett Collection / Depositphotos*)

Ten days before announcing her separation from Carey Hart, P!nk attended Clive Davis' Pre-Grammy Awards Party at the Beverly Hilton Hotel on 9 February 2008. (*Photo by s_bukley / Depositphotos*)

P!nk attended the 52nd Annual Grammy Awards, held at the Staples Centre, Los Angeles, on 31 January 2010, where she performed 'Glitter in the Air', having been nominated for Best Pop Vocal Album for *Funhouse* and Best Female Pop Vocal Performance for 'Sober'. (*Photo by s_bukley / Depositphotos*)

Having reunited with Linda Perry in 2007, P!nk performed 'What's Up?' with her at the Los Angeles Gay and Lesbian Centre's *An Evening with Women* event on 1 May 2010 at the Beverly Hilton Hotel, attending with her husband Carey Hart. (*Photo by Jean Nelson USA / Depositphotos*)

After voicing Gloria and recording 'Bridge of Light' for the soundtrack, P!nk attended the world premiere of *Happy Feet Two* at the Chinese Theatre, Hollywood, on 13 November 2011. (*Photo by s_bukley / Depositphotos*)

The Truth About Love tour was P!nk's last arena tour in Europe to date, visiting The O2 Arena, London, on 25 April 2013. P!nk performed a medley of singles from *Can't Take Me Home*, sporting a leather jacket and full choreography. (*Photo by Steve Bishop*)

P!nk flying over the audience while performing 'So What' has become the grand finale of most of her live shows since *The Truth About Love* tour. (*Photo by Steve Bishop*)

Above: Touring around Europe, P!nk took *The Truth About Love* tour to Prague on 10 May 2013, opening the show with 'Raise Your Glass' while plunging towards the stage on bungee cords. (*Photo by yakub88 / Depositphotos*)

Left: P!nk wore a Hervé Léger dress to the Billboard Women in Music event held in her honour at Capitale, New York, on 10 December 2013. (*Photo by Gregorio T. Binuya, Everett Collection / Depositphotos*)

The 56th Annual Grammy Awards took place at the Staples Centre, Los Angeles, on 26 January 2014. P!nk wore a Johanna Johnson gown to the event, performing 'Try' and 'Just Give Me a Reason', which was nominated for Best Pop Duo/Group Performance and Song of the Year, during the ceremony. (*Photo by Charlie Williams, Everett Collection / Depositphotos*)

P!nk attended the 63rd Annual BMI Pop Awards with her husband Carey Hart on 12 May 2015. At the ceremony, held at the Beverly Wilshire Hotel, she received the BMI President's Award for her outstanding achievement in songwriting and global impact on pop culture and the entertainment industry. (*Photo by Jean Nelson USA / Depositphotos*)

P!nk recorded a cover of Jefferson Airplane's 'White Rabbit' and wrote 'Just Like Fire' for Disney's *Alice Through the Looking Glass*, attending the film's premiere at the El Capitan Theatre, Los Angeles, on 23 May 2016. (*Photo by Elizabeth Goodenough, Everett Collection / Depositphotos*)

At the MTV Video Music Awards 2017, held at The Forum, Inglewood, on 27 August, P!nk performed a medley of her greatest hits before receiving a golden 'moon man' for the Michael Jackson Video Vanguard Award. (*Photo by Jean Nelson USA / Depositphotos*)

Right: P!nk performed 'Beautiful Trauma', suspended on the side of the JW Marriott hotel in Los Angeles, at the 2017 American Music Awards on 19 November, attending the ceremony with her husband Carey Hart. (*Photo by FeatureFlash / Depositphotos*)

Below: On 5 February 2019, P!nk received the 2,656th star on the world-famous Hollywood Walk of Fame, dedicated in the category of Recording at 6801 Hollywood Boulevard, in front of the Hollywood & Highland Complex. (*Photo by FeatureFlash / Depositphotos*)

Above: The *Beautiful Trauma* world tour kicked off in March 2019, with P!nk opening the show performing 'Get the Party Started' while attached by bungee cords to a giant suspended chandelier. (*Photo by Moffly / Depositphotos*)

Left: At the E! 2019 People's Choice Awards, which took place at Santa Monica's Barker Hangar on 11 November, P!nk received the People's Champion Award, arriving with her husband Carey Hart and their two children, Willow and Jameson. During her inspirational acceptance speech, she said: 'I care about decency and humanity and kindness. Kindness today is an act of rebellion. There are people who don't have what you have, help them get it. There is a planet that needs help, it feels good to help. Stop fighting each other and help each other. Get together with your friends and change the fucking world.' (*Photo by FeatureFlash / Depositphotos*)

P!nk opened the 2022 American Music Awards, held at the Microsoft Theatre, Los Angeles, on 20 November, with 'Never Gonna Not Dance Again'. Attending the ceremony with her husband and children, she also performed 'Hopelessly Devoted to You' in tribute to the late Olivia Newton-John during the event. (*Photo by Image Press Agency / Depositphotos*)

Summer Carnival was P!nk's first tour after the COVID-19 pandemic, playing the British Summer Time festival in Hyde Park, London, on 24 and 25 June 2023, where she performed to over 130,000 people with a box office gross of $20.9 million, the largest by an American artist and overall solo act in its history. P!nk and her dancers performed 'Raise Your Glass' while playing with oversized gym equipment such as resistance bands and exercise balls. (*Photo by Steve Bishop*)

In addition to aerial stunts and acrobatics, P!nk's live shows maintain her rock performances, such as during 'Just Like Fire'. (*Photo by Steve Bishop*)

'Last Call' was the first encore during P!nk's 2023 *Summer Carnival* tour, performed while wearing a hooded silver sequin dress. (*Photo by Steve Bishop*)

Discussing *Beautiful Trauma* on *The Elvis Duran Show*, P!nk addressed criticism that she stopped recording R&B music after her debut, *Can't Take Me Home*, citing 'You Get My Love' as an example. She said: 'People say that I abandoned R&B music, but if you actually listen to my records, I've sung R&B my entire career. I mean, if you listen to the last song on this record, "You Get My Love," it's my biggest attempt ever at trying to be one of my heroes, Nina Simone. Some of the best vocals I'll ever do are singing soul music. It's in me. It's there. It's on every record. It's on every record.'

In an interview with *Vulture* magazine in 2023, P!nk shared that the song is hard to sing live. She said: 'I will never do it live. I mean, I would once, but I wouldn't be able to sing for a day or two. It's so high. The bridge is my Whitney moment, I think. "You get my love, baby!" I would die, like, no way. "What are you doing? You're just dumb for even recording that." Did you see *Old School* with Will Ferrell? He does this debate, and he launches into this whole very smart thing and then he's like, "What just happened? I blacked out." That's what it feels like. You leave your body for a minute and then you come back into it, and it's done.'

Bonus Track

'White Rabbit'

Written by Grace Slick
Produced by Andy Dodd
Recorded at Landmark Studio, Nashville and Earthstar Creation Center, California
Duration: 2:43

P!nk recorded a cover of Jefferson Airplane's 'White Rabbit' to promote Disney's *Alice Through the Looking Glass*; the song appeared in the film's trailer in February 2016. Written in 1966 by Grace Slick, the song's title references the white rabbit in Lewis Carroll's original *Alice in Wonderland* story. Slick said the song was intentionally unconventional, responding to the growing 'psychedelic culture' that was becoming mainstream then.

Talking about P!nk's cover to the *Wall Street Journal* in June 2016, Slick added: 'It's good. P!nk has the vocal power, which is all I care about. She sings with power, but it's something more. You sense that if she wanted to, she could open the throttle even more at any time. That coiled energy creates drama and catches the ear.'

In February 2016, Disney released a promotional featurette of P!nk in the studio recording 'White Rabbit,' and talking about *Alice Through the Looking Glass*. In the video, P!nk said: 'I like quirky and I like weird, and this movie is one of the quirkier, more creative stories. This movie is really going to inspire imagination, it's going to be a fun experience. "White Rabbit" is a fun song to sing.' She also confirmed that she would be heading into the studio to write and record an original song for the movie, which resulted in 'Just Like Fire.'

P!nk performed 'White Rabbit' live on *Jimmy Kimmel Live!* in July 2016; however, the song was not included on the *Alice Through the Looking Glass* soundtrack. In October 2017, 'White Rabbit' was officially released as the bonus track for the Japanese edition of *Beautiful Trauma*.

Other Songs

'Today's the Day'

Written by Greg Kurstin and Alecia 'P!nk' Moore
Produced by Greg Kurstin
Recorded at Warner Brothers Studio Lot, Los Angeles
Duration: 3:44
Released as a single in September 2015
Chart Position: Canada: 42; Australia: 11; Germany: 76

A friend of talk show host Ellen DeGeneres, P!nk was asked to write and perform the theme song for season 13 of her hit series, *The Ellen DeGeneres Show*. Co-written and produced by P!nk's long-time collaborator, Greg Kurstin, 'Today's the Day' was released on 10 September 2015. P!nk performed the song live on the show on the same day and was interviewed by Ellen.

Discussing the experience, P!nk said: 'It's the biggest honour in the world. Ellen calls you and asks you to write a song for her. I'm like, "Yes, I will write 50 so that you like one of them." I just wanted it to be happy, because Ellen makes people happy. I pictured Ellen dancing and everyone happy, and I thought, "This is a first for me!" Happiness, it's weird!'

To promote the launch of the new season, a short video featuring P!nk performing the song in the studio with her daughter, alongside clips from Ellen's show, was released in August 2015. The promotional clip went on to win the Outstanding Promotional Announcement—Image award at the 43rd Daytime Creative Arts Emmy Awards in 2016. P!nk learned of the achievement during an appearance on a May 2016 episode of the show while promoting 'Just Like Fire,' where Ellen presented her with the trophy.

'Just Like Fire'

Written by Max Martin, Johan 'Shellback' Schuster, Oscar Holter and Alecia 'P!nk' Moore
Produced by Max Martin, Johan 'Shellback' Schuster and Oscar Holter
Recorded at MXM Studios, Stockholm, Sweden; Wolf Cousins Studios, Stockholm, Sweden and Conway Studios, Los Angeles
Duration: 3:35

Released as a single in April 2016
Music video directed by Dave Meyers
Chart Position: USA: 10; Canada: 11; UK: 19; Australia: 1; Germany: 21

With P!nk having covered Jefferson Airplane's 'White Rabbit' for Disney's *Alice Through the Looking Glass*, she was asked to write an original song for the movie's soundtrack. In an interview with *People* magazine, she expressed her love for the film, saying: 'What's awesome about *Alice Through the Looking Glass* is the whole theme, from the start of the movie, is "Girls can do it, too." She's the captain of her own ship, but it takes her femaleness to be that fierce.'

Co-written and produced by Max Martin, Shellback and Oscar Holter, 'Just Like Fire' was officially released on 15 April 2016, ahead of the movie's soundtrack, which followed in late May. Promoting the song, P!nk held a Facebook Live question and answer session, where she spoke about the creative process.

She said: 'I was one of the lucky few who got to watch the movie. I got to watch it with Willow, and I was inspired by Alice. She's a badass, so the words came very easy. My favourite lyric is, "kick that ceiling," I don't believe there is a ceiling. It's completely different when I write songs for myself, it's 100% narcissistic and self-involved. It's all about my problems. When I write for a movie, it's inspired by their story, and I've actually done it a couple of times, and I've gotten to keep the songs because they were rejected. And I'm really glad, because now they're mine, and I never would have been able to write such a focused song without the movie's inspiration.'

The music video, directed by Dave Meyers, features both P!nk's husband, Carey Hart, and their daughter, Willow. Set in a fantasy world, it shows P!nk hallucinating a giant chess game and tea party. P!nk appeared on *The Ellen DeGeneres Show* to discuss the song and video in May, talking about performing some of its acrobatic scenes. She said: 'The hanging upside-down part is challenging… and it's not a good look! That's why it's not a close-up… people look crazy upside-down!'

'Just Like Fire' was released on CD single exclusively in Australia, where it became her eight #1. In the USA, it peaked at #10 on the Billboard Hot 100, marking her first top 10 hit since 'Just Give Me a Reason.' The song was nominated for Best Song Written for Visual Media at the 59th Grammy Awards in 2017 but lost to another Martin and Shellback collaboration, Justin Timberlake's 'Can't Stop the Feeling!' from *Trolls*.

'Equal Rights'—The Lonely Island featuring P!nk

Written by Andy Samberg, Jorma Taccone, Akiva Schaffer, Raphaël 'SoFly' Judrin, Pierre-Antoine 'Nius' Melki and Yoan 'Odfellow' Chirescu
Produced by Raphaël 'SoFly' Judrin, Pierre-Antoine 'Nius' Melki and Yoan 'Odfellow' Chirescu
Duration: 2:25

American comedy trio Andy Samberg, Jorma Taccone and Akiva Schaffer, better known as the Lonely Island, had worked with various musicians and performers after being hired by *Saturday Night Live* in 2005. In 2016, they launched their second feature-length movie, a mockumentary entitled *Popstar Never Stop Never Stopping*, starring Samberg as Conner4Real, a former boyband member who has gone solo.

In the movie, Conner4Real records and releases a song called 'Equal Rights,' a statement about gay marriage that also takes the opportunity to remind the world he is heterosexual, a parody of the 2012 Macklemore single, 'Same Love.' In addition to guest starring in the movie, P!nk appears on the song, joining Conner4Real on the chorus as she sings, 'I was born this way, you were born your way, gay or straight, straight or gay, it's all OK.'

'Hands'—Various artists—A Song for Orlando

Written by Michael 'BloodPop' Tucker, Julia Michaels and Justin Tranter
Produced by Michael 'BloodPop' Tucker, Mark Ronson and Justin Tranter
Duration: 4:24
Released as a single in July 2016

On 12 June 2016, 49 people were murdered and 53 more injured in a massacre at the LGBTQ+ nightclub Pulse in Orlando, Florida, the deadliest act of violence against the LGBTQ+ community in American history. The following afternoon, songwriter and activist Justin Tranter called the region's primary LGBTQ+ community organisation, The Center Orlando, volunteering help and was told, 'We need as many hands as we can possibly get.'

The following day, Sarah Kate Ellis, CEO of GLAAD, met with Tranter and conceived the idea for a charity single. She told *Billboard*: 'When you hear the song, it talks about hate being the driver here, and that's important because we have to be able to identify what's driving these cruel acts in order to stop them. Artists using their platforms to accelerate acceptance is very powerful.'

In addition to P!nk, 'Hands' features Britney Spears, Adam Lambert, Kacey Musgraves, Gwen Stefani, Jennifer Lopez and Selena Gomez. Proceeds from the single, which was available exclusively on iTunes, were distributed by Equality Florida Pulse Victims Fund, the GLBT Community Center of Central Florida, and GLAAD.

'Setting the World on Fire'—Kenny Chesney featuring P!nk

Written by Ross Copperman, Matt Jenkins and Josh Osborne
Produced by Buddy Cannon and Kenny Chesney
Recorded at Shangri-La, Malibu
Duration: 3:37

Released as a single in July 2016
Chart Position: USA: 29; Canada: 48; Australia: 26

'Setting the World on Fire' is the second single from country singer Kenny Chesney's seventeenth studio album, *Cosmic Hallelujah*, released in October 2016.

In an interview promoting the album, Chesney said: 'When you've made a lot of music and have a certain connection with your audience, you look for different melodies to sing and for songs that really stand out. "Setting the World on Fire" did that for me. My favourite line is "do you think we'll live forever, as we killed another beer." That feeling of two people wanting to live in a moment together forever, knowing things will inevitably change… I love that line. I met P!nk for the first time in the studio when we recorded her vocal. I swear we were in there for about an hour when she got behind the mic and started singing. The hair on my arms literally stood up. She doesn't have a voice… she has a God-given instrument and I feel so fortunate that she wanted to be part of my record. To this day I find it interesting that I hadn't met her until that day in the studio, but if you listen to the voices, it's as if we've been singing together for a really long time.'

Josh Osborne, who co-wrote the Grammy Award-winning 'Merry Go 'Round' with Kacey Musgraves, said the song was inspired by the night of the Grammy ceremony in 2014 when he was sitting in his hotel room drinking champagne with his wife. Talking to *Taste of Country*, he said: 'So many of those images were just stored in my mind, because this whole night in my mind… it was sort of champagne-coloured in my mind, but I'd never really written about it. Ross Copperman started playing that music that became "Setting the World on Fire," and it just already felt emotional, and it felt alive, and it felt like a moment to me. And Matt Jenkins - not knowing my whole story that night with the Grammy stuff - Matt was like, "I have this line I'd written down on a piece of paper about, 'We got drunk on La Cienega Boulevard.' And I don't know what it means, but I love the poetry of a line like that, how real it sounds." And I just was like, "Oh my God." So then in my mind, this song became, "let's just write about that moment, let's just write about that night".'

'Setting the World on Fire' marks P!nk's debut on the USA Billboard country charts, reaching #1 and becoming Chesney's twenty-third single to hit the top spot.

'Lucy in the Sky with Diamonds'—Beat Bugs featuring P!nk

Written by John Lennon and Paul McCartney
Produced by Daniel Johns
Duration: 3:44

In 2016, Netflix launched a new children's animated TV series, *Beat Bugs*, created by Australian director Josh Wakely. Wakely had secured the rights to use The Beatles' music catalogue, using their songs to educate and help teach children life lessons while introducing them to the music.

P!nk was asked to cover 'Lucy in the Sky with Diamonds' for season one of the show, joining artists like Aloe Blacc, Sia, Wesley Schultz and Robbie Williams. Daniel Johns, of the Australian band Silverchair produced the song and provided backing vocals as the character Walter. Other singers on the song include Australian artists such as Gossling as Buzz the fruit fly, Sullivan as Crick, Andy Bull as Jay, Lisa Mitchell as Kumi, and iOTA as Walter.

The soundtrack to season one was released exclusively on Apple Music in August 2016, with a compilation album of songs from seasons one and two released in November.

'Halfway Gone'

Written by Linda Perry and Alecia 'P!nk' Moore
Produced by Linda Perry
Recorded at Kung Fu Gardens, Hollywood
Duration: 3:13

After bumping into Linda Perry in 2007, P!nk wrote and recorded 'Halfway Gone' with her in a one-off session. It was eventually released in November 2017 on the soundtrack to the documentary *Served Like a Girl*, which follows a group of female veterans competing for the crown of Ms. Veteran America.

Linda Perry confirmed to *Rolling Stone* magazine that she and P!nk fell out over 'Beautiful', which was recorded by Christina Aguilera for her album *Stripped*, not just because P!nk wanted the song but also because she had personal issues with Aguilera after 'Lady Marmalade'. She added that, when they reunited years later, they wrote 'Halfway Gone' as well as performing 'What's Up?' together the following year.

Perry said: 'We hadn't seen each other in years. I sat down and said, "Why don't you come by my studio and hang out with me?" And she did. We caught up and it's like, "Do you want to write a song?" "Yeah. Let's write a song." We didn't think much about it, and we just wrote the lyrics. And she at the time was struggling with Carey, so we wrote that song. I asked everybody if I could use the songs, and Alecia said yes. And we parted ways again. She and I, maybe it's not going to be tomorrow, but there will be another time for us, because we're way too creative together. You can just feel it.'

'Waterfall'—Stargate featuring P!nk and Sia

Written by Stargate (Tor Erik Hermansen and Mikkel Storleer Eriksen), Thomas 'Diplo' Wesley Pentz, Sia Furler and Philip 'Jr. Blender' Meckseper
Produced by Stargate (Tor Erik Hermansen and Mikkel Storleer Eriksen)
Recorded at the Stellar Studios, California
Duration: 3:20
Released as a single in March 2017
Music video directed by Malia James
Chart Position: Canada: 86; UK: 47; Australia: 19; Germany: 47

Tor Erik Hermansen and Mikkel Storleer Eriksen, better known as the Norwegian production duo Stargate, have co-written and produced some of the biggest pop hits of the past decade. Their catalogue includes 10 #1 hits on the US Billboard Hot 100, and 11 #1 singles on the UK singles chart, leading to them receiving ASCAP UK's Songwriter of the Year Award in 2007 and ASCAP USA Songwriter of the Year in 2009.

In addition to hits such as 'Irreplaceable' by Beyoncé and 'Beautiful Liar,' her duet with Shakira, the duo produced 'Firework' by Katy Perry, 'Miss Independent' by Ne-Yo, and have worked extensively with Rihanna on songs such as 'Unfaithful,' 'Don't Stop the Music,' 'Take a Bow,' 'Rude Boy,' 'What's My Name?,' 'S&M' and 'Diamonds.'

In 2017, following the trend of producers and DJs having record contracts, RCA Records offered the duo a worldwide artist deal, resulting in 'Waterfall' featuring P!nk and Sia.

A music video was directed for the song, featuring Inka Henriikka and Amalie Lauritzen, two aerial acrobats, skydiving in an indoor flight chamber.

'Need Me'—Eminem featuring P!nk

Written by Alexander 'Alex da Kidd' Grant, Holly B. Hafermann, Jonathan Ingoldsby and Marshall 'Eminem' Mathers,
Produced by Alexander 'Alex da Kidd' Grant
Recorded at Effigy Studios, Ferndale
Duration: 4:25
Chart Position: Canada: 98

Eminem released his album *Revival* in December 2017, featuring another collaboration with P!nk, entitled 'Need Me.' Written about a dysfunctional relationship, Eminem harmonises with P!nk during the second verse.

In an interview on SiriusXM, he said: 'I've always looked at P!nk as kind of a rebel, and I've told her that. I super respect her art and her music and we worked together in the past too. It only made sense for me to have her on that song.'

Unreleased Songs

'Jail Break'

Written by Alexander 'Alex da Kidd' Grant and Alecia 'P!nk' Moore
Produced by Alexander 'Alex da Kidd' Grant
Duration: 3:10

P!nk collaborated with British songwriter and producer Alex da Kidd on 'Jail Break,' having worked with him on Eminem's 'Need Me.' The epic hip-hop power ballad, with a whistle melody at the end of the chorus, sees P!nk calling for a change to her current situation.

Opening with a tag, 'Shut the fuck up, Alex da Kidd is coming,' P!nk sings: 'I'm locked inside my head, my time is ticking down, I'm looking for a way to get out, out of this cage, these walls are caving in, I'm ready for a jail break.'

The demo of 'Jail Break' leaked online in late 2021.

'Headache'

Written by Michael Busbee and Alecia 'P!nk' Moore
Produced by Michael Busbee
Duration: 3:18

Another collaboration with the late Busbee, a demo of 'Headache' leaked online in 2020. On the mid-tempo track, P!nk sings: 'You make me linger in my pain, you're a headache and you're fogging up my brain.'

'Behind Every Man There's a Strong Woman'—Christina Aguilera, P!nk and Elle King

Written by Linda Perry and Christina Aguilera
Produced by Linda Perry
Duration: 5:15

After collaborating on 'Lady Marmalade' and later being embroiled in a public dispute, P!nk and Christina Aguilera reunited on *The Voice*, where they put their differences behind them. Aguilera asked P!nk to join her on a song she had written with Linda Perry entitled 'Behind Every Man There's a Strong Woman'. The song is unreleased but leaked online in late 2025.

P!nk spoke about Christina Aguilera and confirmed the song's existence on *Watch What Happens Live with Andy Cohen* in October 2017. She said: 'We were super young and super new at the whole thing. I think I'm an alpha and she's an alpha, and I'm used to taking my altercations physical and she's used to having them verbal. We just are very different. We are very different. We were very young and new. Women have to learn how to support each other. It's not taught to us on the playground. She's a really sweet person. We made up on *The Voice*, because I hadn't seen her in years and years and years and we became mothers. We grew up and we hugged it out. It's that simple, and I feel so good about that. And also, we did a song together.'

Live Performances

'So Far Away'—P!nk and Paul Mirkovich

Written by Carole King
Duration: 3:15

Singer-songwriter Carole King was inducted as MusiCares Person of the Year in January 2014, honouring her achievements and dedication to philanthropy. At the gala event, a variety of artists performed, including Lady Gaga, Alicia Keys, Gloria Estefan, Jennifer Nettles, and Sara Bareilles.

P!nk was accompanied by her musical director and pianist, Paul Mirkovich, to perform a cover of 'So Far Away' from King's 1971 album, *Tapestry*.

'Over the Rainbow'

Written by Harold Arlen and Edgar Yipsel Harburg
Duration: 3:26

P!nk made her Oscar debut in March 2014, performing a cover of 'Over the Rainbow' at the 86th Academy Awards in tribute to the seventy-fifth anniversary of *The Wizard of Oz*. In honour of the iconic ruby slippers from the film, P!nk wore a red sequin dress and received a standing ovation from the three children of Judy Garland, the late actress who starred as Dorothy and sang the song in the 1939 film.

A press release from the Oscars committee said: 'P!nk is regarded as one of the greatest voices in pop music and one of the best performers of her generation, and we are thrilled to have her join us for a highly anticipated moment on the broadcast.'

'She's Always a Woman'

Written by Billy Joel
Duration: 3:17

'She's Always a Woman' is a complex love song written by Billy Joel in 1977 for his album *The Stranger*, about his then-wife, Elizabeth Weber, who rectified many of his business affairs. P!nk walked down the aisle to the song at her wedding to Carey Hart in January 2006, at the shores of the Four Seasons Resort in Costa Rica, giving the song personal significance to her.

P!nk joined Billy Joel on stage at his SiriusXM Radio Town Hall show in April 2014, telling him before their performance: 'I got to see my dad become happy when your songs came on and we sang them together and it's just it's shaped and painted my whole life. I've always said that Billy is a person that can paint a picture for you with words and it's unique to him. He does that like no one else in the world can do, and it's changed my life. When I sit down to write a song, my first thought is, "This is going to suck and I'm never gonna be Billy Joel."'

'Someday We'll All Be Free' with John Legend

Written by Donny Hathaway
Duration: 3:58

P!nk joined John Legend to perform Donny Hathaway's 'Someday We'll All Be Free' at a special recorded fundraising concert entitled *Shining a Light: A Concert for Progress on Race in America*, filmed on 18 November 2015. Amidst a backdrop of mass shootings and the rise of the Black Lives Matter movement, show producer Ken Ehrlich said the event was 'a celebration of hope... a celebration of humanity.'

'River'

Written by Sarah Grace 'Bishop Briggs' McLaughlin, Ian Scott and Mark Jackson
Duration: 3:38

British singer Bishop Briggs released 'River' in January 2016 on her self-titled EP, where it became a viral hit and later appeared on her 2018 debut album, *Church of Scars*. P!nk first covered the song at her Summerfest concert in Milwaukee on 2 July 2017, adding it to the setlist of her *Beautiful Trauma* tour in 2019. A recording from Wembley Stadium in London, UK, appears on the *All I Know So Far: Setlist* live album.

Talking to BBC Radio 1, P!nk said: 'I'm just a music fan. I'm obsessed with "River" by Bishop Briggs.' In return, Bishop Briggs revealed a tattoo of the P!nk quote—'Kindness is an act of rebellion'—leading P!nk to respond, 'I think my heart just stopped.'

'Stay with Me'

Written by Jimmy Napes, William 'Tourist' Phillips and Sam Smith
Includes an interpolation of 'I Won't Back Down' written by Tom Petty and Jeff Lynne
Duration: 3:17

The gospel-influenced ballad 'Stay with Me' was released in April 2014 by British singer Sam Smith, taken from their debut album, *In the Lonely Hour*, and became their third #1 single on the UK singles chart. The song won Record of the Year and Song of the Year at the 57th Grammy Awards in February 2015.

P!nk came to the UK to promote *Beautiful Trauma* in September 2017, appearing on BBC Radio 1's Live Lounge with host Clara Amfo. In addition to performing 'What About Us,' 'Who Knew' and 'Try,' P!nk covered 'Stay with Me.'

P!nk explained: 'I love their voice so much. I love their songs. I actually was having a little Twitter conversation with them the other day which was very timely. I wanted to tell them, but I didn't. There are songs that come out once in a while that you wish you wrote, and that was one of them.'

'Patience'—Guns N' Roses featuring P!nk

Written by William 'Axl Rose' Bruce Rose, Saul 'Slash' Hudson, Michael 'Duff' McKagan, Steven Adler and Jeffrey 'Izzy Stradlin' Isbell
Duration: 6:15

'Patience' was the lead single from Guns N' Roses' second album, 1988's *G N' R Lies*, reaching #4 on the USA Billboard Hot 100 and charting in the top 20 in the UK and Australia. During their concert on 11 October 2017 at Madison Square Garden in New York City, P!nk joined Guns N' Roses to perform the last part of the song with them. The surprise appearance was as unexpected for P!nk as it was for the audience.

Introducing P!nk, Axl Rose said: 'We're gonna try something, we're gonna bring a friend of ours out here. We didn't even try this, we're just gonna do this off the cuff.' P!nk responded on Twitter after the performance, posting: 'Oh. Yeah. Whatever. No problem', alongside nervous face emojis.

'Everybody Hurts' P!nk and Kelly Clarkson

Written by Bill Berry, Peter Buck, Mike Mills and Michael Stipe
Duration: 3:36

'Everybody Hurts' was released in April 1993, taken from the eighth R.E.M. studio album, *Automatic for the People*. P!nk and Kelly Clarkson performed the song at the American Music Awards in November 2017, opening the show in honour of first responders who had dealt with natural disasters and emergencies across the USA during the year.

Comedian Jamie Foxx introduced the performance, accompanied by his daughter and a group of emergency personnel, saying: 'This year more than perhaps any other in recent history, we needed the power of music to help us escape the news of the day. We needed the power of music to help us heal, from hurricanes, wildfires, hate and hatred-filled violence. 2017 was a year that tested our faith. In these moments of crisis, heroes emerged. As this year comes to a close, we look forward to 2018 with hope. For, even as we mourn those who were lost, we know this: Together, our strength will pull us through. Together, we shall overcome the pain. Together, we can unite as a people and as a nation.'

'Smells Like Teen Spirit'

Written by Kurt Cobain, Krist Novoselic and Dave Grohl
Duration: 4:00

Following unconfirmed rumours that P!nk had covered Nirvana's 'Rape Me' for *M!ssundaztood*, she performed a cover of their defining grunge anthem, 'Smells Like Teen Spirit' on her *Beautiful Trauma* tour.

Originally released as the lead single from their second album, *Nevermind*, in September 1991, Kurt Cobain said he was trying to write the ultimate pop song, taking inspiration from the Pixies for the eventual soundscape.

'We Are the Champions'

Written by Freddie Mercury
Duration: 1:37

'We Are the Champions' is one of the most recognisable Queen songs, appearing on their 1977 album, *News of the World*. P!nk performed a clip of the song at two shows in 2019; her Rock in Rio concert on 5 October and a Formula 1 Grand Prix event on 2 November. A recording of the Rio performance appears on the *All I Know So Far: Setlist* live album.

Songwriting Credits

'Recovering'—Celine Dion

Written by Allen Shamblin, Tom Douglas and Alecia 'P!nk' Moore
Produced by Humberto Gatica and Scott Price
Duration: 3:24
Released as a single in September 2016

Canadian artist Celine Dion sadly lost her husband and manager, René Angélil, to cancer in January 2016, and, at his request, resumed her Las Vegas residency just six weeks later. In May, she recorded and released a cover of Queen's 'The Show Must Go On,' and in July, she told *Entertainment Weekly* about the song.

She said: 'P!nk wrote me a song that I'm freaking out about. You cannot be more excited than me, I'll tell you. I am thrilled not only because I am a fan, but because I know her personally and have met her a few times. She's a genuine person, and it was so generous of her to take the time to write a song for me during the most difficult time of mine.'

Celine performed 'Recovering' at the *Stand Up to Cancer* telecast in September 2016, and on *The Ellen DeGeneres Show*, as well as adding it to her Las Vegas set list. She told the audience ahead of performing it: 'I have received an unexpected gift from someone that I admire tremendously, she is amazing, she is so strong, and I love her. She wrote this song for me, and I will always be very, very grateful. Her name is P!nk.'

P!nk said: 'Celine possesses one of the most incredible voices that I have ever heard. She is like a magic light bulb, walking around emanating light into the world. When I wrote this song, there was such a simple need to it. I know everyone wants to hear Celine wail, I wanted to hear Celine's soul. She is just simply amazing, and getting to write a song for her is one of the biggest honours of my life. I was happy to be a part of her healing, I mean that's huge, that's everything.'

'Sorries'—Andee

Written by Erik Alcok, Pranam Injeti, Khalil 'DJ Khalil' Abdul-Rahman, Kara DioGuardi and Alecia 'P!nk' Moore
Produced by Sébastien Lefebvre
Duration: 3:36

Originally written for *The Truth About Love*, 'Sorries' was recorded by Canadian singer-songwriter, Andee, who appeared on season 5 of the Québecois reality singing TV show, *Star Académie*. It became her second single, released in Canada in October 2014, ahead of *Black and White Heart*, her debut album, released the following May.

P!nk's demo of the song with Kara DioGuardi leaked online in July 2020.

Catalogue Registrations

'Bad News'

Written by Billy Mann, Christian Medice and Alecia 'P!nk' Moore

'No One to Blame'

Written by Tobias Jesso Jr. and Alecia 'P!nk' Moore

11

Hurts 2B Human (2018–2019)

Released:	26 April 2019
Chart Position:	USA: 1
	Canada: 1
	UK: 1
	Australia: 1
	Germany 2

Less than eighteen months after the release of *Beautiful Trauma*, P!nk announced on *The Ellen DeGeneres Show* in February 2019 that she would be releasing her eighth studio album in April, with the first single, 'Walk Me Home,' to be released a few weeks later.

In an interview with Carson Daly for *Today*, P!nk said: 'It's so all over the place, and there are songs that I can't listen to without crying. It came together without me knowing that I was making an album, because I never stopped writing. I put out an album; I went on tour. And then all of a sudden, I thought 'I should put out an EP, because I have these songs that I think are great,' but then I realised I had 20 songs, and I had to put an album.'

She added: 'I've asked a lot of people in my time to collaborate with me, and I get a lot of "no's"… I'm good with "no." But this time I got green lights. I got to sing with Chris Stapleton, which will be one of the greatest honours of my life. I got to try writing songs with Billy Joel. I got to work with Dan Reynolds again, from Imagine Dragons, and Ryan Tedder, and collaborate with Khalid, Wrable, and Cash Cash.'

The album's first single, 'Walk Me Home,' premiered on 20 February 2019, with P!nk including it as part of a greatest hits medley live at the BRIT Awards in London that evening. At the ceremony, she received the award for Outstanding Contribution to Music, a category which was reinstated for the first time since 2012, when Blur had received the honour.

Hurts 2B Human was named after her collaboration with Khalid, with P!nk telling iHeart Radio that she tries to name her albums after something that resonates with her. She explained: 'I always name an album after a song that... I try to find the one that encompasses or just resonates the most with me. Either where I'm at or where I think the world is at, or usually where I'm at – I'm very narcissistic when it comes to writing and creating. As you get older, your parents get older, that's incredibly painful to experience. And being a mother sometimes is incredibly painful. Everyone likes to talk about the beautiful bits but being a wife can be incredibly painful. Also, the point of that song was "I've got you."'

Using photography from Andrew Macpherson, the artwork was designed to look like watercolour paintings by Jeri Heiden and Niek Steinhardt of Smog Design Inc.

As a result of the proximity to its predecessor, and that promotion would be limited because of her *Beautiful Trauma* world tour, P!nk was warned by her record label that it might not be as commercially successful. She told *Billboard* magazine: 'Our whole conversation was, "Don't beat yourself up if it doesn't do as well as the last one."' This was not the case; the album went to #1 in nearly all her major markets, selling over 95,000 copies in its first week in the USA alone.

Album Tracks

'Hustle'

Written by Jorgen Odegard, Dan Reynolds and Alecia 'P!nk' Moore
Produced by Jorgen Odegard
Additional Production by Dan Reynolds
Recorded at The Village Studios, Los Angeles
Duration: 2:55
Chart Position: Australia: 69

'Hustle' was co-written with Dan Reynolds, the lead singer of American band Imagine Dragons, alongside Jorgen Odegard, who produced two tracks on their fourth studio album, *Origins*. The album opener was released on 28 March 2019 as a promotional single alongside pre-orders for *Hurts 2B Human*, with a lyric video simultaneously premiering on YouTube.

Against an infectious swing-inspired beat and repeated finger clicks, P!nk lets a partner know that he mistook her love for weakness, saying, 'I guarantee I won't repeat this, no, don't hustle me.'

'(Hey Why) Miss You Sometime'

Written by Max Martin, Johan 'Shellback' Schuster and Alecia 'P!nk' Moore
Produced by Max Martin and Johan 'Shellback' Schuster
Recorded at MXM Studios, Los Angeles and MXM Studios, Stockholm, Sweden
Duration: 3:23

'(Hey Why) Miss You Sometime' is the only collaboration with Max Martin and Shellback on *Hurts 2B Human*, with P!nk asking an ex-lover why she misses them even though the relationship was toxic.

The song features multiple pop culture references, including Jack Daniels whiskey, the movie *Titanic*, country singer Johnny Cash and fast-food restaurant McDonald's.

'Walk Me Home'

Written by Nate Ruess, Scott Harris and Alecia 'P!nk' Moore
Produced by Peter Thomas and Kyle Moorman
Recorded at Roundhead Studios, Auckland, New Zealand
Duration: 2:59
Released as a single in February 2019
Music video directed by Michael Gracey and Stuart Bowen
Chart Position: USA: 49; Canada: 17; UK: 8; Australia: 11; Germany: 33

The anthemic 'Walk Me Home,' co-written with Scott Harris, known for his work with Shawn Mendes, and Nate Ruess, who duetted with P!nk on 'Just Give Me a Reason,' sees her finding hope through love and connection in uncertain times. Backstage at the BRIT Awards 2019, where she performed the song for the first time as part of a greatest hits medley, P!nk told Capital FM: 'This adulting thing is a lot. And it's better shared with a loved one.'

A fan of the movie musical *The Greatest Showman*, P!nk approached the film's director, Michael Gracey, to shoot the music video for the song. In a behind-the-scenes featurette of her shooting the video, P!nk said: 'It's going to be really, really, possibly the most beautiful thing I've ever done. There's a lot of dancing and a lot of partners, but it's just me. It's very hard to explain with words... you're going to have to see it and take it in. But it's a magic trick, essentially. It's going to be the most visually stunning thing I think I've probably ever done.'

The video, which pays homage to scenes from classic musicals such as *Singing in the Rain*, premiered the following month. Filmed on the Universal backlot in California, it shows P!nk dancing alone in a red evening dress, supported by invisible silhouettes. The imagery portrays the feeling of being alone, even in the presence of others.

In April, shortly after the release of *Hurts 2B Human*, a second music video for 'Walk Me Home' was released on P!nk's YouTube channel starring London-based drag collective Sink the Pink in a lip-sync battle, shot at Bethnal Green Working Men's Club. P!nk posted on her social media: 'This is the best lip sync battle I've ever seen! Feast your eyes!'

'Walk Me Home' became another global hit single for P!nk, reaching #11 in Australia, where it was certified 4x Platinum. It reached the top 10 in the UK singles chart and topped the radio airplay chart in March 2019. In the USA, it peaked at #49 on the Billboard Hot 100 but became her tenth #1 on the Adult Pop Songs radio airplay chart.

'My Attic'

Written by Julia Michaels, Ilsey Juber and Freddy Wexler
Produced by The Struts (Jakob Jerlström and Ludwig Söderberg)
Recorded at Wolf Cousins Studios, Stockholm, Sweden and Roundhead Studios, Auckland, New Zealand
Duration: 3:02

'My Attic' is a stripped-back ballad, co-written by Julia Michaels and produced by Swedish duo The Struts. The song uses the metaphor of a messy attic to explore P!nk's emotional interior, and the combination of fear and hopefulness that comes with letting her guard down and letting someone in.

Adam Lambert chose to record the song for his 2023 album of cover versions, *High Drama*. Before performing the song at a concert in London, he told the audience: 'We tend to go through things and we sweep them under the rug. We don't process these emotions, and this metaphor is "My Attic". In my attic, I keep all those things that I haven't dealt with. I put them in a box, put some tape on it, label it, and stick it upstairs, so it's still in my house, but I don't want to look at it. We all have things that we go through, we all have wounds, and with this song, it allows me to be vulnerable and share those things with you.'

'90 Days' featuring Wrabel

Written by Steve Robson, Alecia 'P!nk' Moore and Stephen Wrabel
Produced by Steve Robson and Stephen Wrabel
Recorded at Roundhead Studios, Auckland, New Zealand
Duration: 3:50
Wrable appears courtesy of Big Gay Records
Music video directed by Remi Bakkar

'90 Days' was co-written with singer-songwriter Wrabel, who also features on the track. The song's title refers to the commonly believed myth that it takes twenty-one days to form a habit and ninety days to break one. P!nk said on *The Ellen DeGeneres Show* that she discovered Wrabel through his video for 'The Village,' saying that the song and video made her cry. She said: 'His dream is to make an album, and I hope that this is what does it for him.'

Talking to *GEM* magazine, Wrabel said: 'The day I met P!nk and went over to her studio to work on our ballad, '90 Days,' was a very surreal and dreamy moment for me. I walked out of my apartment and there was a Cadillac outside to pick me up and drive me to the studio. I remember calling my grandma and asking her, "What the heck is happening in my life? How is this real?" I was so emotional the whole ride there. As we were working on our song, I had this idea for P!nk and me to harmonise on an ad-lib. I thought it'd be really cool but I was kind of scared to ask her. I mean, she's freaking P!nk! When I finally had the guts to ask her, she loved the idea and we went for it. After the studio session, I just sat there with my knees up and my head in my knees, like a turtle in his shell, and I started to sob. She gave me the kindest hug and said, "You can cry, babe. It's all good." You grow up wanting to do something and you hope that it becomes true one day, but you don't know if it ever will. Having had that experience is definitely one of the biggest and precious moments.'

A music video for the single, opening with P!nk talking about her husband Carey Hart on *The Ellen DeGeneres Show* and showing the highs and lows of her relationship, premiered on 18 June 2019. P!nk posted on Instagram that the video was released as a surprise, directed and filmed by her backing dancer, Remi Bakkar, during tour stops in Portland and Detroit. She said: 'It's shot just for fun, just because we wanted to, and I hope you love it.'

Wrabel went onto tour with P!nk during her 2019 Beautiful Trauma world tour dates in Europe, where he joined her on stage to perform '90 Days.'

'Hurts 2B Human' featuring Khalid

Written by Teddy Geiger, Scott Harris, Anna-Catherine 'Uffie' Hartley, Alexander 'Xplicit' Izquierdo, Alecia 'P!nk' Moore and Khalid Robinson
Produced by Jorgen Odegard
Recorded at Record Plant, Los Angeles
Duration: 3:23
Khalid appears courtesy of Right Hand Music Group/RCA Records
Music video directed by Alissa Torvinen
Chart Position: Canada: 87; UK: 61; Australia: 48

'Hurts 2B Human,' a duet with Texan singer and labelmate Khalid, is the album's title track, released as the album's third promotional single on 22 April 2019. A lyric video for the song premiered on YouTube the same day, featuring AI avatars of P!nk and Khalid created by the website Genies.

In an interview with *Entertainment Weekly*, P!nk said that she wrote the song and felt it needed Khalid to appear on it. He agreed to the collaboration because his mother is a fan of hers. She said: 'I've crossed over. Someone I think is my age will walk up to me in an airport and be like, "Hey! My mum loves you!" And I'm like, "Fuck! I mean thank you!"'

She elaborated on the song saying: 'When this song happened, it hit a string in me that just resonates. I feel like in 2019 if you're present and not totally escaping your feelings and you're looking around at what's going on in the world, especially this country, it hurts. It fucking hurts your heart. If you choose to remain open-hearted, then it's just going to hurt for a while. I think that's a good thing because that's what creates change and I think we're starting to see change and see people show up and fight back. Also, being a woman and Khalid being an African American male in America, it fucking hurts. But I think it's a really hopeful song.'

An official music video for the song, directed by Alissa Torvinen, premiered on 18 September 2019. Torvinen described the video as 'telling a story of human experience and connectedness.' It shows a large apartment block, taking viewers into the living spaces of a diverse range of residents, including both P!nk and Khalid, who cross paths in the hallway towards the end of the video.

In a behind-the-scenes video at the music video shoot, P!nk said: 'It hurts to be human when there's something happening that's out of your control and you feel powerless. When a dictator decides that a certain people shouldn't belong. It hurts to be human when you're a woman and a bunch of old white men decide that they know better than you about your own body. It hurts to be human when racism exists. When the divide between class is so wide that the rich get richer and the poor have no chance of ever getting out of the cycle that they're in. It hurts to be human when you don't know what to tell your children about their future and what the world's gonna look like.'

Khalid added: 'For me, it's an acknowledgement of all of the hardships that I feel that we are all going through, especially on society right now. There's a lot of decisions that have been made that have affected the majority. The people who are making the decisions are a little outdated. Their viewpoints are outdated; mind frames are outdated.'

'Hurts 2B Human' charted on download sales after its release in April, peaking at #19 on the USA Billboard Pop Digital Songs chart. Although the song received limited radio airplay in Italy in September, coinciding with the music video's release, it was not released as an official single.

'Can We Pretend' featuring Cash Cash

Written by Cash Cash (Jean-Paul Makhlouf, Alex Makhlouf and Samuel Frisch), Ryan Tedder and Alecia 'P!nk' Moore
Produced by Cash Cash (Jean-Paul Makhlouf, Alex Makhlouf and Samuel Frisch) and Ryan Tedder
Recorded at The Village Studios, Los Angeles
Duration: 3:44
Cash Cash appears courtesy of Big Beat/Atlantic Recording Corporation
Released as a single in June 2019
Music video directed by Jon Jon
Chart Position: Canada: 99; UK: 88; Australia: 99

'Can We Pretend' is a nostalgic electro-pop mid-tempo track about escaping current reality and reminiscing about life before social media, referencing when P!nk was 22. The song was written with Ryan Tedder, with music from DJs Jean-Paul Makhlouf, Alex Makhlouf and Samuel Frisch, known collectively as Cash Cash.

In the lyrics, P!nk references President Donald Trump, who was elected in 2016 (and again in 2024), singing: 'Can we pretend that we both like the president?' In an interview with *USA Today*, she said: 'I think he's a joke. I think it's also a joke how divided we've all become, and he's been a catalyst for division. Look, I was raised by a Vietnam vet, Air Force person who had me marching on Washington since I was three years old. I believe in patriotism being that you defend your ideals. We have one of the worst leaders that this country has ever had, so you have to speak out about it. People say, "You should just shut up and sing," but it's like, "What do you do? Are you in politics? Why does your opinion matter more than mine?" I'm a citizen of the United States, and I will continue to speak out until I'm in my next lifetime as a puppy. Yes, I would like to come back as my dog.'

Talking about the song's creation to *EDM.com*, Cash Cash said: 'We always loved P!nk's voice so we were just inspired being able to collaborate with such a legendary artist. She wrote the lyrics and vocals with Ryan Tedder. They sent them to us and we built the music in about a week. Then we mixed and mastered it and that was that. We got a little nostalgic with it and ended up blending one of our custom synth sounds we used in our song "Take Me Home," which worked out really well in the song. It's always fun to revisit a sound you've used in the past to try and build on it, modify it, or just take inspiration from it.'

A lyric video for the song was released on 11 April 2019 to promote the album, followed by an animated music video on 28 June, when it became the album's official second single. Directed and drawn by Jon Jon, the video's storyline was co-created by The GoldenBoyz (Nick Florez and RJ Durell). Jon Jon said: 'P!nk had a strong message that she wanted to convey with this animated music video and it was a blast to bring it to life, in warp speed, with my line and shape style with limited spots of colour.'

'Can We Pretend' charted in the top 100 in the UK, Australia and Canada, backed by a remix EP containing mixes by MOTi, Hook n Sling, Yves V and Bart B More. The song became P!nk's seventh #1 on the USA Billboard Dance Club Songs and entered the top 10 on the Billboard Adult Pop Airplay chart. It also reached the airplay top 5 in France and Germany.

'Courage'

Written by Greg Kurstin, Sia Furler and Alecia 'P!nk' Moore
Produced by Greg Kurstin
Recorded at Echo Studio, Los Angeles and Earthstar Creation Center, California
Duration: 4:20

'Courage' is a soaring power ballad, co-written by Sia, who previously collaborated with P!nk on 'Waterfall,' released by Stargate in March 2017. The song served as the theme for the live-action movie adaptation of *Knights of the Zodiac*, titled *Saint Saiya: The Beginning* in Japan, premiering in April 2023.

In 2020, Sia released a companion album to her movie, *Music*, entitled *Music: Songs from and Inspired by the Motion Picture*. The album featured the single 'Courage to Change,' which includes an interpolation of 'Courage.'

'Happy'

Written by Teddy Geiger, Sasha Sloan, Steph Jones and Alecia 'P!nk' Moore
Produced by Oscar Görres
Recorded at Wolf Cousins Studios, Stockholm, Sweden; MXM Studios, West Hollywood; The Village Studios, Los Angeles and Earthstar Creation Center, California
Duration: 3:01

An introspective song about body image, self-esteem, and self-acceptance, 'Happy' is P!nk's first collaboration with Swedish producer Oscar Görres. Max Martin and Johan 'Shellback' Schuster discovered Görres, and he gained recognition for his work on DNCE's 2016 album *DNCE* and MARINA's 2019 album *Love + Fear*, as well as working on songs for both Britney Spears and Taylor Swift.

Talking to *USA Today*, P!nk shared that the song is deeply personal, referencing the lyric, 'Since I was 17, I've always hated my body and it feels like my body's hated me.' She said: 'The reason is because I've always had this very tomboy, very strong gymnast body, but actually at 17 I had a miscarriage. And I was going to have that child. But when that happens to a woman or a young girl, you feel like your body hates you and like your body is broken, and it's not doing what it's supposed to do. I've had several miscarriages since, so I think it's important to talk about what you're ashamed of, who you really are and the painful shit. I've always written that way.'

'We Could Have It All'

Written by Greg Kurstin, Beck Hansen and Alecia 'P!nk' Moore
Produced by Greg Kurstin
Recorded at Echo Studio, Los Angeles and Earthstar Creation Center, California
Duration: 4:33

The dramatic 'We Could Have It All' is the album's second collaboration with Greg Kurstin, written about missed opportunities and the potential of what could have been. Written in 2015, the song features contributions from Beck, who penned P!nk's 2003 single 'Feel Good Time' with William Orbit.

Kurstin had previously worked with Beck as a member of his live band before becoming a full-time songwriter and producer. He later produced Beck's 2017 album, *Colors*. In a 2016 interview with ASCAP, Kurstin reflected on his work with Beck, saying: "I was touring with him, which was a great experience, but I had to break the news that I didn't want to tour anymore, and I wanted to pursue what I'm doing now. And that was a long time ago. But it was cool to have him sort of follow some of the stuff that I did and want to come around and work with me in this new capacity.'

'We Could Have It All' also features drums by Foo Fighters drummer Taylor Hawkins, who died in March 2022. In 2023, P!nk was invited by his bandmate Dave Grohl to perform at a tribute concert in Los Angeles.

'Love Me Anyway' featuring Chris Stapleton

Written by Allen Shamblin, Tom Douglas and Alecia 'P!nk' Moore
Produced by Alecia 'P!nk' Moore
Additional Production by Sal Oliveri and Simon Gooding
Recorded at Grand Central South, Tennessee and The Village Studios, Los Angeles
Duration: 3:09
Chris Stapleton appears courtesy of Mercury Nashville
Released as a single in September 2019
Chart Position: USA: 96

A country-tinged ballad, 'Love Me Anyway' features country singer-songwriter Chris Stapleton and was produced by P!nk. In interviews promoting *Hurts 2B Human*, P!nk described working with Stapleton as a tremendous honour, explaining her admiration and respect for him and his music. Stapleton and P!nk went onto write and record 'Just Say I'm Sorry' together, the album closer on 2023's *Trustfall.*

In 2023, whilst promoting *Trustfall*, P!nk reflected on their collaborations, saying: 'Chris Stapleton is one of the best singers to me that's ever lived. He's effortless. I don't know if you all heard him sing the National Anthem, but I was upset. I was upset. I was offended. Really. He just doesn't move. And then that comes out. I'm like, "What's that like?" And he's the nicest guy. He's a "one take wonder" and he's like, "Is that like what you were thinking?" And "Is that what you thought you wanted? Because I can do whatever." I'm like, "I know you can do whatever." And he's just so humble and he loves to collaborate outside of his genre, which is what I love to do as well, because I use pop as like an umbrella.'

She added to *Vulture* magazine in 2023: 'I'm always surprised when I hear myself on the radio. I hear "Love Me Anyway" with Chris Stapleton, from *Hurts 2B Human* sometimes, and it always makes me stop, and I just get this dumb happy look on my face. I'm also one of his biggest fans, so that might be why. I can't believe that people like that say "yes." He's one of the gentlest souls you would ever meet, and he is kind, and he loves collaborating, and he's so freaking talented.'

'Love Me Anyway' was released as a single in the USA and Canada, peaking at #20 on the Billboard Adult Pop Airplay chart and #52 on the Billboard Country Airplay chart. The duo performed the song live at the 53rd Annual CMA Awards in November 2019.

'Circle Game'

Written by Greg Kurstin and Alecia 'P!nk' Moore
Produced by Greg Kurstin
Recorded at Echo Studio, Los Angeles; Henson Recording Studios, Hollywood and Earthstar Creation Center, California
Duration: 4:53

'Circle Game' is a reflective ballad contemplating the passage of time and the inevitability of change, with its title referencing Joni Mitchell's 1970 song of the same name. Written by P!nk and Greg Kurstin, the song explores her relationship with her father, James T. Moore, who was in remission from cancer at the time, and her reflections on being a parent herself.

In an interview with *Entertainment Weekly*, P!nk said the song was inspired by a Father's Day post she shared on Instagram in June 2018, talking about the day she announced her marriage was over in 2008. Following intrusive questions from the paparazzi, she called her father who came and helped fight 'monsters in her closet' for her.

Discussing her relationship with her father and other thoughts behind the song, P!nk said: 'My dad had cancer last year. He was my first hero. He was my God when I was a little girl. He's who taught me to fight for what I believe in. He's a big part of me. It's hard when you get to our age and all your friends' parents start getting older and some are passing on, and it's a really painful thing to go through. It's scary for me. Even though I'm this 39-year-old mother of two and I'm walking through the world with my head up and my shoulders back, at the end of the day I miss my dad and I want my dad to come and fight back for me sometimes. He's older now and I have to take care of him. It's just that part of life and it's inevitable. "Circle Game" is about growing up and still feeling like that little girl, waiting for my dad to fix my problems and realising that's not the way it is anymore. And now that I have children, it just changes when you look at your kids. I'm like, "Wow, I'm your person." There's a beautiful weight in that that just makes you reflect.'

'The Last Song of Your Life'

Written by Billy Mann and Alecia 'P!nk' Moore
Produced by Billy Mann and Alecia 'P!nk' Moore
Recorded at Earthstar Creation Center, California
Duration: 4:53

'The Last Song of Your Life' sees P!nk seeking authenticity from a friend, asking them to imagine it's their final opportunity to share their truth. The song was co-written and produced by Billy Mann, continuing their record of collaborating on some of P!nk's most meaningful songs.

Bonus Track

'More'

Written by Michael Busbee and Jetta John-Hartley
Produced by Michael Busbee
Recorded at Roundhead Studios, Auckland, New Zealand and Henson Recording Studios, Hollywood
Duration: 3:50

'More' is a bonus track on the Japanese edition of *Hurts 2B Human*, written and produced by Michael Busbee, who wrote 'Try,' with British singer-songwriter, Jetta.

The song is the last collaboration between P!nk and Busbee, as he sadly died aged 43 in September 2019, just weeks after being diagnosed with Glioblastoma.

In July 2023, Apple Music asked country singer-songwriter Madeline Edwards to cover the song as part of their 'Lost & Found' project. In addition, they also released the original demo of 'More,' performed by Busbee and Jetta.

Other Songs

'Bennie and the Jets'—Elton John featuring P!nk and Logic

Written by Elton John and Bernie Taupin
Produced by Justin Tranter, Daniel Crean and Wes Period
Recorded at Westlake Recording Studios, West Hollywood
Duration: 3:11
Logic appears courtesy of Def Jam Recordings

In April 2018, Elton John released an album of his biggest hits recorded by other artists, entitled *Revamp: Reimagining the Songs of Elton John and Bernie Taupin*. In addition to P!nk and Logic, the album features Mary J. Blige, Lady Gaga, Coldplay, Ed Sheeran, Florence + the Machine, Demi Lovato, Sam Smith, Miley Cyrus, and more.

P!nk and Logic's re-recording of 'Bennie and the Jets,' subtitled the '2018 Version,' opens the album, featuring sampled vocals from Elton's original recording.

Elton, who approached most of the artists directly for the project, said: 'It's always a huge compliment when an artist loves your song enough to take the time and effort to rework it. As songwriters, Bernie and I are thrilled when singers we admire and respect as much as those on *Revamp* choose to add their own unique twist in the process. It means that our music is still relevant and ultimately that our songs continue to reach new audiences. We're humbled and thank them all for their generosity.'

'A Million Dreams'

Written by Benj Pasek and Justin Paul
Produced by Greg Wells, Joseph Trapanese, Justin Paul and Alan Lacamoire
Recorded at The Village, Los Angeles and Electric Lady Studios, New York City
Duration: 2:43
Chart Position: USA: 90; Canada: 80; UK: 11; Australia: 26; Germany: 70

The success of *The Greatest Showman* movie, starring Hugh Jackman, Zac Efron and Michelle Williams, led to Warner Brothers Records commissioning new versions of the songs, performed by some of the world's biggest pop stars, for an album entitled *The Greatest Showman – Reimagined.*

P!nk was approached to cover 'A Million Dreams' and recorded the song alongside her daughter, Willow, whose reprise is also included. Other artists featured on the album, released in October 2018, include Kelly Clarkson, Sara Bareilles and Panic! at the Disco.

In a video of the recording session, P!nk tells Benj Pasek and Justin Paul, the film's songwriters: 'I grew up listening to *Annie* and no one has done this for me, for my heart, since I was a little girl - and to have her finally have something like this? You made our favourite movie ever.'

P!nk recorded a new version of the song in 2020, featuring the Ndlovu Youth Choir, to raise money for UNICEF's Changemaker campaign. She said: 'It was an honour to collaborate with the Ndlovu Youth Choir on this new version of "A Million Dreams." Although we were thousands of miles apart due to the pandemic, we were connected by UNICEF's lifesaving mission of putting children first. Join me in supporting UNICEF by donating to their lifesaving work around the world.'

In September 2025, P!nk and Willow appeared as special guests at Hugh Jackman's *From New York, with Love* concert at Radio City Music Hall. Introduced by Jackman, they performed both 'A Million Dreams' and P!nk's 'Who Knew' together as a trio.

Unreleased Songs

'Amnesia'

Written by Greg Kurstin and Alecia 'P!nk' Moore
Produced by Greg Kurstin

Registered on ASCAP in 2019, 'Amnesia' was written during sessions for *Hurts 2B Human.* A 10-second clip of the song leaked online in November 2023, with P!nk singing: 'Help me now remember, you me and together.'

Live Performances

'The Star-Spangled Banner'

Written by John Stafford Smith and Francis Scott Key
Duration: 2:12

A tradition in the USA, P!nk performed a cover of 'The Star-Spangled Banner' at the Super Bowl LII before the New England Patriots vs. Philadelphia Eagles game in February 2018.

P!nk revealed she had the flu during the performance, removing a throat lozenge just before singing. She posted on Instagram: 'Trying to practice the flu away. I've been waiting to sing this song since 1991 when I saw my idol, Whitney Houston, own this song. And now, my chance has finally come. And it just so happens that this chance comes when I have two small Petri dish kids who literally cough into my mouth and rub their snot on my cheek. You can't write this stuff I swear!'

'Jolene'

Written by Dolly Parton
Duration: 3:30

P!nk first performed a cover of Dolly Parton's iconic 1973 classic 'Jolene' at the MusiCares Gala 2019, where Dolly was awarded 'Person of the Year.' Dolly said at the event: 'It's been such a thrill for me tonight to see all these great artists that are singing songs that I've written and been part of.'

A few years later, P!nk was asked to induct Dolly into the Rock and Roll Hall of Fame at the thirty-seventh annual induction ceremony on 5 November 2022. P!nk said: 'There are few finer songwriters, male or female, that have ever lived. She's one of the greatest storytellers of her time - of any time.'

P!nk joined Dolly, Brandi Carlile, Sheryl Crow, Annie Lennox, and Pat Benatar for the show's encore performance of 'Jolene.'

'The Christmas Song' featuring Willow Sage Hart

Written by Robert Wells and Mel Tormé
Duration: 2:36

P!nk and her daughter performed a cover of the Christmas classic, 'The Christmas Song' in November 2020 for *The Disney Holiday Singalong*, which aired on ABC in the USA for the holiday season. Hosted by Ryan Seacrest, the show featured performances of Christmas classics from people's respective homes in response to the COVID-19 pandemic. In addition to P!nk, the show featured Katy Perry, Adam Lambert, Andrea Bocelli, BTS and Michael Bublé.

'The Christmas Song' is commonly subtitled 'Chestnuts Roasting on an Open Fire' or 'Merry Christmas to You,' and was made famous in 1946 when Nat 'King' Cole recorded it.

Songwriting Credits

'Broken and Beautiful'—Kelly Clarkson

Written by Christopher 'Marshmello' Comstock, Steve Mac, Johnny McDaid and Alecia 'P!nk' Moore
Produced by Christopher 'Marshmello' Comstock and Steve Mac

Duration: 3:39
Released as a single in March 2019

Johnny McDaid and Steve Mac worked with P!nk and dance producer Marshmello on 'Broken and Beautiful.' In late 2018, the song was recorded by Kelly Clarkson for the soundtrack to *UglyDolls*, an animated film about a line of dolls. In addition to performing songs on the soundtrack, Kelly voices the lead character, Moxy, a pink UglyDoll, full of confidence, hope and curiosity.

'Courage to Change'—Sia

Written by Greg Kurstin, Sia Furler and Alecia 'P!nk' Moore
Produced by Greg Kurstin
Duration: 4:52
Released as a single in September 2020

Australian singer-songwriter Sia wrote extensively with P!nk for *Hurts 2 B Human*, including the album track, 'Courage.' In September 2020, Sia released 'Courage to Change,' featuring an interpolation of the P!nk song, as a single from the companion album to her movie, *Music*, entitled *Music: Songs from and Inspired by the Motion Picture*.

Catalogue Registrations

'Casualty'

Written by Greg Kurstin, Sia Furler and Alecia 'P!nk' Moore

'Two Souls'

Written by Dan Reynolds, Kristine 'K.Flay' Flaherty and Alecia 'P!nk' Moore

'Big Sur Family Workshop'

Written by Greg Kurstin and Alecia 'P!nk' Moore

'Bliss'

Written by Greg Kurstin and Alecia 'P!nk' Moore

'Dive'

Written by Greg Kurstin, Sia Furler and Alecia 'P!nk' Moore

'You Need Me'
Written by Greg Kurstin, Sia Furler and Alecia 'P!nk' Moore

'Look Up'
Written by Greg Kurstin, Sia Furler and Alecia 'P!nk' Moore

'Entitled Girls'
Written by Steve Mac, Johnny McDaid and Alecia 'P!nk' Moore

'Whoa'
Written by Pharrell Williams and Alecia 'P!nk' Moore

'Searching for a Heartbeat'
Written by Butch Walker and Alecia 'P!nk' Moore

'I Sing'
Written by Corey Britz, Justin Derrico, Alecia 'P!nk' Moore and Mia Celeste Dyson

'Motorboat'
Written by Corey Britz, Justin Derrico, Alecia 'P!nk' Moore and Travis Lee Ference

'Overpriced Smoothie'
Written by Corey Britz, Justin Derrico, Alecia 'P!nk' Moore and Travis Lee Ference

'Silver Lining'
Written by Corey Britz, Justin Derrico, Alecia 'P!nk' Moore and Travis Lee Ference

'Over and Over'
Written by Askjell Solstrand, Lauren Frawley, Summer Overstreet, Gabe Reali and Alecia 'P!nk' Moore

12

All I Know So Far: Setlist (2009–2021)

Released:	21 May 2021
Chart Position:	USA: 13
	Canada: 8
	UK: 4
	Australia: 2
	Germany: 5

Having worked with Michael Gracey, director of *The Greatest Showman*, for the 'Walk Me Home' music video, P!nk's manager suggested they collaborate on a documentary film showing her life on the road while raising a family. The resulting movie, *All I Know So Far*, was purchased by Amazon and released exclusively on their Prime Video platform on 21 May 2021, with a live album and soundtrack to the documentary, *All I Know So Far: Setlist*, being made available simultaneously.

The documentary follows P!nk on the *Hurts 2B Human* world tour, culminating in her performance at Wembley Stadium in London, UK.

The soundtrack features eleven highlights recorded across the concerts on 29 and 30 June 2019, as well as her 2009 performance of 'Bohemian Rhapsody' from the Sydney Entertainment Center and 'We Are the Champions' from Rock in Rio 2019.

In addition, the album features two new songs—'All I Know So Far,' written as a title track for the documentary, and 'Cover Me in Sunshine,' a duet with her daughter, Willow Sage Hart.

The cover artwork shows the audience during one of P!nk's sold-out nights at Wembley Stadium, with a photo of her sitting and being kissed by her son Jameson Moon Hart, superimposed onto the stage.

Album Tracks

'All I Know So Far'

Written by Benj Pasek, Justin Paul and Alecia 'P!nk' Moore
Produced by Greg Kurstin
Co-Produced by Benj Pasek, Justin Paul and Alecia 'P!nk' Moore
Recorded at No Expectations Studios, Los Angeles and P!nk's Studio, Santa Barbara
Duration: 4:36
Released as a single in May 2021
Music video directed by Dave Meyers
Chart Position: USA: 74; Canada: 30; UK: 39; Australia: 25; Germany: 75

'All I Know So Far' is the theme song from P!nk's Amazon documentary of the same name, released as a single in May 2021. The autobiographical anthem sees P!nk singing about growth, perseverance, and motherhood, dedicating it to her daughter, Willow. The song was written by P!nk with musical theatre composers Benj Pasek and Justin Paul, who wrote the hit Broadway musical and movie *Dear Evan Hansen*, and *The Greatest Showman*.

In an interview with *USA Today*, P!nk said: 'I'm a total theatre nerd. And I'm like, who better than Benj and Justin? So I called them up and we wrote a song on Zoom.'

The lyrics are based on dialogue from the documentary, with the chorus taking inspiration from something P!nk's father, James T. Moore, would say to her when she was younger. She said: 'I remember looking at him in the front seat and him going, "Honey, you just put your head back, spit in the wind, and show them what you got." And he raised me that way. I mean, he was a Vietnam vet. He was tough, and he raised me like that, but he was also a poet, a folk singer and he knew the language of the trees. He gave me all of that. He was always so proud of me.'

Dave Meyers directed the music video for the song, featuring P!nk passing on part of her life story to her daughter, Willow, including her tumultuous relationships with her mother and husband, and the lessons she learned along the way. The video stars Cher as God, actress Judith Light as P!nk's mother, her husband Carey Hart, and their children.

Cher said: 'I'm so proud to be in P!nk's video. She is a great artist and has made it through the jungle to be "P!nk" on her own terms. In my way, this is my struggle to be who I am. In many ways, it's every woman's struggle. This song might be her best, and the video is beyond.'

P!nk said: 'Dave Meyers and I are back together again. Since this song is sort of the story of my life and a letter to my daughter, making this video with Dave after we did our first video together 22 years ago is a really special full circle moment. He's truly a genius and I am full of gratitude for our friendship and to experience all the times we've been able to work together.'

'Cover Me in Sunshine' featuring Willow Sage Hart

Written by Maureen 'Mozella' McDonald and Amy Allen
Produced by Ludvig 'A Strut' Söderberg
Recorded at House Mouse Studios, Stockholm, Sweden and P!nk's Studio, Santa Barbara
Duration: 2:36
Released as a single in February 2021
Music video directed by Alecia 'P!nk' Moore and Willow Sage Hart
Chart Position: Canada: 60; UK: 52; Australia: 6; Germany: 7

'Cover Me in Sunshine' was recorded during the COVID-19 pandemic, co-written by Amy Allen, who contributed to two USA Billboard Hot 100 #1 singles in 2018—'Back to You' by Selena Gomez and 'Without Me' by Halsey—and Mozella, a prolific songwriter who co-wrote 'Wrecking Ball' for Miley Cyrus, and worked extensively on Madonna's 2015 album, *Rebel Heart*. Willow Sage Hart, P!nk's daughter, is credited as a guest on the song, providing vocals throughout the chorus.

Whilst production and recording were handled by A Strut in Stockholm, Sweden, P!nk and her daughter recorded the song at home. She posted on Instagram that the song would be released as a Valentine's Day present to fans, saying: 'We all know this year has been different and challenging and at times, terrifying and tumultuous, angsty and all the things, and I personally find comfort in music. I find comfort in song. But we have this song called "Cover Me in Sunshine" that we recorded at home because it made us feel happy and so we're going to put it out for no other reason than that we hope that the song makes you feel happy. We thought we'd put it out around Valentine's Day as a big ol' hug and a kiss from us to all y'all.'

A music video was released, featuring home footage of P!nk and Willow enjoying outdoor activities, such as riding horses and collecting eggs from their chickens. P!nk said: 'My baby girl and I recorded a song and made a video together! We hope it brings you joy and sweetness and sunshine.'

P!nk and Willow performed the song at the 2021 Billboard Music Awards, as she received the ICON award, as well as on the *Summer Carnival* tour throughout 2023 and 2024.

13

Trustfall (2020–2023)

Released:	17 February 2023
	1 December 2023 (Tour Deluxe Edition)
Chart Position:	USA: 2
	Canada: 1
	UK: 1
	Australia: 1
	Germany: 1

While sessions for *Trustfall*, P!nk's ninth studio album, officially began in 2021, she had already been working on music intermittently during 2020, including learning how to record her vocals at home. During interviews to promote *All I Know So Far*, which were carried out via video conferencing, she revealed that she had started thinking about the album but that it was 'very early.'

In May 2021, P!nk was honoured with the Icon Award at the Billboard Music Awards, saying: 'It feels good to be out, it feels good to be out of my sweatpants!' During the ceremony, she performed a medley of hits, including 'Cover Me in Sunshine' with her daughter, Willow, 'All I Know So Far,' 'Get the Party Started,' 'So What' 'Blow Me (One Last Kiss),' 'Who Knew,' 'Just Like a Pill' and 'Just Give Me a Reason.' When asked about a new studio album, P!nk remained tight-lipped, simply confirming she had started work.

In July 2022, P!nk released a surprise one-off single, 'Irrelevant,' included on the deluxe tour edition. By that point much of the album was complete. In addition to reuniting with frequent collaborators, such as Billy Mann, Max Martin, Greg Kurstin, Stephen Wrabel and Teddy Geiger, *Trustfall* expands her eclectic soundscape through new collaborations with David Hodges, Fred Again, The Lumineers and First Aid Kit.

Unlike most of her previous albums, where P!nk co-wrote nearly every song, *Trustfall* also sees her taking a different approach by accepting songs from other songwriters. Talking to Cody Rigsby during the *Trustfall* album release livestream, she explained: 'It was totally different. I used some of the best advice I ever got from my first record company president, L.A. Reid. He said, "I know you are a songwriter, and you're going to have to prove yourself over and over and over again. But never get in the way of a good song. Never let your ego get in the way of a good song." And so I, for the first time really, was accepting a lot of other people's words. And I'm glad I did it, because they're my words, too. Just like my words become your words. I found, for like a quarter of the album, a way to get out of my own way.'

P!nk also emphasised her desire to continue creating albums. She said: 'I'm proud of it as a body of work. People say that the general public do not listen to albums anymore. But I don't actually think that's true. I think we put on an album when it's time to cook dinner and have a glass of wine. I miss the experience of getting my cassette tape or my vinyl and unfurling it and looking for personal handwriting and lyrics and a secret message and having that time alone in your room where no one's screaming at you.'

The album's tracklist was carefully curated to reflect her intent, opening with 'When I Get There,' a ballad about death and the afterlife. Speaking to *Billboard* magazine, P!nk explained: 'I feel like we're all in this constant state of overwhelm, and so we put our feelings away just so that we can get through a day. I wanted to find a way back to the truth and the authentic feelings. So, opening the album with that, instead of like, "Hey, let's ease into each other," it's like, "No, no. Sit down. I want to talk to you. We're gonna clear all the bullshit away and have a conversation." That's how I am as a person. If you ask me how I am, how much time do you have? So "When I Get There" as an album-opener was my way of saying, "Let's talk about real stuff."'

The album's title came from its second single, which resonated deeply with P!nk's current thoughts about the world. A 'trustfall' is most often used in team-building sessions, where one person falls and relies on the rest of the team to catch them and stop them from falling.

In an interview with *iNews*, P!nk said: 'Life is just a fucking trustfall. It's like you feel like you're falling backwards and you don't know where the ground is sometimes. The world that we live in demands a lot of trust from us. We trust that we can safely participate in elections. We trust that our rights are going to stick around. We trust that we can drop our kids off at school.'

In the album credits, P!nk included an acrostic poem for *Trustfall*, suggested by her daughter. Each letter represents just one or two words: 'Truth,' 'Reflection,' 'Uncertainty,' 'Security,' 'Terror,' 'Faith,' 'Acceptance/Audacity,' 'Letting go,' 'Love.' She added: 'I think finding words is my life's work. And it doesn't matter how many you choose – it's always hard, especially when you want to be deeply seen and understood.'

Trustfall was another global hit for P!nk, reaching #1 in the UK, Australia, Canada and Germany, just missing out on the top spot in the USA. She also announced her first tour since COVID-19, the *Summer Carnival* tour, which opened in the UK in June 2023, travelling through Europe and North America. In October 2023, a smaller version of the tour played in arenas across the USA as the *Trustfall* tour (with similar staging) before the show headed to Australia and New Zealand in early 2024. It returned to Europe for a second leg, concluding with a second leg in both arenas and stadiums in the USA and Canada.

Album Tracks

'When I Get There'

Written by David Hodges and Amy Wadge
Produced by David Hodges
Recorded at Sleepwalker Studios, Los Angeles
Duration: 3:20
Released as a single in February 2023
Chart Position: USA: 82; Canada: 94; UK: 44

In August 2021, P!nk's father, James T. Moore, passed away at the age of 75 after being diagnosed with prostate cancer. *Trustfall* opens with 'When I Get There,' a deeply personal song about death and the possibility of an afterlife, which she dedicated to his memory.

David Hodges, formerly of Evanescence, and Amy Wadge, who has worked extensively with Ed Sheeran, wrote the song and submitted it to P!nk's label, unaware of the personal resonance it would have for her. She told Zane Lowe on Apple Music 1: 'It came to me when my dad was sick. And I said, "This is my song. This has to be my song. This is my song." And I was able to play it for him before he died. And it's just a beautiful thing.'

She later told *People* magazine: 'I felt like it was a gift. I wouldn't be able to write that song yet. I haven't unpacked that suitcase yet. I don't think I will for a while, but it's such a simple, beautiful song, and I love the idea that he might be somewhere nice. I've lost a lot of people in my life. But this time, I lost my dad and a dear friend within eight months of each other, and I just wonder where they went. I want to think they're somewhere. It's a sweet idea.'

'When I Get There' was released as a single with a lyric video on Valentine's Day, before the album's release. P!nk posted on Instagram: 'Sometimes love leaves us too soon. On Valentine's Day, I cherish the love I have that I can touch, and the love I have in my heart for those who have gone on to the next adventure. This one's for you, Daddy, Sir.'

P!nk told Howard Stern on his SiriusXM show that she likes to believe in the afterlife, saying: 'Before he died, I asked him what he'd like to come back as, and he said, "Well, I'm a pilot honey, so I'd like to be a bird of flight." I went home and it was during COVID, so I wasn't around a lot of people, I was nervous to be around my kids so I quarantined away from them. I had both doors open where I was staying, and I heard a commotion and looked on the dining room table, and there was a hawk. It was staring at me and I was like, "Oh my God, dad." And he flew out onto the banister, turned around and looked at me and turned his head sideways and off he went. Every time I walk out of my house this hawk follows me all the way, anywhere I'm going, until I get where I'm going, and then he flies away, so I'm a believer.'

'Trustfall'

Written by Fred 'Fred Again' Gibson, Johnny McDaid and Alecia 'P!nk' Moore
Produced by Fred 'Fred Again' Gibson and Johnny McDaid
Recorded at Fieldwork Studio, London, UK and Fieldwork Studio, Los Angeles
Duration: 3:57
Released as a single in January 2023
Music video directed by Georgia Hudson
Chart Position: USA: 82; Canada: 24; UK: 14; Australia: 19; Germany: 17

'Trustfall' is the title track and second single from the album, written and produced by British singer-songwriter-producer Fred Again and Johnny McDaid of the Irish band Snow Patrol, who also collaborated with P!nk on 'What About Us.' Fred Again had previously worked on 'Shotgun' by George Ezra, before collaborating with artists such as Ed Sheeran, XCX, and Stormzy.

P!nk said the synth-laden, euphoric pop song was written and recorded in the summer of 2022 over a few days spent working with Fred and McDaid. Speaking to Cody Rigsby on the *Trustfall* album release livestream, she explained: 'I came into the room with that in my head, and I just feel like in order to be a human being in this world today, it requires a lot of trust. It requires trust to get out of bed in the morning, and drop your kids off at school, and participate in elections, and have an opinion, and have a vagina, and all the things. It's hard for so many groups of people right now. "Trustfall" is two things – I feel like we're all falling backwards and we don't know where the ground is, it's an unsettling feeling like you don't know when to brace. But it's also that freedom of falling and letting go completely and trusting and having faith in the universe that it's going to take care of you, and that there's enough beautiful people around you to catch you. And it's everything that my life is about.'

For the music video, P!nk reunited with Georgia Hudson, who directed 'What About Us' and the unreleased video for 'Revenge' featuring Eminem. P!nk said: 'I did "What About Us" with Georgia Hudson and then her and I had kind of a falling out. I thought of her again for "Trustfall" and was like, "Do you want to work with me again?" She was crying because she was so happy to be able to put a period on the end of a sentence.' The music video opens with P!nk asking, 'Are you gonna fall? Is someone supposed to catch you? Or do you catch yourself? There will be something worth falling for.'

With choreography by Ryan Heffington, the concept was inspired by the director's personal experiences. In a behind-the-scenes video, Hudson explained:

'This is a really honest story that I've pulled from my own life about re-finding the courage to love again after you've had a little bit of heartache. We wanted to create a really gritty human message about transformation, about turning the dark into light and doing the damn scary thing. It always impresses me with Alecia how much trust she gives to me, she is like: "Take the song. Digest it. How does it make you feel now? Let's make other people feel like that, too!"'

To promote the song and album, P!nk performed 'Trustfall' on *The Graham Norton Show* in the UK, collaborating with French acrobat and choreographer Yoann Bourgeois to create a visual effect inspired by weightlessness. The song became another hit for P!nk, peaking in the top 20 in the Netherlands, Switzerland, Austria, Ireland and the UK, reaching #14. In Germany, it spent 38 weeks on the singles chart and reached #1 on the airplay chart, helping P!nk set the record for the most songs by a female artist to reach the top.

'Turbulence'

Written by Matthew Koma and Madison Love
Produced by Matthew Koma
Recorded at P!nk's Studio, Santa Barbara
Duration: 3:26

'Turbulence' is another song gifted to P!nk during the creation of *Trustfall*, reassuring the listener that life's challenges are comparable to turbulence during a flight.

During a press junket in the UK, P!nk said: 'I think we're all walking around with this low-level trauma after the pandemic. "Turbulence" is a song about anxiety and it's almost like I'm having a conversation with my kid about it. My favourite line is, "And when you say that you can't, I will watch you dance through this turbulence." And that makes me want to cry about trying to help Willow through the world as it is now. It's daunting, so daunting. Willow is a worrier. She's an internal processor. And she's also allergic to injustice.'

On Apple Music 1, P!nk elaborated: 'I love "Turbulence" because it's... I played it for my friend's teenager and she was just reduced to tears and I knew that it was speaking to her anxiety, the kind everybody has. And I just, I hope that that song helps a little because it's such a nice idea. It's, you know, as bumpy as it gets, as scary as it gets. It's just turbulence. But I'm such a terrible flyer!'

'Long Way to Go' featuring the Lumineers

Written by Jesse Shatkin, Alecia 'P!nk' Moore, The Lumineers (Wesley Schultz and Jeremiah Fraites), John 'Mikky Ekko' Sudduth and Maureen 'Mozella' McDonald
Produced by Jesse Shatkin, Alecia 'P!nk' Moore, The Lumineers (Wesley Schultz and Jeremiah Fraites) and Simon Gooding

Additional Production by David Baron
Recorded at Sun Mountain Studio, Boiceville
Duration: 3:09
The Lumineers appear courtesy of Dualtone Music Group

P!nk approached American folk band The Lumineers to collaborate on a song for *Trustfall*, having been a fan since their 2012 debut single, 'Ho Hey.' Together, they co-wrote 'Long Way to Go,' with Jesse Shatkin, Mikky Ekko and Mozella, with the band's Wesley Schultz joining P!nk on vocals for the song.

Although P!nk had not previously collaborated with Jesse Shatkin as a songwriter or producer, the two had known each other since she recorded 'Blow Me (One Last Kiss)' for *The Truth About Love*. Shatkin had previously worked as an engineer for Greg Kurstin, who introduced him to Sia in 2013, leading to him collaborating with them on the hit single, 'Chandelier.'

During the *Trustfall* album release livestream, P!nk told Cody Rigsby: "The Lumineers are awesome. And Wes's voice and my voice, I thought, would be really cool. And I've known Jeremiah for a long time. We've been threatening to work together. And you just never know. It's all about timing.'

The Lumineers joined P!nk to perform 'Long Way to Go' live during her *Summer Carnival* concert in Nashville on 22 September 2023.

'Kids in Love' featuring First Aid Kit

Written by Ludvig 'A Strut' Söderberg, Jakob Jeriström and Klara Söderberg
Produced by Ludvig 'A Strut' Söderberg
Recorded at House Mouse Studios, Stockholm, Sweden
Duration: 2:47
First Aid Kit appear courtesy of Columbia Records

'Kids in Love' is an acoustic, nostalgic song about the personal growth that can come from early relationships. The song features Swedish folk duo Johanna and Klara Söderberg, best known as First Aid Kit, co-written by half of the group. In an interview with *Billboard* magazine, P!nk was asked about the lyric, 'If you don't fuck up, then you'll never learn,' saying: 'I learn through experiential fuckery. I mean, that's my whole life. I have to remember that as a parent, also. I have to remember that.'

On working with First Aid Kit, she added: 'I've been a fan of theirs for so long. And then I went to the 2019 BRIT Awards and they gave me this ridiculous award, and I got to sing with Dan Smith from Bastille. And we're hanging out at the after-party, and these girls were there, and Dan introduced them - and I heard him wrong, so I didn't know it was First Aid Kit. So, I was thinking they were some band that I didn't know about! I was like, "What kind of music do you make?" And they were nice about it. And I was like, "What's the name of your band again?" They're like, "First Aid Kit." I was like, "Shut... the front... door.

I'm your biggest fan." It was a full turnaround. It was like, "P!nk didn't know who the fuck they were," and then I was like, "No, you don't understand! I've been listening to you forever! You're from Sweden!" I was like, "Do you think like we can all start a band! Dan can be the singer, and I'll learn drums!" So, we started a band in our heads - me, First Aid Kit and Dan from Bastille. I think that'd be a cool band. But I just wanted to work with them, because they're awesome. They're my new Indigo Girls.'

'Never Gonna Not Dance Again'

Written by Max Martin, Johan 'Shellback' Schuster and Alecia 'P!nk' Moore
Produced by Max Martin and Johan 'Shellback' Schuster
Recorded at House Mouse Studios, Stockholm, Sweden; Kallbacken Studios, Stockholm, Sweden and MXM Studios, Los Angeles
Duration: 3:44
Released as a single in November 2022
Music video directed by Alecia 'P!nk' Moore and The GoldenBoyz (Nick Florez and RJ Durell)
Chart Position: USA: 99; Canada: 29; UK: 19; Australia: 64; Germany: 86

A fun, feel-good dance-pop track about living in the moment and celebrating life, 'Never Gonna Not Dance Again' was the first single from *Trustfall*. Co-written by Max Martin and Shellback, who first collaborated with P!nk on *I'm Not Dead*, she told *ABC News* that the song is more than just a reaction to the COVID-19 pandemic, where clubs and bars were closed and concerts cancelled, despite writing it over FaceTime.

She said: 'It's about how the only thing I want to do is find joy. I don't want to worry anymore. You can take everything I have, but you can't take my joy. I'm never gonna be in a situation that I don't say how I really feel and say "I love you" when I want to, and hug when I want to, and laugh when I need to, and cry when I need to and dance when I need to. I just want to find authentic joy.'

P!nk recalled to *Music Week* that she approached the duo with the song title, and a very clear brief in mind: "I think it's really fun for them when someone comes with an idea, like, "This is what I want, it's very specific, it's called 'Never Gonna Not Dance Again,' and it has to be the best song we've ever made! No pressure." After the fact, Shellback was like, "I actually think this might be my favourite production I've ever worked on!" I said, "See, you're welcome!"'

The song was selected as the album's lead single to provide levity, with P!nk telling Cody Rigsby on the *Trustfall* album release livestream: 'It's still an honest song. It's still talking about real stuff, but it's just a fun thing. I was like, "This song is kind of like... like my formula, isn't it? It's kind of cheesy." And then by the end of the song, I'm like, "I don't care. I feel happy when I hear that. I feel happy by the time this song is over." We all have such low-level trauma that we're walking around with that, for survival, we can't deal with at all times. But sometimes we just have to dance and stop it. Stop beating ourselves up and each other.'

The song, which references Whitney Houston's 'I Wanna Dance with Somebody,' was released alongside its music video on 4 November 2022, with P!nk simultaneously announcing her European *Summer Carnival* 2023 tour dates. The music video, directed by P!nk with Nick Florez and RJ Durell, who previously worked on 'Beautiful Trauma,' sees her skating and causing havoc in a grocery store.

A teaser campaign was launched for the song, allowing fans in the USA to call a telephone number to find out more about P!nk's mock product line, 'Vicious Bitches Chips'es,' humorously described as a 'spicy AF' alternative to 'basic bitch chips.' Upon calling the number, fans heard a clip of 'Never Gonna Not Dance Again.'

'Runaway'

Written by Edvard Førre Erfjord and Clementine Douglas
Produced by Greg Kurstin
Recorded at No Expectations Studios, Hollywood
Duration: 2:42
Released as a single in July 2023
Music video directed by Brad Comfort

'Runaway' shares its title with the *I'm Not Dead* album track. Edvard Førre Erfjord, who worked on UK #1 singles 'Shout Out to My Ex' and 'Black Magic' for British girl group Little Mix, wrote 'Runaway' with singer-songwriter, Clementine Douglas; the song was produced by Greg Kurstin.

Douglas shared on Instagram: 'Me and Edvard met over Zoom last year and wrote this song. We loved it and felt it was special, such an honour to have it on P!nk's album.'

An official lyric video premiered on 7 June 2023, featuring archival footage of Cher, Jamie Lee Curtis, Jane Fonda and the USA National Aerobic Champions, directed by Brad Comfort. 'Runaway' was released to German radio as the third single from *Trustfall* the following month but did not chart in the top 100.

'Last Call'

Written by Billy Mann, Alecia 'P!nk' Moore and Pete Wallace
Produced by Billy Mann
Co-Produced by Pete Wallace
Recorded at Earthstar Creation Center, California; Turtle Sound Studios, Weston; Pen to Platinum Studios; Justin Derrico Studios & Aaron Sterling Studios
Duration: 4:04

'Last Call' is a country-inspired 'campfire song,' serving as a poignant reminder to seize the moment and not miss opportunities to make amends. The song, a collaboration with Billy Mann, was one of the first written for the album, alongside 'Never Gonna Not Dance Again.'

Posting on Twitter about 'Last Call,' Mann wrote: 'I love this song and I have a few other favourites on this album, too! If you play guitar, it's an easy one to learn - 4 chords. P!nk can do it.'

'Hate Me'

Written by Greg Kurstin and Alecia 'P!nk' Moore
Produced by Greg Kurstin
Recorded at No Expectations Studios, Hollywood
Duration: 3:20

'Hate Me' sees P!nk addressing her experience of being portrayed as a villain while refusing to let the other party adopt the role of passive victim. In interviews to promote *Trustfall*, P!nk explained that she wrote from the perspective of all women villainised by society, triggered by an argument she had with her husband, Carey Heart.

In an interview with *USA Today*, she said: 'It was a bad one. "Hate Me" is sort of the female experience to me. This will be a polarising statement, but men tend to villainise women, and it's usually the women who take care of them and take most of their shit. I felt, in a way, my father did that to me, and my husband does that to me sometimes, and I will not stand for it. I will not be the villain in your story. You will not be a victim around me. You will take accountability for your life and your choices and I will take accountability for mine. Can you tell I feel things really deeply? Can you imagine being my husband? That night I played him the song. We weren't even speaking, and he giggled and said, "You're welcome." I tried to write what it feels like to be the woman in the equation. Whether that's how society treats us or villainises us, whether it's our boss, father, or husband, it's infuriating. I'm tired of being the villain.'

'Lost Cause'

Written by Stephen Wrabel, Sam de Jong and Sam Romans
Produced by Sam de Jong
Recorded at P!nk's Studio, Santa Barbara
Duration: 3:28

'Lost Cause' is a reflective ballad about feeling disconnected in a relationship, co-written and produced by Sam de Jong. One of the first songs picked for the album, P!nk said it resonated deeply with her, explaining that the lyrics reflected a conversation she once had with her husband, Carey Hart.

In an interview with *Billboard* magazine, she said: 'Carey came to me a long time ago - at a good moment, when we weren't arguing - and said, "Hey, when we argue and you say really mean things, it hurts me and I really need you to stop." I was blown away… like, "Whoa, what a beautiful thing to do, Carey, to bring that up at a time where everything's going well." Time moves on and you both get mean after a while, and the world is mean. And I'm like, "You can call me a loser, but just don't tell me I'm unredeemable." Everybody is redeemable. Unless they're gone - unless they're in the dirt. I don't believe old dogs can't learn new tricks.'

'Feel Something'

Written by Teddy Geiger, Ian Franzino, Jason Evigan and Nate Mercereau
Produced by Teddy Geiger, Afterhrs (Ian Franzino and Andrew Haas), Jason Evigan and Nate Mercereau
Recorded at P!nk's Studio, Santa Barbara
Duration: 3:04

'Feel Something' is a slow, introspective ballad about taking risks in love to feel alive, with P!nk singing, 'I gave my heart to the wolves, and they tore it open, I did it again and again and again, and I got nothing, but I'll do it again and again and again till I feel something.'

The song was written and produced by Teddy Geiger, who worked on 'Hurts 2B Human,' with Afterhrs, who worked extensively with One Direction. Jason Evigan, who has written for Maroon 5, Dua Lipa and Kelly Clarkson, also worked on the song with multi-instrumentalist, Nate Mercereau.

'Our Song'

Written by Jesse Shatkin, Jessica 'HARLOE' Karpov and Maureen 'Mozella' McDonald
Produced by Jesse Shatkin and Jessica 'HARLOE' Karpov
Recorded at The Ribcage, Los Angeles and Santa Ynez Studio, Santa Ynez
Duration: 2:54

'Our Song' was given to P!nk by Jesse Shatkin during the sessions where they recorded 'Long Way to Go.' The song started life as a piano melody written by HARLOE, with additional work from Shatkin and another of his collaborators, Mozella, who had co-written 'Cover Me in Sunshine.'

On Instagram, HARLOE wrote: 'A true bucket list moment! Co-wrote and co-produced "Our Song" for P!nk. So much gratitude and love for this journey.'

In February 2024, during her first *Summer Carnival* date in Sydney, Australia, an audience member went into labour during P!nk's performance of 'Our Song,' causing her to pause the show. P!nk said: 'Someone's having a baby! Is it Alecia or Alex being born? I feel like we all shouldn't be looking. Everyone give her privacy! She didn't just have the baby, right? Is the baby here? No? Okay! Congratulations! Wow! "Our Song," that was the one that did it! I wouldn't have called that one, I thought it would have been like "Get the Party Started" or "Never Gonna Not Dance Again," that's so exciting! Good luck, you're going to do great. This music should not be your rolling out song!'

'Just Say I'm Sorry' featuring Chris Stapleton

Written by Chris Stapleton and Alecia 'P!nk' Moore
Produced by Greg Kurstin
Recorded at No Expectations Studios, Hollywood
Duration: 3:33
Chris Stapleton appears courtesy of Sound Records/Mercury Records Nashville

'Just Say I'm Sorry' was written with Chris Stapleton, who duetted with P!nk on 'Love Me Anyway,' taken from 2019's *Hurts 2B Human*.

Talking with radio presenters Maxwell Jones and Crystal Rosas on Z100 New York, P!nk said: '"Just Say I'm Sorry" is a poem I wrote for Carey. And I read him the poem, and five minutes later Chris and I had a song. I was like, "You know you have to sing with me, right?" He was like, "Oh, are you sure you want me to?" I'm like, "Dude, yeah. Yes." And the third line... I would have never written the third line. It was his. It's, "Just say I'm sorry... it's not the hardest thing to do." But it feels like it, although I believe in the power of an authentic apology. And it's the three R's, for me - it's regret, remorse, and resolution. People think apologising is giving your power away. It's actually taking it back because you're saying, "I'm not afraid to be vulnerable in front of you. That's how strong I am." I will apologise. I apologise to my kids every day. I apologise to my employees. I apologise when I'm wrong. I'll apologise when I'm not. But man, it's so hard for some people to say, "I'm sorry." The closest "I'm sorry" I ever got from my dad was, "I'm sorry you're so sensitive." And I was like, "Dude, that's generational. That's not an apology. That's not it, Dad. You gotta do better."'

Tour Edition Bonus Tracks

'Dreaming' P!nk, Marshmello and Sting

Written by Christopher 'Marshmello' Comstock, Nick 'Digital Farm Animals' Gale, Gordon 'Sting' Sumner,
Produced by Christopher 'Marshmello' Comstock and Nick 'Digital Farm Animals' Gale
Contains a portion of 'Fields of Gold' written by Sting
Duration: 2:50
Released as a single in October 2023
Chart Position: Canada: 64; UK: 99; Germany: 93

Whilst on the *Summer Carnival* tour, P!nk continued recording new music and reunited with Marshmello, following their work on 'Broken and Beautiful,' to collaborate on a song he was working on with Sting. 'Dreaming' is an uplifting, house-influenced track that samples Sting's 1993 single 'Fields of Gold,' featuring vocals from both P!nk and Sting.

On Instagram, Sting confirmed that 'Dreaming' was Marshmello's idea, saying: 'I always like it when a different mind takes one of my songs and adds something of their own to it. I never feel that possessive. I'm always interested to know where it can go.'

On bringing P!nk and Sting together on the song, Marshmello said: 'This is the most unexpected collaboration any of us ever thought, or maybe the world, might think.'

P!nk added: 'It's beautifully random - different people from different places coming together to make music. Music makes my heart happy. To meld all of the worlds… it's fun. You can take something and make it new again.'

In a press release, P!nk's record label confirmed that 'Dreaming' would be the first of two new singles to feature on a special tour deluxe edition of *Trustfall*, alongside live recordings of six songs from the *Summer Carnival* tour.

'Dreaming' charted in the top 100 in the UK and Germany based on download sales, and reached #9 on the USA Billboard Dance/Electronic Songs chart.

'Irrelevant'

Written by Ian Fitchuk and Alecia 'P!nk' Moore
Produced by Ian Fitchuk
Recorded at P!nk's Studio, Santa Barbara
Duration: 3:52
Released as a single in July 2022
Music video directed by P!nk and Brad Comfort
Chart Position: Australia: 73

On 24 June 2022, the Supreme Court overturned Roe v. Wade, effectively allowing abortion bans across the USA. P!nk commented on Twitter: 'Let's be clear: if you believe the government belongs in a woman's uterus, a gay person's business or marriage, or that racism is okay – then please in the name of your Lord, never fucking listen to my music again. And also fuck right off. We good?'

Following her comment, she received angry messages from right-wing and anti-abortion trolls. Less than a month later, she shared: 'Woke up. Got heated. Wrote song. Coming soon.'

The next day, she released 'Irrelevant,' her first collaboration with songwriter and producer Ian Fitchuk, who had worked with Kacey Musgraves on her album *Golden Hour*.

In a press release for the song, P!nk said: 'As a woman with an opinion and the fearlessness to voice that opinion, it gets very tiring when the only retort is to tell me how irrelevant I am. I am relevant because I exist and because I am a human being. No one is irrelevant. And no one can take away my voice.'

A few days after the song's release, a music video directed by P!nk and Brad Comfort premiered on YouTube. The video features images of past civil rights movements alongside present-day marches for #MeToo, Black Lives Matter, climate justice, LGBTQIA+ equality and reproductive rights. It also includes images of controversial politicians, including Rudy Giuliani, Donald Trump and the Supreme Court Justices who voted to overturn Roe v. Wade.

All proceeds from the song were donated to When We All Vote, Michelle Obama's nonpartisan voting initiative.

The song was included on the *Trustfall* special tour deluxe edition.

'All Out of Fight'

Written by Fred 'Again' Gibson, Johnny McDaid and Alecia 'P!nk' Moore
Produced by Fred 'Again' Gibson and Johnny McDaid
Recorded at Fieldwork Studio, London, UK and Fieldwork Studio, Los Angeles
Duration: 3:32
Released as a single in December 2023
Music video directed by David Spearing

'All Out of Fight' is another collaboration between P!nk, Fred Again and Johnny McDaid. It was released on the special tour deluxe edition of *Trustfall* in December 2023 and was sent to radio in certain countries to promote the release. The song's lyrics explore the complexities of a relationship ending, reflecting on making peace with saying goodbye as exhaustion sets in.

A story-based music video for the song, directed by David Spearing, was released simultaneously, starring Drew Lipson and Cailyn Rice. They play a couple experiencing milestones, such as moving in together, before one of them falls ill with cancer. Despite their struggles, they continue to fight, demonstrating their love for one another through acts of kindness.

In the UK, 'All Out of Fight' charted at #23 on the Singles Sales chart in December 2023 and reached #17 on the Singles Downloads chart.

Other Songs

'One Too Many'—Keith Urban with P!nk

Written by Mich 'Cutfather' Hansen, PhD (Peter Wallevik and David Davidsen), James 'Boy Matthews' Norton and Cleo Tighe
Produced by Keith Urban, and Mich 'Cutfather' Hansen and PhD (Peter Wallevik and David Davidsen)
Additional Production by Dan McCarroll

Recorded at Henson Recording Studios, Los Angeles and P!nk's Studio, Santa Barbara
Duration: 3:25
Released as a single in September 2020
Music video directed by Dano Cerny
Chart Position: USA: 52; Canada: 22; UK: 40; Australia: 6

'One Too Many' was written by Danish-Norwegian songwriters Cutfather and PhD, alongside British songwriters Boy Matthews and Cleo Tighe. Australian country singer Keith Urban chose it for inclusion on his eleventh studio album *The Speed of Now Part 1*, released on 18 September 2020.

Talking about the song to *Billboard* magazine, he said: 'My co-executive producer Dan McCarroll sent the song to me, and I loved it 100%, top to bottom. It was written as a duet. P!nk is just someone I've always loved. I've always loved her voice. She's so diverse in her abilities to tell a story. That's really what she's great at. She's blessed with one of the greatest voices. She's a singer's singer. And I just thought, "Man, I wonder if she would love this song?" and sent it to her and she hit me back. And it was on. She had to record her vocals remotely in California. And that wasn't an unusual thing... the unusual thing was then shooting a video remotely and piecing all that together, that was a bit more challenging.'

P!nk confirmed in an interview with the *Wall Street Journal* in 2021 that she recorded the vocals herself at home, a skill she learned during the pandemic. She said: 'I learned how to use GarageBand and record myself. For a 40-year-old girl to learn how to be alone and record for the first time in her life, even though it was just GarageBand, it was a huge accomplishment for me because I'm usually at the whim of engineers and producers. To be able to do it on my own - I did the Keith Urban duet that we did, I recorded "Cover Me in Sunshine," I recorded "All I Know So Far," recorded the Rag'n'Bone Man single and all these other things. It just felt so empowering and liberating.'

'One Too Many' became the sixth single from the album, released on 16 September 2020. That same day, a live performance of the song aired during the 55th Academy of Country Music awards, with P!nk pre-recording her part in what became known as their 'Two Room Duet.' On the album's release date, Urban performed the song for Amazon's *The Speed of Now Part 1* showcase, featuring P!nk on video behind him. Footage filmed for this performance was reused in December when he performed the song on the finale of *The Voice*.

The music video for the song was also filmed remotely. Directed by Dano Cerny, it also premiered on 18 September, featuring Urban using a sofa as a life raft as he floats, while P!nk is shown sitting alone on a beach. 'One Too Many' was a commercial success, reaching #6 in Australia, where it was certified 4x Platinum, and reached #10 on the USA Country Airplay and Hot Country Songs charts.

'Anywhere Away from Here'—Rag'n'Bone Man and P!nk

Written by Rory 'Rag'n'Bone Man' Graham, Ben Jackson-Cook, Mark Crew, Dan Priddy and Simon Aldred
Produced by Mike Elizondo
Co-Produced by Rory 'Rag'n'Bone Man' Graham and Ben Jackson-Cook
Recorded at Phantom Studios, Gallatin and P!nk's Studio, Santa Barbara
Duration: 3:58 (Radio Edit – 3:42)
Released as a single in April 2021
Music video directed by Joe Connor and Tim Mattia
Chart Position: Canada: 88; UK: 9; Australia: 43

P!nk initially heard 'Human,' the first single from British singer Rag'n'Bone Man's major label album of the same name, while visiting the UK in 2017. Expressing her love for him, P!nk was invited to record vocals for a duet version of 'Anywhere Away from Here,' which he wrote and recorded for his second album, *Life by Misadventure,* in 2021. His solo version features on early vinyl pressings of the album instead of the duet.

In a press release, P!nk said: 'I had already fallen in love with his voice, and when we met in person I quickly learned he has a beautiful soul, too. Since then, I knew I wanted to work with him one day. "Anywhere Away from Here" couldn't be a better song for us to sing together. I'm so honoured to be a part of this collaboration.'

Rag'n'Bone Man added: 'This song is an honest reflection of wanting to disappear from uncomfortable situations - about the vulnerabilities that we all face. It's an honour to have P!nk on this record and I'm so glad she is able to be a part of it.'

The duo shot a music video for the song in early 2021, with UK scenes directed by Joe Connor and Tim Mattia directing P!nk in the USA. Rag'n'Bone Man's scenes were filmed at the Duke of York's Theatre in London, which remained closed to the public until October 2021 due to the COVID-19 pandemic. In the video, the theatre becomes overgrown with cornfields as animals take to the stage.

The song was released as a single in April 2021, ahead of the album's May release. At the BRIT Awards in May 2021, Rag'n'Bone Man performed the song with the Lewisham and Greenwich NHS Choir while P!nk's recording from the music video played on screen behind them. This special version of the song was released to raise money for the UK National Health Service Charities Together fund, helping it reach the official UK top 10.

Prior to the performance P!nk, who was unable to visit the UK due to COVID-19, told Hits Radio: 'I love Rory so much. I was so happy he asked me to sing with him, I would do anything he wanted, I love him to pieces. And I love our song.'

During her *Summer Carnival* date at the Aviva Stadium in Dublin, Ireland, in June 2024, Rag'n'Bone Man joined P!nk on stage to perform the song.

'(I Can't Get No) Satisfaction'—Dolly Parton featuring P!nk and Brandi Carlile

Written by Mick Jagger and Keith Richards
Produced by Kent Wells
Recorded at Kent Wells Productions, Nashville; Sound Stage Studios, Nashville; Soundstruck Studios, Nashville; No Expectations Studios, Los Angeles (P!nk) and Northern Lights, Maple Valley (Brandi Carlile)
Duration: 3:58

After being invited to join the Rock and Roll Hall of Fame in 2022, Dolly Parton initially declined, saying that she was a country singer, not a 'rock star.' Deciding to change that to live up to the honour, she began recording an album of rock covers with some of her favourite performers. Both P!nk and Brandi Carlile join Dolly on her cover of the classic Rolling Stones song, '(I Can't Get No) Satisfaction,' on the aptly titled album *Rockstar*.

Originally written and recorded in 1965, the song became the fourth UK #1 for the Rolling Stones and is often considered one of the world's greatest songs of all time. Dolly told *Billboard* that she originally wanted Mick Jagger to join her on the song, saying: 'I love the Rolling Stones. I've always wanted to do the song "Satisfaction." That's one of my husband's favourite songs.'

When their schedules couldn't align for the album's deadline, Dolly added: 'I thought, "Well, if you're not going to sing that with me, I'm going to get some girl power going here!"'

Unreleased Songs

'Still Alive'

A 10-second clip of the country-influenced 'Still Alive' leaked online in October 2023, alongside snippets of two other songs from the *Trustfall* sessions. Included was a clip of 'All Out of Fight,' which was officially released on the tour deluxe edition of the album in December.

In the clip, P!nk sings: 'And your head feels inside out, when your lungs won't hold all the air that you need, that's how you know you're still alive.'

'Choose You'

A 10-second clip of ballad 'Choose You' leaked online in October 2023, featuring P!nk singing: 'Cause it's just what you do with love, no one's ever held me like you, love, and even when we're breaking in two.'

Live Performances

'The Pretender' with Foo Fighters

Written by Dave Grohl, Taylor Hawkins, Nate Mendel and Chris Shiflett
Duration: 5:20

In March 2022, Foo Fighters band member Taylor Hawkins died just hours before he was due on stage with the group in Bogotá, Colombia, having complained of chest pains. In June, Hawkins' family and the rest of Foo Fighters announced there would be two tribute shows in his memory, one at Wembley Stadium in London and one at the Kia Forum in Inglewood, California.

In addition to having played on P!nk's song, 'We Could Have It All' from *Hurts 2B Human*, P!nk said Foo Fighters, including Hawkins and his bandmate, Dave Grohl, always supported her career. She said: 'Taylor was the sweetest. He was just a soulful, loving, supportive man. Him and Dave were always so supportive to me in live settings where other bands were like, "What the fuck is she doing here?" I loved him, I loved that man.'

Grohl invited P!nk to join the line-up at the California concert, which took place on 27 September 2022. Introducing her to the stage, he said, 'This is the part where all of Taylor's good friends come up and play.' She joined the rest of Foo Fighters to perform 'The Pretender' from their 2007 album, *Echoes, Silence, Patience & Grace*.

'Barracuda' with Nancy Wilson from Heart

Written by Ann Wilson, Nancy Wilson, Roger Fisher and Michael Derosier
Duration: 4:38

American rock band Heart, led by sisters Ann and Nancy Wilson, released 'Barracuda' in 1977 from their third album, *Little Queen*. The song was inspired by a cover of Joni Mitchell's 'This Flight Tonight' by Scottish band Nazareth, with whom the group were touring in Europe.

Guitarist and co-vocalist, Nancy Wilson, became friends with Taylor Hawkins, and had asked him to play drums on her 2021 solo album, *You and Me*. Dave Grohl introduced Wilson as 'a rock hero to all of us, also from Seattle' at the Taylor Hawkins tribute concert in California, before adding, 'Who can sing a Heart song? P!nk!' The duo went on to perform 'Barracuda' live together.

'Somebody to Love'

Written by Freddie Mercury
Duration: 5:58

'Somebody to Love' was written by Queen's Freddie Mercury and released on the band's 1976 album, *A Day at the Races*. The song was one of the only tracks

Taylor Hawkins stepped out from behind the drums to sing during a Foo Fighters show, including at some of the last concerts he performed with the group.

Queen's Brian May and Roger Taylor performed the song at both tribute concerts to Hawkins, with P!nk joining them on vocals at the California show, stepping in at the last minute to fill in for another artist who had COVID-19.

'Hopelessly Devoted to You'

Written by John Farrar
Duration: 3:30

P!nk performed a cover of the ballad 'Hopelessly Devoted to You' at the American Music Awards in November 2022. The song, from the movie *Grease*, was chosen to honour Olivia Newton-John, who starred in the film and sadly passed away in August of that year.

In an Instagram post, following her death, P!nk said: 'I met her maybe three times - and she was an absolute angel. One of the loveliest, kindest, lights from within a human being I have ever met. Kindness personified. May she Rest in Peace and may her family be held in love and light during this difficult time.'

She added to ABC: 'I had the pleasure of being around her several times, and she was as darling as you would imagine. She was such an icon, and it's a really big honour to be able to sing her music.'

'Make You Feel My Love'

Written by Bob Dylan
Duration: 2:40

'Make You Feel My Love' was written by Bob Dylan and released as the lead single from Billy Joel's third greatest hits album in August 1997, reaching #50 on the USA Billboard Hot 100. Dylan's recording followed a few months later, appearing on his thirtieth studio album, *Time Out of Mind*, with a further recording by Garth Brooks charting in 1998, appearing on the soundtrack to the movie, *Hope Floats*.

However, the song's commercial peak came from British singer Adele, who released the song as the fourth single from debut album, *19*, in October 2008. During the 2020 COVID-19 quarantine, P!nk taught herself how to play 'Make You Feel My Love' on piano, premiering a performance on Instagram. She added her cover to select dates of the *Summer Carnival* world tour, telling *60 Minutes* in 2023: 'I can play halves of songs. One of my favourite songs is "Make You Feel My Love" and I played this every day during COVID. I played it every day until I was good enough to go on stage and play an instrument.'

'Nothing Compares 2 U'

Written by Prince Rogers Nelson

BBC Radio 2's *Piano Room – P!nk Live*
P!nk featuring the BBC Concert Orchestra
Arranged by Stevie Blacke
Duration: 4:42

Trustfall – Tour Deluxe Edition (2023) Live
P!nk with Brandi Carlile
Arranged by Paul Mirkovich
Duration: 5:05

P!nk chose 'Nothing Compares 2 U,' written by the late Prince and made famous by Irish singer, songwriter and activist, Sinéad O'Connor, as her cover of choice for her November 2023 BBC Radio 2 Piano Room special, where she was accompanied by the BBC Concert Orchestra.

Sinéad O'Connor passed away on 26 July 2024. When P!nk opened her USA Summer Carnival tour days later, she asked Brandi Carlile, one of her support acts, to join her to perform the song in tribute.

Introducing the song, P!nk told the audience: 'When I was a little girl, my mom grew up in Atlantic City and I used to go down to the Ocean City Boardwalk with my ten dollars and I would make a demo tape... I would make a little cassette tape and imagine it was my demo for the record company. And it would always be either "Greatest Love of All" by Whitney Houston or "Nothing Compares 2 U" by Sinéad O'Connor. So, in honour of Sinéad, and in honour of my very, very talented friend Brandi Carlile, I asked her if she would come out here and sing this song with me.'

An official recording of P!nk's live performance with Carlile appears on the *Trustfall* Tour Deluxe Edition.

'Heartbreaker'

Written by Geoff Gill and Cliff Wade
Duration: 5:30 ('Just Like Fire'/'Heartbreaker' Medley)

'Heartbreaker' was the second single from American rock star Pat Benatar's debut album, *In the Heat of the Night*, released in October 1979. Not to be confused with P!nk's song of the same name (which was a B-side to her 2006 single 'Stupid Girls') a cover of Benatar's classic was included as part of a medley with 'Just Like Fire' on the 2003 *Summer Carnival* tour.

Pat Benatar and her husband, Neil Giraldo, who were supporting P!nk during the USA leg of the tour, joined her on stage to perform the song together at the SoFi Stadium, Inglewood, California, on 5 October 2023.

An official live recording of the 'Just Like Fire'/ 'Heartbreaker' medley appears on the *Trustfall* Tour Deluxe Edition.

'You Oughta Know'

Written by Alanis Morissette and Glen Ballard
Duration: 3:30

'You Oughta Know' was the lead single from Alanis Morisette's iconic 1995 album, *Jagged Little Pill*, which inspired a generation of female singer-songwriters, including P!nk. At *ELLE* magazine's 6th Annual Women in Music Celebration in May 2015, P!nk told *E! News* that she was there to see Alanis perform, as she is a huge fan, adding: '*Jagged Little Pill* is one of the best albums ever made in my opinion.'

Alanis Morissette joined P!nk on stage on 5 October 2023 to perform a duet version of 'You Oughta Know' during P!nk's *Summer Carnival* tour at the SoFi Stadium, Inglewood, California. After the song, they hugged as P!nk said: 'I love you so much it hurts... This woman changed everything. She changed everything.'

'When I Fall in Love'

Written by Victor Young and Edward Heyman
Duration: 5:00

'When I Fall in Love' was written in early 1952, with a recording by Doris Day reaching #20 on the USA Billboard Top 200 that summer, and a 1956 cover by Nat King Cole peaking at #2 on the UK singles chart.

In July 2025, after having dinner with her mother, Judy, at the Amore Restaurant in Sarasota, Florida, P!nk asked if she could perform an impromptu set. Accompanied by the restaurant's in-house pianist, Eddie Tobin, she sang a cover of 'When I Fall in Love', telling diners that it made her mother happy. She later took over the piano herself to serenade the audience with her version of 'Make You Feel My Love'.

'Hopeless War' featuring Willow Sage Hart

Written by Jonathan Clay, Zach Chance and Justin Levine
Duration: 2:18

Days after dispelling rumours that she had separated from her husband, P!nk stepped in as the special guest host of *The Kelly Clarkson Show* in March 2026, launching its Women's History Month celebrations. Two planned shows in Mexico, which had been due to take place in April 2026, were cancelled due to 'logistical issues', prompting P!nk also to deny rumours that she would take over the show permanently, following Clarkson's previous announcement that this would be her final season.

Opening the show with her own version of *Kellyoke*, P!nk performed a cover version of a song at the start of each episode. Monday's Broadway special featured a duet with her daughter, Willow Sage Hart, who joined her on 'Hopeless War' from the coming-of-age musical *The Outsiders*. Discussing the choice, P!nk explained that she had relocated her family to New York to give Willow more opportunities to see and study theatre, adding that they had recently seen *The Outsiders* together.

'Let Me Believe' with Shoshana Bean

Written by Shoshana Bean, Melissa Fuller and Chris Gelbuda
Duration: 2:45

Broadway actress Shoshana Bean appeared as one of the guests on P!nk's first episode hosting *The Kelly Clarkson Show*, where she promoted her solo album *Only Smoke*. P!nk joined Bean for a duet of 'Let Me Believe', a song Bean wrote in Nashville about the end of her relationship.

'lighthouse'

Written by Kelly Clarkson, Jesse Shatkin and Aben Eubanks
Duration: 2:22

For her second episode as guest host of *The Kelly Clarkson Show*, P!nk paid homage to her friend, covering 'lighthouse' from Kelly's tenth studio album *chemistry*. Released in 2023, Clarkson wrote 'lighthouse' about her divorce from Brandon Blackstock, who died in August 2025, having described it as 'the saddest song I've ever written'.

P!nk said: 'It is such a powerful song, it is also an insane song to cover. I don't think people should cover Kelly Clarkson, but the brave few try!'

'Die on this Hill'

Written by Sienna Spiro, Omer Fedi and Michael Pollack
Duration: 1:51

P!nk chose two songs she had already covered for her third and fifth days hosting *The Kelly Clarkson Show*, performing 'River' by Bishop Briggs and 'Time After Time' by Cyndi Lauper. For her fourth episode, she performed British singer-songwriter Sienna Spiro's 2025 single 'Die on This Hill'. She told viewers that Spiro discovered the chords to the song while learning Queen's 'Bohemian Rhapsody', adding, 'which is why we love it'.

Epilogue

Despite having released three successful albums since 2013—*Beautiful Trauma*, *Hurts 2B Human* and *Trustfall*—P!nk has long made it clear that her priority is to be a legendary touring performer rather than someone who is chasing hit singles. Although 'Trustfall' was undoubtedly a radio hit internationally, stations in the USA were more reluctant to add it to playlists, leading to 'Runaway,' the third single from *Trustfall*, only being released in select territories.

However, as of November 2024, P!nk's *Summer Carnival* tour had been seen by more than 4.8 million people worldwide, becoming the seventh highest-grossing tour by a female artist in history and her biggest tour to date.

In 2013, despite having a recent radio hit with 'Just Give Me a Reason,' she told *Billboard* magazine: 'I keep my head to the dirt and I just fucking pound the pavement. And I'm in a stable of show horses, of prized ponies, and I learn from the best. You can't compare anybody to the Tina Turners and the Chers and the Sades and the Janet Jacksons - yet. And to me, they're touring artists, they're lifelong legendary touring artists. Bette Midler. These are my gods. I'm not after having a radio hit, I'm after making people cry in concert.'

She added that Roger Davies, who helped resurrect Tina Turner's career and turned her into a legendary touring act, is responsible for helping her. She said: 'He saw something in me for whatever reason, and I was willing to do the work. It's sort of like paint by numbers with him - if you do this, this, this, this and that, then you'll become a touring artist. It's what has kept me around, being a touring artist, for sure. So, while I come up with who I am and what I want to say, and live my life, he has helped me figure out how to turn that into something that's - I don't want to say lucrative. Something that's successful, that is a formula that works.'

Following the resurgence of Las Vegas as a venue for more current acts to host residencies—which started with Britney Spears in December 2013 and has gone on to include the likes of Mariah Carey, Christina Aguilera, Jennifer Lopez,

Kelly Clarkson, Janet Jackson, Shania Twain and Adele—P!nk has expressed her desire to have one too. She said: 'I would like to have the best show that Vegas has ever seen, and I think that I can. For a performer like me, to have a stage that doesn't have to travel... you can do so much!'

After taking a break from touring in 2025 and revealing on Instagram that it had been a difficult year, which ended with her undergoing neck surgery, 2026 got off to a better start when P!nk was nominated for the Rock and Roll Hall of Fame, in her first year eligible. She said: 'I never ever fit neatly into a box. That was kind of the whole point. This nomination isn't mine; it's ours. It's for every one of us who ever felt like an outsider or underdog and found something in this music that made them feel less alone.'

With P!nk's passion for songwriting and a second album from You+Me completed but currently unreleased, there is no doubt that she will continue to grow her legacy. After all, she told *60 Minutes* in 2023: 'When they say a woman has to slow down, become smaller, take up less space, calm down... no, absolutely not. Who says? Why can't we ride it until the wheels fall off? That's what I plan on doing!'

APPENDIX

Tours

No Strings Attached Tour

*NSync with support from P!nk
9 May 2000–1 August 2000
USA—51 Dates

Setlist
'Most Girls'
'Split Personality'
'Stop Falling'
'You Make Me Sick'
'There You Go'

The Party Tour

2 May 2002–18 December 2002
USA and Canada—36 Dates
UK and Europe—5 Dates
Japan—3 Dates
Australia and New Zealand—11 Dates

Band
Jason Chapman, Cassandra O'Neal, Mylious Johnson, Rafael Moriera, Janis Tanaka, Cassandra O'Neal and Janis Tanaka

Setlist
'Get the Party Started'
'M!ssundaztood'
'18 Wheeler'
'What's Up?'
'Dear Diary'
'Respect'
'I Love You'/ 'You're All I Need to Get By'
'Janie's Got a Gun'
'You Make Me Sick'
'Just Like a Pill'
'Lonely Girl'
'Numb'
'Summertime'/ 'Piece of My Heart'/ 'Me and Bobby McGee'
'Family Portrait'
'My Vietnam'
'Eventually'
'There You Go'
'Don't Let Me Get Me'

Support Acts
Candy Ass, The Kennedy Soundtrack, Lucky 7

Try This Tour
19 February 2004–5 May 2004
UK and Europe—32 Dates
Australia—11 Dates

26 June 2004–22 August 2004 (Summer Tour)
UK and Europe—31 Dates, including festivals

Band
Jason Chapman, Adriana Balic, Mylious Johnsonn, Rafael Moriera, Leah Rose Randi and Brandee Adams

Dancers
Lindsey Blaufarb, Kemba Shannon and Addie Yungmee

Setlist
'Can't Take Me Home'
'There You Go'
'Split Personality'
'Most Girls'
'Lady Marmalade'
'I Wanna Rock'
'Don't Let Me Get Me'
'18 Wheeler'
'Family Portrait'
'Just like a Pill'
'Respect'
'My Vietnam'/ 'Misery'/ 'Eventually'
'Summertime'/ 'Me and Bobby McGee'/ 'Piece of My Heart'
'Feel Good Time'
'God Is a DJ'
'Oh My God'
'Trouble'
'Last to Know'
'Try Too Hard'
'Unwind'
'Welcome to the Jungle'
'Get the Party Started'

Setlist (Summer Tour)
'Don't Let Me Get Me'
'Trouble'
'What's Up'
'Respect'
'Save My Life'
'Last to Know'
'Eventually'
Medley: 'Summertime'/ 'Me and Bobby McGee'/ 'Piece of My Heart'
'There You Go'
'Just like a Pill'
'Try Too Hard'
'Unwind'
'Family Portrait'
'18 Wheeler'
'Misery'
'Numb'
'Get the Party Started'

I'm Not Dead Tour

17 June 2006–29 July 2006 (Club Tour)
USA and Canada—18 Dates

8 September 2006–10 June 2007
UK and Europe—32 Dates
Australia and New Zealand—11 Dates

8 January 2007–29 March 2007 (Supporting Justin Timberlake)
USA and Canada—37 Dates

23 June 2007–11 September 2007 (Summer Tour)
UK and Europe—31 Dates, including festivals
United Arab Emirates—1 Date
Africa—3 Dates

Band
Jason Chapman, Mark Schulman, Justin Derrico, Adriana Balic, Janis Tanaka, Stacy Campbell and Jenny Douglas-Foote

Dancers
Clare Turton, Ruth Inchaustegui-Prince and Reina Hidalgo

Setlist (Club Tour)
''Cuz I Can'
'Trouble'
'Just Like a Pill'
'Stupid Girls'
'Who Knew'
'Family Portrait'
'18 Wheeler'
'Lonely Girl'
'I'm Not Dead'
'Don't Let Me Get Me'
'There You Go'
'What's Up?'
'Leave Me Alone'
'The One That Got Away'
'Dear Mr. President'
'Get the Party Started'

Setlist
''Cuz I Can'
'Trouble'
'Just Like a Pill'
'Who Knew'
'I'm Not Dead'
'Lady Marmalade'
'Stupid Girls'
'There You Go'
'God Is A DJ'
'Fingers'
'Family Portrait'
'Redemption Song'
'The One That Got Away'
'Dear Mr. President'
'What's Up?'
'U + Ur Hand'
'18 Wheeler'
'Don't Let Me Get Me'
'Leave Me Alone'
'Nobody Knows'
'Get the Party Started'

Support Acts
Marion Raven, Gary 'Mudbone' Cooper, Nadirah X, Infernal, The Androids, Lili, Sorgente, Lââm, Kamera, Vanilla Ninja and Matt Nathanson

Setlist (Supporting Justin Timberlake)
''Cuz I Can'
'Trouble'
'Just Like A Pill'
'Who Knew'
'Stupid Girls'
'Family Portrait'
'Dear Mr. President'
'U + Ur Hand'
'Don't Let Me Get Me'
'Leave Me Alone (I'm Lonely)'
'Get the Party Started'

Setlist (Summer Tour)
''Cuz I Can'
'Trouble'
'Just like a Pill'
'Who Knew'
'Stupid Girls'
'I'm Not Dead'
'Family Portrait'
'My Vietnam'
'Last to Know'
'Try Too Hard'
'Me and Bobby McGee'/ 'Mercedes Benz'/ 'Piece of My Heart'
'Lonely Girl'
'Don't Let Me Get Me'
'18 Wheeler'
'Dear Mr. President'
'What's Up'
'Leave Me Alone (I'm Lonely)'
'U + Ur Hand'
'Get the Party Started'

Funhouse Tour

24 February 2009–20 December 2009
UK and Europe—41 Dates
Australia and New Zealand—58 Dates
USA and Canada—12 Dates
UK and Europe—40 Dates

Director and Executive Producer
Baz Halpin

Band
Paul Mirkovich, Mark Schulman, Justin Derrico, Eva Gardner, Kat Lucas, Jessy Greene, Stacy Campbell and Jenny Douglas-Foote

Dancers
Alison Faulk, Leo Moctezuma, Reina Hidalgo, Nikki Tuazon, Addie Yungmee, Sebastien Stella and Dreya Weber

Setlist
'Bad Influence'
'Just Like a Pill'
'Who Knew'
'Don't Let Me Get Me'
'I Touch Myself'
'Please Don't Leave Me'
'U + Ur Hand'
'Leave Me Alone (I'm Lonely)'
'So What'
'Family Portrait'
'I Don't Believe You'
'Dear Mr President'
'Trouble'
'Babe I'm Gonna Leave You'
'Sober'
'Bohemian Rhapsody'
'Funhouse'
'Crazy'
'Get the Party Started'
'Glitter in the Air'

Funhouse Summer Carnival Tour

29 May 2010–25 July 2010
UK and Europe—34 Dates, including festivals

Band
Jason Chapman, Mark Schulman, Justin Derrico, Eva Gardner, Kat Lucas, Stacy Campbell and Jenny Douglas-Foote

Dancers
Nikki Tuazon and Addie Yungmee

Setlist
'Get the Party Started'
'Funhouse'
'Ave Mary A'
'Who Knew'
'Bad Influence'
'Just Like a Pill'
'Please Don't Leave Me'
'Sober'
'I'm Not Dead'
'Unwind'
'I Don't Believe You'
'Dear Mr. President'
'Mean' with Butch Walker
'My Generation'/ 'Basket Case'/ 'Roxanne' with Butch Walker
'What's Up?'
'Try Too Hard'
'U + Ur Hand'
'Leave Me Alone (I'm Lonely)'
'So What'

The Truth About Love Tour

13 February 2013–31 January 2014
USA and Canada—26 Dates
UK and Europe—25 Dates
Australia and New Zealand—46 Dates
USA and Canada—40 Dates

Director and Executive Producer
Baz Halpin

Band
Jason Chapman, Mark Schulman, Justin Derrico, Eva Gardner, Kat Lucas, Stacy Campbell and Jenny Douglas-Foote

Dancers
Tracy Shibata, Colt Prattes, Reina Hidalgo, Khasan Brailsford, Janelle Ginestra,

Loriel Hennington, Remi Bakkar and Jimmy Slonina

Choreography
Golden Boyz (RJ Durell and Nick Florez); Dreya Weber

Setlist
'Raise Your Glass'
'Walk of Shame'
'Just Like a Pill'
'U + Ur Hand'
'Leave Me Alone (I'm Lonely)'
'Try'
'Wicked Game'
'Just Give Me a Reason'
'Trouble'
'Are We All We Are'
'How Come You're Not Here'
'Sober'
'The Great Escape'
'Who Knew'
'Time After Time'
'Fuckin' Perfect'
'Most Girls'/ 'There You Go'/ 'You Make Me Sick'
'Slut Like You'
'Blow Me (One Last Kiss)'
'So What'

Beautiful Trauma World Tour

1 March 2018–2 November 2019
USA and Canada—46 Dates
Australia and New Zealand—42 Dates
USA and Canada—43 Dates
UK and Europe—27 Dates
Brazil—1 Date

Director and Executive Producer
P!nk and Baz Halpin

Band
Jason Chapman, Mark Schulman, Justin Derrico, Eva Gardner, Adriana Balic, Jessy Greene, Stacy Campbell and Jenny Douglas-Foote

Dancers
Tracy Shibata, Remi Bakkar, Khasan Brailsford, Reina Hidalgo, Shannon Holtzapffel, Jeremy Hudson, Madelyne Spang, Justin Lutz and Anthony Westlake

Choreography
Golden Boyz (RJ Durell and Nick Florez); Loriel Hennington

Setlist
'Get the Party Started'
'Beautiful Trauma'
'Just Like a Pill'
'Who Knew'
'Revenge'
'Funhouse' / 'Just a Girl'
'Smells Like Teen Spirit'
'Secrets'
'Try'
'Just Give Me a Reason'
'I'm Not Dead'
'Just like Fire'
'What About Us'
'For Now'
'Barbies'
'I Am Here'
'Fuckin' Perfect'
'Raise Your Glass'
'Blow Me (One Last Kiss)'
'So What'
'Glitter in the Air'

Summer Carnival Tour/Trustfall Tour

7 June 2023-20 November 2024
UK and Europe—21 Dates

USA and Canada—23 Dates
USA and Canada—18 Dates (*Trustfall* Tour)
Australia and New Zealand—20 Dates
UK and Europe—17 Dates
USA and Canada—16 Dates (*Trustfall* Tour)
USA and Canada—16 Dates

Director and Executive Producer
P!nk and Baz Halpin

Band
Jason Chapman, Brian Fraiser-Moore, Justin Derrico, Eva Gardner, Adriana Balic, Stacy Campbell, Nayanna Holley and Dani Moz

Dancers
Tracy Shibata, Khasan Brailsford, Reina Hidalgo, Shannon Holtzapffel, Jeremy Hudson, Madelyne Spang, Christian Sanchez, Marley Tré Webster, Mo Armstrong and Jake Hinga

Choreography
Luke Broadlick, Alison Faulk, Anthony Bartley and Charlie Bartley

Setlist
'Get the Party Started'
'Raise Your Glass'
'Who Knew'
'Just Like a Pill'
'Try'
'What About Us'
'Turbulence'
'Make You Feel My Love'
'Just Give Me a Reason'
'Fuckin' Perfect'
'Just Like Fire'
'Please Don't Leave Me'
'Cover Me in Sunshine'
'Kids in Love'
'When I Get There'
'I Am Here'
'Irrelevant'
'No Ordinary Love'
'Runaway'
'Trustfall'
'Blow Me (One Last Kiss)'
'Never Gonna Not Dance Again'
'Last Call'
'So What'

Bibliography

Books

Walker, B. and Diehl, M. (2011) *Drinking with Strangers: Music Lessons from a Teenage Bullet Belt*. New York: William Morrow & Co.

Magazines & Newspapers

The Advocate magazine
The Associated Press newspaper
American Songwriter magazine
Arena magazine
Billboard magazine
Blast magazine
Blender magazine
Canoe magazine
Café magazine
The Canadian Press magazine
City Life newspaper
Cosmopolitan magazine
The Courier Mail newspaper
The Daily Telegraph newspaper
Details magazine
Diva magazine
ELLE magazine
Entertainment Weekly magazine
The Face magazine
The Financial Times newspaper
Get Out! magazine
GEM magazine
GQ magazine
GenQ magazine
The Herald Sun newspaper
Hit Parader magazine
Hot Press magazine
The Independent newspaper
The Irish News newspaper
The Ledger newspaper
The Los Angeles Times newspaper
NME magazine
Manchester Evening News newspaper
Music Connection magazine
Music Week magazine
The New York Times magazine
People magazine
The Philadelphia Inquirer newspaper
The Press of Atlantic City newspaper
Q magazine
Redbook magazine
Rolling Stone magazine
Seventeen magazine
Songwriter Universe magazine
Spin magazine
Studio magazine

The Sydney Morning Herald newspaper
The Telegraph newspaper
Time magazine
The Torontoist newspaper
Tribe magazine
USA Today newspaper
Variety magazine
Vulture magazine
Wall Street Journal newspaper
The Washington Post magazine
Women's Health magazine

Websites

AOL Music—aol.com
ASCAP—ascap.com
Audacy
Buzzfeed—buzzfeed.com
Consequence
drDrew.com—drdrew.com
Idolator—idolator.com
Instagram—instagram.com
iNews
MassLive
News.com.au
Official Charts Company UK
Orange
Popmatters—popmatters.com
Promonews
Spotify—spotify.com
Stereogum—stereogum.com
Taste of Country—tasteofcountry.com
VladTV
Yahoo! Music—music.yahoo.com
X [formerly Twitter]—x.com

Radio, TV and Podcasts

60 Minutes
ABC
Alice 97.3
Apple Music 1
Behind The Music: P!nk
BBC News
BBC Radio 1
Capital FM
CBS News
Driven
Heart Radio UK
Friday Night with Jonathan Ross
Good Morning America
Hollywood at Home
iHeart Radio
Howard Stern
Jabba's Morning Glory
Jimmy Kimmel Live!
The Kyle and Jackie O Show
Making the Video
MTV
MTV News
MusicMusic Canada
NextTribe
NPR
On the Record: P!nk – Beautiful Trauma
Oprah
The Queen Latifah Show
Planet Rock
SiriusXM
Today
The Tonight Show with Jimmy Fallon
VH1
Who's Talking to Chris Wallace?
XFM
Z100 New York

About the Author

Steve Bishop is a pop music aficionado, renowned as the UK's leading Britney Spears expert and author of *Britney Spears: Song by Song*. Steve's passion extends beyond Britney to other icons, including P!nk, Cyndi Lauper and Lady Gaga. With an impressive collection of memorabilia and deep knowledge of the genre, Steve's work celebrates the artistry and impact of these pop legends, offering fellow fans a deeper understanding and appreciation of their favourite music and its cultural significance.

Thank You

I can't believe I have completed a second book in the *Song by Song* range! This book is dedicated to my family and friends, including my parents (Cheryl and Colin), my siblings and their families (Cat, Anthony, Luke, Jem, Macie and Hadley) and my lover, James. A special thank you to everyone who supported *Britney Spears: Song by Song*, especially my friends and colleagues at West London College.